D0044570

E. Bronson Ingram

E. Bronson Ingram

Complete These Unfinished Tasks of Mine

Martha Rivers Ingram

Hillsboro Press

PROVIDENCE PUBLISHING CORPORATION

FRANKLIN, TENNESSEE

TENNESSEE HERITAGE LIBRARY

Printed in the United States of America

05	04	03	02	01		1	2	3	4	5

Library of Congress Catalog Card Number: 2001091854

ISBN: 1-57736-216-0

Cover design by Gary Bozeman

Permission to reprint portions of the article from *Advantage Magazine*, April 1987, has been granted by the publisher.

In the appendix, courtesy of the St. Paul Companies Archive, is reprinted a portion of "Men of Vigor," the *Saint Paul Letter*, April 1953, pages 7–10. It describes Charles and Frederic Bigelow.

Hillsboro Press
PROVIDENCE PUBLISHING CORPORATION

238 Seaboard Lane Franklin, Tennessee 37067

800-321-5692

www.providencehouse.com

To

the Ingram Scholars of Vanderbilt University

and

all Ingram Associates worldwide

past, present, and future

CONTENTS

PREFACE

rskine Bronson Ingram II, my husband of almost thirty-seven years, was a very complex, private man. Although he was often in the public eye in his later years, he was never comfortable there. He much preferred to keep his life and his business affairs out of the spotlight. As you'll see, his sense of responsibility and his strong desire to make a contribution to society put him into several highly visible public roles, which he carried out in his typically excellent way.

I feel as though Bronson as a young person was really rather shy, and strangely enough, even as he became older and more successful, he still was rather shy. Sometimes people mistook that for arrogance or standoffishness. I like the way that his longtime friend John Alden Rodgers described it: people tended to "misread" Bronson. He was not very good at small talk; he just did not do very well at cocktail parties or large social gatherings. If you could get him one on one, however, you'd have a memorable conversation. He had a lot of insecurities, and I know of them as only a wife would know of them. But he had a lot of strengths that he recognized in himself. And he was a loyal friend. If you asked any of his really good friends—whether they were childhood friends such as Jake Wallace and Ed Nelson or later friends such as Joe Wyatt and Arnold Palmer—he would do anything for them, and they, in turn, were very, very loyal to him. He was a paragon of virtue in many ways—honest and dependable—and he was a man with some real flaws, including his famous temper, that made him the person he was.

Bronson rarely verbalized his innermost feelings, but his responses and reactions to adversity provide some insight into his character. If everything had gone along perfectly, I wonder if he would have ever thought to spend time with Vanderbilt or INROADS. I wonder if he would have had to do the self-examination that makes one stop and ask, "How did these things happen, and what can I do about them now that they've happened?"

Bronson led an incredibly full life as a husband, father, brother, friend, businessman, civic leader, and sportsman. For the most part he and I tended to live in the present with an eye toward the future, and our involvement in day-to-day activities left little time for thinking about the past. To help me recall specifics of Bronson's life, I reviewed his personal calendars from 1975 to 1994. There were many notations for business meetings and civic activities, yet there were many notations for "duck hunting with the boys," travel destinations, golf dates, and fishing on the *Patsea IV, V,* or *VI* or on the Moisie River. Despite all of his demanding activities and commitments, he tried to keep some balance in his life by taking time off for rest and relaxation. He could say with Izaak Walton, "I have laid aside business, and gone a-fishing," and he could add a-golfing, a-hunting, and a-traveling.

June 15, 2001, marked the sixth year since Bronson's death, and on November 27, 2001, he would have celebrated his seventieth birthday. With this book I hope to give as complete a picture of Bronson as possible. To that end, I have asked others to contribute their stories or comments about him. In several instances I have been able to include Bronson's own words from letters he wrote or interviews he gave or speeches he delivered.

At one point after the Ingram Scholarship Program at Vanderbilt University got under way and after he knew that he was seriously ill, he told me, "If I don't make it through this illness, I hope that the thing I'll be remembered for is the Ingram Scholarship Program. I think that may be one of the most worthwhile things that we've done." That is why I've dedicated this book to that group as well as to the Ingram Associates, who helped make all of this possible.

The subtitle, *Complete These Unfinished Tasks of Mine,* comes from a poem that Bronson found among his mother's things after she died. He liked the poem and its sentiment, and it sums up his call to his family, his friends, his associates at Ingram Industries and Ingram Micro, the Ingram Scholars, and many others. (I must add that Bronson never would have used the word "dear" about anything, so I chose not to include it in the subtitle.) Here is the poem, "Turn Again to Life" by Mary Lee Hall:

If I should die and leave you here a while,
Be not like others, sore undone, who keep
Long vigil by the silent dust and weep.
For my sake turn again to life and smile,
Nerving thy heart and trembling hand to do
That which will comfort other souls than thine;
Complete these dear unfinished tasks of mine,
And I, perchance, may therein comfort you.

ACKNOWLEDGMENTS

Many people helped me make this book a reality: My children—Orrin, John, David, and Robin—shared their stories of life with Dad.

Bronson's sisters, Alice Hooker and Patricia Hart, provided details of family history and of the early Bronson.

Maryanne Davidson, Bronson's secretary of many years, was on hand for the greater part of Bronson's life. She knew dates, places, and people—and she knew the real Bronson as perhaps few people did.

Many other friends, family members, and business associates—too numerous to list here—told of their experiences with Bronson.

D. B. Kellogg guided me through the entire writing process, from getting my thoughts down on paper and organizing them to preparing the final draft of the manuscript. She also conducted interviews, collected and reviewed letters and newspaper clippings, and sorted through photos. Her patience and persistence were remarkable.

Keel Hunt of the Strategy Group began conducting interviews not long after Bronson's death to be used someday in a biography of Bronson. Many of them have been incorporated here.

Bill Carey permitted me to have access to some audiotapes he compiled as he was writing his book on Nashville businesses, *Fortunes, Fiddles & Fried Chicken*.

Andrew B. Miller and his capable staff at Providence House Publishers have put all of this material together into this tribute to Bronson and his legacy.

CHAPTER 1

Beginnings

*Life has taught us that love does not consist in gazing at each other
but in looking together in the same direction.*
—Antoine de Saint-Exupéry

G race talked me into it. It was the winter of 1957, and I was a senior at Vassar. One of my friends from Nashville, Grace Ward (now Hall), asked if I would have a blind date with a friend of her boyfriend, Ed Nelson. I already had a date that weekend, and I was reluctant to break it. Grace said, "Oh, Martha, you better break it. You're really going to like this man, and you're going to be so sorry if you don't." The young man I was supposed to go out with that weekend was someone I had been out with quite a bit, and I knew it was going nowhere. I did the unaccustomed thing for me, which was to break the date, and went to New York with Grace. That was where I met Bronson Ingram for the first time.

Several Nashvillians had made the trip, and one of them was John Jay Hooker, who had ordered two limousines to take the group around town. We went to all the glamorous places. We saw *My Fair Lady* with Rex Harrison and Julie Andrews, which had just opened. We went to a restaurant called Chez Vito that had lots of red velvet and strolling violinists. We heard Edith Piaf sing plaintive French songs at Versailles, a Midtown night club. For a senior in college who had been treated to lots of beer and pizza on dates, the experience was quite extraordinary.

On Saturday morning, Bronson and I were walking around town and he said, "I need to stop in here at my tailor. I've got something that is basted, and they need to be sure it's right before they seam it up the rest of the way." Going to a tailor with a date was another unusual experience for me. (By the way, he had that sport coat until the day he died, and it still buttoned.)

Back at school, away from all the excitement of New York, I thought, *Now, wait a minute. I think I really like this man, but do I just like him or his lifestyle?* I decided I liked both, but I got very little feedback from him—only a postcard or two. I thought that was the end of it.

After graduation in the spring, I returned to my hometown of Charleston, South Carolina, and worked for my father at WCSC-AM/FM and WCSC-TV. I was the eldest of three children, and he was more or less training me to take over the business for him someday. In addition to my daytime duties, I chose to be the disc jockey for a classical radio show on my father's FM station. I was on from 7:00 to 11:00 each evening and called my program "Music from the Masters." I even lowered my voice and used the pseudonym of Elizabeth Crawford because some listeners might think it was inappropriate for the owner's daughter to hold that position. I was responsible for all of it, including writing the introductions and selling spots to advertisers. In what little spare time I had I went on dates with several young men.

Grace invited me later that summer to visit her in Nashville, and I did. She said, "I'm going to fix you up with Bronson Ingram again. You all had a good time, and I think, long term, you all might go places." I had a date with him the first night and was to have had a date the second night with Franklin Jarman, whom I had never met. He was of the Genesco family. Grace was very interested in fixing me up with someone in Nashville because she and I were good friends, and she thought it would be nice if our relationship continued by me moving to Nashville.

At the end of the evening, Bronson asked, "What are you doing tomorrow night?" I replied, "I have a blind date tomorrow night with Franklin Jarman." He said, "Do you mind if I call him and just simply tell him you're already taken?" I thought that was a splendid thing for him to do, and we went out a second time. I never even met Franklin until several months later.

I sailed with Bronson a couple of times that summer in Minnesota, where his family had a summer home, and I didn't think it was fun at all. He yelled like Captain Bligh. He was so competitive, he wanted everything to be done just so. I grew up around water and sailboats, but not that kind of sailboat and certainly not with the competitive sailing pressures that he was used to. My legs ended up bruised from the sideboards that I had to sit on as we tilted from one side, leaned one way, and then came about and leaned the other way. After one weekend, my father glanced at my legs and said, "How in the world did you get so black and blue?" I explained to him about the sailing, and he asked, "Are you sure you want to go around with a man who puts you into a boat that gets you so black and blue?" I decided that our relationship was probably better off without

Bronson, just before we were married.

me in his sailboat, and Bronson agreed. I became a fierce spectator instead of a crew member.

Bronson sometimes flew himself to Charleston to see me. The first time I ever flew with him, he was in the company's twin-engine Cessna 310. As he was getting ready to go back to Nashville, he asked if I wanted to go with him, and I decided to accompany him. We took off, and I could tell that my parents were absolutely frantic that I was going off into the wild blue yonder with this man they hardly even knew. They were doubly shocked when we turned up again about an hour later. We ran into a bank of thunderstorms and couldn't get through. Bronson did not have an instrument rating, and he knew enough to turn around and come back before we got totally in trouble. I think my parents somehow felt that if he was cautious enough to come back, they wouldn't worry too much about me flying with him again.

My brother, John Rivers Jr., is ten years younger than I, so he was not yet a teen when Bronson and I started dating. He was paying closer attention to my dating life than I realized. He remarked, "Bronson often flew his plane to Charleston. It was amazing how often the plane had some kind of mechanical difficulty, and he had to stay another day."

Others were noticing, too. Bronson's father and I were alone at breakfast one morning at their Tyne Boulevard home. It was April of 1958 when he suddenly looked up from his *Tennessean* and said, "You know, it gets expensive letting Bronson fly our Cessna to Charleston so often to see you. Sometimes he gets stuck there in bad weather, and we have to send Elmour [Meriwether, the pilot] to help get him and the plane back. It's damn inconvenient. Why don't you just marry my son and be done with it?" "Mr. Ingram," I replied, "he's not yet asked me." Shaking his head and smiling, Mr. Ingram said, "Well, then he's a damn fool!" At least I knew that Bronson's father would approve of me—if Bronson ever got around to asking.

In May when I came back to Nashville for the Iroquois Steeplechase, Bronson did ask me to marry him. He started out by saying, "I want to come over to Charleston to visit you next weekend [the weekend following the Steeplechase]." I told him, "I have another gentleman friend coming from Atlanta then." He paused. "I don't want you going out with anyone else." I said, "You don't have any rights to me, but you could have." He hesitated, then said, "Oh, my God, I think I know what this means." I said, "Well, it's up to you." He said, "Then you would marry me if I were to ask you?" I answered, "Yes, but don't ask me if you don't mean it." He said, "Well, will you?" and I said, "Yes."

I was staying at his parents' house. The next morning when I got up, he was already outside, wandering around, looking stricken. At age twenty-six, almost twenty-seven, he found that he had gotten himself engaged. I don't think he had ever really thought

about it, and suddenly, here he was with a fiancée. I saw him down by the creek, and I went to join him there. I said, "You know, what you asked me last night is something nobody else knows about. You look so pale and so stricken by all this. If you'd like to back out, it's okay." He said, "Oh, no, I really want to go forward with it." He must have been awake most of the night thinking, *Oh, my God, what have I done?*

My parents, Mr. and Mrs. John Minott Rivers, announced our engagement in June. We planned the wedding for October 4, to be held in Charleston.

The newly married Mr. and Mrs. E. Bronson Ingram, October 4, 1958.

Mr. and Mrs. O. H. Ingram (Bronson's parents), Bronson and Martha, and Mr. and Mrs. John M. Rivers (Martha's parents).

My brother, John, recalled: "We took a family trip to the West Coast. Five family members and twenty-seven suitcases piled in a station wagon. I kept calling Bronson 'Burnside,' and Martha talked about him throughout the whole trip." I guess I could be excused for talking about him so much, since we had not been engaged long. We made the trip that summer after my sister's graduation from Vassar.

On Saturday, October 4, 1958, Bronson and I were married in St. Philip's Protestant Episcopal Church at 8:30 P.M. The Reverend S. Grayson Clary and Bishop Thomas Neely Carruthers of the Diocese of South Carolina officiated. That church was meaningful to my family. My father had been senior warden several times, and my mother was much involved in the women's activities.

Elizabeth (then called Betty Craig), my sister, was maid of honor, and Mrs. Vernon Reese Loucks (Ann Thomas), who had been my roommate at Vassar, was matron of honor. The bridesmaids were Mrs. Frederic Bigelow Ingram (Barbara), Bronson's sister-in-law; Mrs. Henry Williamson Hooker (Alice) and Mrs. Henry Rodes Hart (Patricia), Bronson's sisters; and Grace Ward (my Nashville friend from Vassar who introduced us in the first place).

Frederic (Fritz), Bronson's brother, was best man. The groomsmen and ushers were Henry Williamson Hooker and Henry Rodes Hart, both brothers-in-law of Bronson; Fraser Robin Bigelow, Bronson's cousin; John Jay Hooker Jr.; Edward Gage Nelson; Johnson Bransford (Jake) Wallace; John Minott Rivers Jr., my brother; Thomas Pinckney Rutledge Rivers and George Lamb Buist Rivers Jr., my cousins; Brownlee Owen Currey Jr.; Scott Crabtree; John Alden Rodgers; and Frank Prince Macartney.

Following the ceremony, the reception was held at my parents' home, 20 Church Street, near the Battery in the old section of town. The formal garden, lighted with side sconces and crystal chandeliers, was decorated to resemble a large ballroom. A string ensemble provided the music.

Many friends and family members were able to attend. Mr. Ingram chartered a plane to take people from Nashville to Charleston. This partial list gives some idea of the people who were there, in addition to the wedding party: Mr. and Mrs. James C. Ward Jr., Mr. and Mrs. Jack M. Bass, Jack M. Bass Jr., Mr. and Mrs. J. C. Bradford, Mr. and Mrs. John S. Bransford Jr., Edith Caldwell, Mr. and Mrs. Allen Cargile, Mrs. Brownlee O. Currey, Emily Fletcher, Mr. and Mrs. Minos Fletcher Jr., Horace Hill, Mr. and Mrs. W. F. Howard, Mr. and Mrs. Andrew H. Mizell III, Mr. and Mrs. Ralph Owen, Mr. and Mrs. Eldon Stevenson, Mr. and Mrs. Hamilton Wallace, Mr. and Mrs. William Waller, and Ryan Richardson.

John Alden Rodgers vividly recalled the event: "I don't know how many people Mr. Ingram took on that airplane, and people came from all over the country. They took over the Fort Sumter Hotel, a big hotel right there on the Battery. Mr. and Mrs. Rivers had the reception at

The wedding party: (left to right) John M. Rivers Jr., Frank Macartney, Ed Nelson, Brownlee Currey Jr., John Jay Hooker Jr., Barbara Ingram, Scott Crabtree, Patricia Hart, Jake Wallace, Grace Ward, Dr. Thomas Rivers, Bronson, Martha, Henry Hooker, Betty Craig Rivers, Ann Thomas Loucks, Rodes Hart, Alice Hooker, Buist Rivers Jr., and Bobby Bigelow.

their house. It rained so hard that everybody felt sorry for everybody else, but we all had a lot of fun.

"The next morning I walked by the cashier's office at the hotel. Mr. Ingram was on his way to play golf, but he had stopped in the cashier's office to go over his account. He was sitting down in a chair, the cashier wasn't there, so I walked in and shook hands with him and said what a great time we had and how wonderful everything was. He had a stack of checks that was deep, right in front of him, and he was looking through them. He said, 'Hmmm, this is really something. Everybody had a good time, didn't they?' I said, 'Yes, sir.' He kind of shook his head and grinned. I said, 'Have a good game, Mr. Ingram. See you later.' He was a very generous fellow."

Despite the rain, we had a wonderful wedding, and we left for our honeymoon that evening. We went to Acapulco, where Bronson became so ill (Montezuma's Revenge) that after three days we had to return to Nashville. Of course, when we got back from what was supposed to be a week-long honeymoon in three days, even our families thought, *Oh, gosh, it must all be over.* But he soon recovered his health, and we moved into a house on Evelyn Avenue.

Looking back, I guess it was a fairly precipitous courtship, but we had very similar backgrounds, we had very good, solid educations, and we had fun together. Our biggest difference was that he was Presbyterian, and I was Episcopalian. We thought we could get beyond that. Like any newly married couple, we had a lot to learn about each other, but we looked forward to the years ahead. Neither of us could have predicted how low the lows or how high the highs we would experience together.

CHAPTER 2

A Family of Doers

Well done is better than well said.
—Benjamin Framklin

The Ingram family tree had no roots in Tennessee when Orrin Henry (Hank) Ingram brought his new bride to Nashville in 1928, the year of their marriage. The former Hortense Bigelow was born July 26, 1906. She was the daughter of Alice Fraser of Richmond, Quebec, and Frederic R. Bigelow of St. Paul, Minnesota. Hortense's father was president of St. Paul Fire and Marine Insurance Company. Hank Ingram was born June 26, 1904, in Eau Claire, Wisconsin, the son of Erskine Bronson Ingram and Louise Coggeshall Ingram. His grandfather, for whom he was named, was a pioneer in the lumber industry of Wisconsin and an early investor in the Weyerhaeuser Timber Company. (See the appendix for more details of family histories.)

The family's purchase of the Thomas Henry Company, a textile concern in Nashville, represented a new business opportunity since the timber business in Wisconsin was phasing out, according to Alice Hooker, Bronson's sister. Apparently, Hank Ingram had some experience with textiles because an article in the *Tennessean*, published on December 13, 1936, reported that his "first job during summer vacations, while attending Wharton School of Finance (Univ. of Penna.), was setting up machinery in a textile mill in Phila."

Hank and Hortense met at the University of Minnesota. Alice explained, "Mother had left Vassar after spring vacation of her senior year. She had to care for her mother, Alice Bigelow, who was dying and, in fact, died in 1927. Mother never received a degree. I'm not sure why Dad was at the university because he had graduated from Wharton."

In July 1998, the late Sam Fleming, a longstanding family friend, invited Bronson's and my children to his home to tell them a bit about their grandfather: "Hank worked mentally all the time. Hank had a lot of money for those times, and he really didn't have to work." Alice commented that "during the depression, Daddy didn't have new money that was lost. I think he lent a lot of people money. He helped them through the hard times. He was very private about his business affairs, but he was generous with his friends who were in dire straits."

Hank Ingram was not one to be idle, despite having a comfortable financial situation. This letter from him to Mrs. Ingram, postmarked February 4, 1934, and written from the Roosevelt Hotel in New York, gives some indication of Mr. Ingram's attitude toward his early business venture:

Dear Mrs. I—

It is now twelve bells and Brother [Ernest] Jones and I are just getting up. We were both all in and the long sleep has remade us.

We are going to Ted Martin's for dinner and will of course meet his new wife.

To-morrow and Tuesday will be full days and we hope to place some more business. So far between us we have sold nearly 250,000 lbs. Would like to hit 400,000 before we get home. It was a great pleasure to land nearly every merino account in New England in our competitors backyard. The best of all is that the mill is loaded for <u>blue</u> February.

Working on a deal with Ellis Leach which sounds too good to be true—yarn for Chevrolet-Pontiac fabrics. The yarn is 12/1 and 24/2 25% wool 25% mohair 50% cotton which should be right up our alley. They would furnish the wool and mohair and allow us cost plus a handsome profit if we can make the yarn to suit them, and I can't see why we can't do it. <u>The quantity is only 500,000 lbs!!</u>

Wish you would ask J. C. about the newspaper deal. We should get going on it. I'll call you Tuesday or Wednesday night to find out about it.

We will probably be here Monday and Tuesday—Reading (Abe Lincoln Hotel) Wednesday & possibly Thursday. Then down the valley and home by Saturday I hope.

I miss you all a lot—the boys & girls (Alice—Eileen & H). Glad Mr. Fritz enjoyed the burning cotton.

Lots of love,

Hank

(The poor-hardworking-longsuffering-

ever-willing—your humble servant??—Mr I)

By 1936, Mr. Ingram had reorganized the Thomas Henry Company, had renamed it Ingram Manufacturing Company with two subsidiaries—Ingram Spinning Company (merino yarn) and Tennessee Tufting Company (tufted fabrics)—and was a director of the Tennessee Railroad and a member of the advisory board of American National Bank. He was only thirty-two.

The next year, 1937, the textile company had employee relations issues, so Mr. Ingram closed it down. He retained only the Tennessee Tufting Company, which remained in whole or in part in the Ingram family until the 1960s. It was not thriving in the late 1930s, however, and Mr.

O. H. Ingram, Bronson's great-grandfather, a lumberman and an early investor in Weyerhaeuser Timber Company.

Ingram decided to explore other businesses.

The petroleum industry caught his attention. People were beginning to recover somewhat from the effects of the depression and were buying automobiles. U.S. industry was gradually increasing production. War in Europe seemed more than likely. The demand for petroleum was there. Mr. Ingram, Fred Koch, and another partner established Wood River Oil and Refining Company, and they built a 7,500-barrel-a-day refinery at Wood River, Illinois (not far from St. Louis), completing it in 1939. The company had producing properties in Oklahoma and Kansas and a pipeline gathering system.

Transportation of the product on the rivers proved to be inadequate, and to provide better service to customers, Wood River Oil entered the river transportation business with Wood River Oil Barge Company in 1942. This aspect of the business was right down Mr. Ingram's waterway. He had a deep love of water and boats, and his love affair with barges lasted until his death. Four years later, Ingram Products Company acquired the river fleet of Wood River Oil Barge Company.

Mrs. O. H. Ingram, Bronson's great-grandmother, April 25, 1896.

In 1950, the partners of Wood River Oil and Refining Company sold their interests to Sinclair Oil and Refining Company. The refinery had reached production of 30,000 barrels per day.

Mr. Ingram reentered refining operations in 1953 with Ingram Oil and Refining Company, under the control of Ingram Products Company. A company brochure stated: "The acquisition of a tank farm, 145 acres of land, and dock facilities at New Orleans, Louisiana, provided the framework for a completely new refinery. Completed in 1954, this new 12,000 barrel-per-day refinery is equipped with the most modern refining equipment." The next year, 1955, Ingram Products Company sold its fleet to Ingram Barge Company, a newly organized company.

While Mr. Ingram was keeping his eye on the family's business interests, Mrs. Ingram was occupied with the running of the family itself. They had four children: Fritz (born in 1929), Bronson (born in 1931), Alice (born in 1933), and Patricia (born in 1935). Both Fritz and Bronson were born in St. Paul because Mrs. Ingram went home for their births.

Left: Alice Fraser Bigelow, Bronson's grandmother.

Right: Frederic R. Bigelow, Bronson's grandfather.

Sam Fleming observed: "I don't think Hank ever carried a personal checking account. Hortense did everything. He didn't want anybody to know about his business affairs, and they were carried out at First Trust Company Bank in St. Paul for a long time. He and Hortense were very close together. Hortense was the 'business manager' of his personal life. She managed everything for the household. Family decisions were made by Hortense."

Bronson's sister Patricia Hart described her and her siblings' growing-up years: "Our parents expected the four of us to work hard, and there was not a whole lot of praise. Sports were always a big part of the family. They frowned on our staying inside; we were not allowed *not* to be busy. We all have strong personalities and are a little opinionated. If we were scrapping on the floor, our parents would let us do it unless we were about to kill each other.

"They always taught that we were very fortunate and with that went obligations. We were to give time and talents. We are doers." All of the children grew up to take an active role in civic affairs.

Patricia added, "We weren't given any money when we were growing up. We didn't expect toys, but we had bountiful Christmases. Of course, they were organized Christmases."

Mr. and Mrs. Ingram seemed intent on making sure that their children were not spoiled, and they all became productive, useful citizens. They were brought up with good values and certainly privilege, but I would not consider them overly indulged. The Ingrams adored their children, but both being from the Midwest, they were no-nonsense parents. They were less effusive about the good things and more vocal about the bad things. It was as if they said, "Look, if you're doing it right, we're not going to talk about it. We'll let you know when you make a mistake."

They were different from my parents, who told me how wonderful and special I was from the day I was born. The Ingrams lived as though they thought their children were special, but they did not do what I call the southern thing—provide constant reinforcement and maybe too much in some cases. As Bronson and I had children, he tended to follow his parents' pattern, and I tended to follow my parents' pattern. Just ask our children!

There was a definite difference in the way my in-laws interacted with their children and the way my parents interacted with their children, yet both sets of parents ended up producing positive results. The Ingram children have done quite well, and so have my siblings and I. The message is: there is no one way to raise children.

Bronson received most of his pre-college education at schools in Nashville. He entered Parmer School in 1937 and remained there until 1941. Because of the downturn in the Tufting Company's business, Mr. and Mrs. Ingram considered living full time in St. Paul, so the children went to school there from September 1941 to June 1942; Bronson attended St. Paul Academy. The harsh Minnesota winter convinced the Ingrams that Nashville was the place to live no matter what business they were in. Mr. Ingram looked out the window one snowy morning and said, "Hortense, only an Eskimo or a damn fool would live here on purpose. Let's move back to Nashville." (She evidently agreed, as long as she could keep a house in Minnesota for the summers. She retained a lovely home on White Bear Lake until she died.) Bronson then entered Montgomery Bell Academy in 1942, where he stayed until 1946. In that year, Mr. Ingram sent him to Andover. Bronson's friend Jake Wallace commented, "I would say he went to Andover because his father told him that's where he was going. Period. Not a subject for serious debate or maybe even any debate at all." Bronson did well at Andover, but he was homesick and missed his friends. His parents allowed him to come back to Montgomery Bell in 1947, and he graduated from there in 1949. He was on the tennis team from 1947 to 1949, and the yearbook noted: "Bronc—burns up the tennis courts and wheels a two-toned green Olds about town—strictly a good guy."

The Ingrams bought a house on Tyne Boulevard, and they had enough property to keep a pony in a fenced-in area. At that point there were few houses on the street. During World War II, they bought a cow, and Bronson's job was to milk it, so they could provide their own milk and butter.

Having four children of their own meant that the Ingram house was always filled with youngsters. Bronson's group of friends included Jake Wallace, John Alden Rodgers, Ed Nelson, Bill Bailey, Bill Howard, and John Bransford. They played the typical backyard basketball and football and occasionally went to the movies. They looked out for each other from their early years to their later years, loyal to the end.

Erskine Bronson Ingram, Bronson's grandfather, circa 1910–15.

Jake Wallace's parents, Hamilton and Ann Wallace, became very good friends of Mr. and Mrs. Ingram, and the boys went to school together. Jake said, "We would go places on the bus. The bus went down Belle Meade Boulevard, and Bronson lived just a short hop off of the bus line down on Tyne, and I lived just a short distance from the bus line down at Sutherland Avenue, so it was very easy for us to ride the bus to the movies together on Friday night. In those days, even if you were only nine or ten years old, it was safe to do those kinds of things and your parents let you do them."

Above: Erskine Ingram and his son, Hank, Eau Claire, 1937.

Left: Hank Ingram and his mother, Louise.

He described the young Bronson: "Bronson was just as intense a little boy as he was when he grew up. Bronson was a guy who was stubborn. He was not very big. Bronson grew a lot once he got into high school. [He eventually reached six feet in height.] When he was eleven, twelve, thirteen years old, he was pretty small, but he was forever getting in fights. It was unbelievable. He had what I would describe as a pugnacious side to him as a young boy, although he lost more often than he won in those endeavors.

"I've often thought of the literally hundreds of people that we know who are born into a good economic situation who really do nothing about it. And to me, I think, they just live off of the largesse of their ancestors. I think Bronson was an interesting guy because he worked hard always. It really didn't make any difference if we were talking about school or whether we were talking about hobbies. Whatever it was, Bronson was always very intense and very anxious to always do the best he could do, and that frankly created some of the interesting confrontations because people that didn't do their best really Bronson had very little time for. He was disdainful of somebody who was not putting out up to their capabilities—whether it be sports or you name it. I think there needs to be an award given for the person that was born into means who did more with his life than circumstances would ever had imagined that he needed to. Bronson would certainly come to my mind as being about the best I know of."

Above: Bronson and his great-grandmother Fraser, June 1933.

Opposite page: Hank Ingram and Bronson on the Great Lakes, July 1936.

Discipline was strict in the Ingram household. John Alden Rodgers recalled, "Mr. Ingram had a set of rules, and

Patricia, Alice, Bronson, and Fritz.

he wanted everybody to abide by them. And they pretty well did. I think Mr. Ingram was fair as long as you behaved. The same with Mrs. Ingram. She was a disciplinarian. She had a set of rules, and she expected you to behave whether you were her child or me as their guest. One time we were going down West End Avenue, and she was taking us to the movie downtown. We passed a car that I knew, and I rolled the window down and said, 'Hey! Hello!' She turned around and said, 'Will you close that window and sit down? Don't holler out of my car window!' She got me. I didn't say a word the rest of the day. They just had their sets of rules and expected people to abide by them—and we did. Bronson was a trusted friend—from the first time I met him to the last time I saw him."

The children's respect for—and certain knowledge of—their parents' discipline probably explains why the children got into little serious trouble. But they did have their lapses. Two of Bronson's more serious transgressions involved a car.

John Alden Rodgers was not a participant, but he knew what happened. "I guess we were in high school, old enough to have a

Left: Alice and Patricia, Fritz and Bronson, early 1940s.

Below: Fritz, Bronson, Alice, and Patricia riding at White Bear Lake, 1940.

driver's license. Bronson's father had gotten a brand new Oldsmobile. It was green in color. Somehow Bronson talked his father out of the keys that night. He called me and said, 'Do you want to go for a ride?' That meant more than around the block. I said, 'No.' I don't know what I had going on, but I missed this ride. He took the car out from Tyne, out to Chickering, and going down Chickering, he was probably going a little fast. Chickering and Old Hickory dead-end down there. He didn't make the stop. He takes this car down a barrier, down into a ditch. I don't think his father ever got over that."

In another instance, on Christmas Eve, Bronson was driving, and other boys were in the car with him. He was pulled over for speeding, and the police put him in jail. They called his father, but his father left him there overnight. Bronson's sister Patricia recalled, "That was a grim Christmas Day. There was no joy in the house, and our father was livid. Of course, being so young, I didn't know what was going on at the time. I didn't learn until years later what really happened."

For years, Mr. Ingram kept an office in St. Paul, and he took the entire family to their house at White Bear Lake for the summers. Mrs.

Ingram's sister, Eileen Bigelow, lived in the area year-round, and she had a farm with horses. All of the Ingram children learned to ride, starting with ponies, when they were six or seven years old. It was almost like summer camp because there were so many activities to keep the youngsters busy. The White Bear Yacht Club offered tennis, sailing, and golf with fine teaching professionals. They could fish from the Ingrams' boat. Mrs. Ingram probably spent most of her days shuttling children from one place to the other.

The whole family loved sports. Mrs. Ingram was not a participant, but she was a fierce spectator and encouraged the children in their activities. Alice said, "All of us were competitive in sports, but it was not out of balance. The theory was to expose us to all of these various things. When our southern friends visited us there, they were thunderstruck at the activities and the level of constant activities. We rode horseback, played golf and tennis, and sailed. Then we water-skied, fished, and played in the water. They asked us when we ever stopped to rest. We didn't."

Bronson's sport of choice during those summers would have been sailing. The lakes around Nashville are not really big enough to do the kind of sailing that he was doing. It needed the vastness of White Bear Lake. He started in a little X boat, then moved up to C and E class scows. For the E scow he needed two to three crew members; there was a weight

Above: Classes of Montgomery Bell Academy, 1943–44; Bronson is on the far right of the first row.

Opposite page: Bronson at the Woodhill Horse Show, 1946. (Photo by his aunt, Eileen Bigelow.)

Above: Bronson and his crew of the Sailfish IV.

Right: Frank Macartney, seated, and another crew member who helped Bronson win trophies at inland lake regattas.

Opposite page: Young Bronson relaxing in his sailboat.

limit as to the number of pounds on board. Two of his good friends at White Bear Lake were Frank Macartney and Bob Ordway (who died of polio while he was at Yale).

He sailed against Buddy Melges (a crew member for Bill Koch when he won the America's Cup in 1992) and other people of that high caliber. He won many races at regattas, for example, the Class E Pine Lake Yacht Club Perpetual Challenge Trophy in 1951. He was racing for the White Bear Yacht Club, and his racing number was W–20.

The Ingram family, 1951 or 1952.

Ed Nelson knew Bronson from the age of seven or eight, and he was involved with everything from sports and school to business with him as they grew older. He said of the Ingram children: "They were all very good athletes. In looking at how they performed in their sailing, sailing is not an easy task for a child, and these children, all of the Ingram family, graduated from these small X boats and C boats on up to E boats and requiring more crew and more skill and a lot of work. You'd be out maybe four hours working, but when you got back to the dock, all of those sails would be neatly folded and put into sailbags and the boat was secured. There was never an incomplete event." He added, "Everything in the Ingram household was shipshape."

If Bronson's sport of choice was sailing, Mr. Ingram's sport of choice was playing golf. He liked to fish, too, but nothing else approached his love of golf. In his later years, Bronson's love of golf probably equaled that of his father. Mr. Ingram became an early member of the Augusta National.

Sam Fleming knew the details. "Shortly after the establishment of the Augusta National Golf Club in 1932, Brownlee Currey and Peck

Owen joined and from time to time took friends there from Nashville. After the war, World War II, the Club came on hard times and was seeking qualified members. On Brownlee's and Peck's recommendations, invitations were sent by Bobby Jones, who was the president, to Edwin Craig, Jay Ward, Hank Ingram, and myself. The initiation was $1,000 and dues $100 a year."

Only Mr. Ingram and Sam Fleming accepted. On several occasions Mr. Ingram took friends from the Belle Meade Country Club on his plane to Augusta—Brownlee, Peck, Ham Wallace Sr., Jay Ward (my friend Grace's father), Dr. Joe Hibbitts, Jimmy Tupper, and George Livingstone (Belle Meade's golf pro).

Later Eldon (Steve) Stevenson also became a member of Augusta; he was a friend of Dwight Eisenhower. Alice said that "Mr. Stevenson played golf with Daddy every week. They would bet 25 or 50 cents and act as if it was $1 million."

In 1960, Mr. Ingram, Steve Stevenson, and Sam Fleming built the Tennessee Cottage at Cliff Roberts's urgent insistence. They equally divided the cost of $105,000, and Augusta National retained ownership.

Sam Fleming recalled one particular event while some of the Nashville men were at Augusta: "Hank had a phone call, came back, and announced: 'My refinery in Louisiana is burning up. But don't get upset. We are fully insured. However, unfortunately, the insurance is held by the St. Paul Fire and Marine [Hortense Ingram's family business]!'"

The Augusta membership was very important to Mr. Ingram, and he was pleased when Fritz became a member. Bronson was not invited to join until after his father's death. When Cliff Roberts wanted to find someone to run the tournament (the Masters) and the club, he was getting on in years. He asked Sam Fleming to check with the Ingram brothers. Sam said, "I contacted them, and Cliff had said it wouldn't take but six months of their time. They were touched, but of course, they turned it down."

Bronson spent his first year of college at Vanderbilt, where he was on the tennis team. He transferred to Princeton in his sophomore year (1950), and he played on the golf team there. He belonged to the Republican Club and Tiger Inn. He roomed with Dick Strassner, Bob Cowan, and Joe Masi.

In the summer following their sophomore year in college, Ed Nelson and Bronson drove from Nashville to Texas to California, then through the Northwest, across the country, to Minnesota. Mr. Ingram let them borrow his 1950 Oldsmobile and his Standard Oil credit card. They arrived safely at White Bear Lake, and Ed said, "I remember sitting at the dinner table and Mr. Ingram passed around a partial payment check [for the sale of Wood River Oil and Refining]. It was either the picture or the check, and it was a very large check. It was the only time I ever saw him display any kind of anything to do with money."

Bronson in his uniform as a supply corps officer in the navy.

Such displays were atypical of the whole family. Bronson always had the feeling that the family's wealth could go away if he didn't take care of it. He never considered himself a wealthy man nor did he ever aspire to be known as a wealthy man. He told me that one of the most horrifying things that happened to him at Princeton occurred when somebody introduced him as Moneybags. He said he was so embarrassed because his family, although they were really quite prosperous, never discussed being anything other than average people. They didn't want to appear to have a dime more than their friends down the street.

Bronson graduated in 1953 with a degree in English from Princeton. Almost immediately after graduation, he entered the navy; he had been in the NROTC since September 1949. At that point in time, young men were still required to join a branch of the armed forces, and Bronson's tour of duty occurred during what the naval reporting forms called the "Korean Emergency" (June 25,

1950, to January 31, 1955). The date of his commission was June 15, 1953, as an ensign. (Ironically, the date of June 15, forty-two years later, would prove to be another milestone for Bronson.) Twenty months of his tour were devoted to sea duty, and four months to continental U.S. duty.

The USS Cambria, *the ship on which he served.*

Leaving White Bear Lake on June 25, Bronson reported for duty on June 29 at Bayonne, New Jersey. There he would be in the Naval Supply Corps School until October 23. Then he was on board the *USS Cambria* from November 2, 1953, until February 28, 1954.

His posting from March 1, 1954, to February 28, 1955, included Navy Yard Overhaul; Underway Refresher Training, GTMO; Amphibious Training, Little Creek, Virginia; and Unit of U.S. Sixth Fleet and Transport Division 24. Collateral duties as of June 1954 were Audit Board, Postal Board, Bonds Office, Income Tax, and Insurance. He was appointed a lieutenant, junior grade, in the Supply Corps in December 1954. Again on the *Cambria*, he was in the Mediterranean from September 1954 to February 1955. As of February 28, he was Assistant for Disbursing, Ship's Store Officer, and "S" Division Officer. His last day of service was June 7, 1955. No wonder Bronson later told me he considered his training in the Supply Corps to be the equivalent of a graduate school course in business. He said he learned about business in general, inventory control, including keeping inventory fresh, and billing. The training turned out to be a huge asset to him from a business point of view.

An unfortunate event happened while he was on board ship, yet it could have been much worse. He contracted polio—what the doctors called a mild case—although he told me of the spinal tap that was done with severe pain to him. The only residual effects were that his left arm was slightly smaller and his left arm was never as strong as his right arm. When he was wearing a shirt, it was not noticeable. He was very right handed, but occasionally, the left arm's weakness bothered him and he complained, "That damn polio." His friend Bob Ordway had polio at the same time but died of it, and his death deeply affected Bronson. He mentioned it to me on more than one occasion: "Why him? Why not me?"

Both of Bronson's parents were involved in the community, and one of Mrs. Ingram's civic activities was the Junior League, which in those days focused on children who had polio. Alice had this vivid memory: "When I was a little girl, the Junior League had a Palm Sunday paper sale. They went door to door, raising money to support the Crippled Children's home. Mother took me and Patricia along with her. It was just expected that we were to take responsibility in the community." Mrs. Ingram's children learned that lesson well from her.

Alice continued, "Mother didn't sit back; she had no southern flower mentality. It was not her frame of reference. She said what she thought." Mrs. Ingram served on several boards of organizations and was invariably the treasurer. She had an uncanny ability with figures, and as Alice said, "The men were always stunned that she had such a grasp of finance." Mrs. Ingram was one of the first women to take an active role with the United Way, Travellers Rest, and Cheekwood in the early days.

Mr. and Mrs. Ingram emphasized the importance of education to their children and took steps to assure that quality education was available in Nashville for others' children. Mrs. Ingram was a founder of Ensworth and Harpeth Hall. Mr. Ingram was on the Vanderbilt Board of Trust, and he worked with Montgomery Bell Academy and supported it when it was in financial distress.

Sam Fleming summarized some traits that Bronson and his father shared, and the list is a good way to briefly illustrate what Bronson was like to live with or work with:

Both were invariably on time and expected others to be.

Both got upset, but didn't stampede when things went wrong, but rather grew stronger and more determined to work things out and usually did.

Both were justifiably proud, but not egotistical or arrogant; generous but wouldn't countenance any part of being imposed upon. They absolutely rebelled when anybody tried to impose upon them.

Both loved boats.

Both were willing to help others, but expected those being helped to help themselves and make a contribution to the community.

They didn't seek after glamour and preferred to live well, but not ostentatiously.

When they were upset, they had a short fuse, usually expressed in some profanity.

Both were extremely proud of their children and made family gatherings a priority. However, both were strict disciplinarians.

Both never forgot White Bear Lake and the professional that taught all of the family the fundamentals of golf.

Both had great integrity.

Dictum Neum Pactum (translated "My Word Is My Bond") has been the motto of the London Stock Exchange. It most assuredly would apply to both Hank and Bronson throughout their entire lifetimes.

Joe Wyatt, now chancellor emeritus of Vanderbilt University, would not have the opportunity to know Mr. Ingram and did not meet Bronson until he was in his early fifties. Yet he observed, "His father was a very accomplished businessman and a decision maker, and I believe really pushed Bronson hard on the business side. He gave him a lot of support, but he left him to make the decisions to succeed or fail. Once he thought Bronson was ready to go, he turned him loose. He was very much influenced by his parents. His mother, I would say from what Bronson shared with me, the social consciousness. His father, on being fair, being trustworthy, when you give your word you keep it, whether it is written down on a piece of paper or not. That kind of ethic as well as style."

And that is the man I married.

CHAPTER 3

Nashville to New Orleans . . . and Back Again

Why is it that great men always have to go early?
—Groucho Marx

B ronson assumed a position in his father's business after he left the navy. By early November 1955, he had been assistant treasurer for Ingram Products Company for two months. A management committee consisting of Fritz, Bronson, Mr. Ingram, Andrew Mizell III, and Jim O'Neill held planning meetings each Monday morning.

Andy Mizell had joined the company as a credit manager but swiftly moved into the position of vice president and chief operating officer of Ingram Oil. Bronson worked directly with him, and they focused on developing the retail business by opening and operating service stations. The Nashville office was at Sixty-third and Centennial at that time (an oil terminal is there now). The company had been refining fuel and transporting it and selling it to other stations, and as Andy said, "We reluctantly started in the retail business because we would be competing with ourselves." Fritz and Jim O'Neill in New Orleans focused on the refining efforts. There was a third office in St. Paul, primarily to take care of banking needs and to provide a place to work in the summer.

The oil business was demanding. Andy Mizell recalled, "Of the last year that I was in that business, I spent more than six months in the air. I loved the business, but the pace was a killer. We traveled all the time. I can remember one specific day having breakfast in New

Orleans, flying to Washington and Baltimore and having meetings there, and flying back to New Orleans for supper."

Bronson started thinking of himself as an oil man, and his duties multiplied. By November 1956, he was secretary/treasurer of Ingram Oil and Refining Company and oversaw sixty-five employees in the operation of fifteen company-owned service stations in five states. He was supervising the construction of additional stations and helped with wholesale sales through six terminals. Eventually, the company built truck stops complete with bunk rooms, showers, and a restaurant, which was innovative for the time. He was also a director of Ingram Barge Company. He and Andy Mizell and Andy's wife, Yolanda, even worked on the design of the Ingram logo, still in use today. The old Wood River logo was their starting point.

In 1957, all of the Ingram operations, except the service station operation, moved to New Orleans. Bronson continued to live in Nashville until early 1959, after we had married, and then we, too, made the move. Mr. Ingram never lived permanently in New Orleans, but he would stay over sometimes on his boat, the *Patsea II.*

Mr. Ingram insisted on everyone being on time—no matter what. John Donnelly, who became the credit manager of Ingram Oil after Andy Mizell, recalled: "Mr. Ingram ran his life, I think, by the clock and the calendar. If you were going to fly down to New Orleans with him, you made sure you were there thirty minutes ahead of schedule because he was known to have absolutely left people who were not there promptly."

Andy Mizell was on hand for one incident involving Bronson. "Bronson and I had been up late working on something. Mr. Ingram and I were at the airport, on the plane. But there was no Bronson. Mr. Ingram said, 'Where is Bronson?' I said, 'He'll be here in two minutes.' Mr. Ingram sat there looking at his watch. He always sat in the same seat: a rear seat on the starboard side. I said, 'I can see the car coming now.' It was a two-door gray Olds. But time was up. Mr. Ingram said, 'George, let's go! Start the engines.' So they shut the door and started the engines, even though Bronson had driven right up to the plane. I convinced Mr. Ingram to open the door for him."

Mrs. Ingram christening the M/V Hortense B. Ingram.

I can tell you from firsthand experience that Bronson was forever afterward the same way; he could not abide people who were late—and he let them know it.

By 1961, Bronson was vice president and/or treasurer and director for Ingram Barge, Ingram Oil, Ingram Trading Company de Venezuela, and General Properties, Inc. He was involved with general supervision, policy and planning, and special financial planning. His development as an oil man seemed to come to a screeching halt, however, when Mr. Ingram merged Ingram Oil Company and Refining with Murphy Oil Company in that year. For all practical purposes Bronson was out of a job—no more oil and no more service stations.

We returned to Nashville, and Bronson worked directly with Mr. Ingram. The emphasis was on the barge line, which had not been sold. He admired his father very much, and in many ways his father was his mentor. He literally sat in Mr. Ingram's office and did as his father said, "Just sit and listen, son." He was getting more "graduate" courses in business.

John Donnelly recalled that about that time, Fritz and Bronson created Ingram Brothers with a petroleum engineer, Cliff Shaw. "Cliff Shaw was the limited partner, and Fritz and Bronson were the general partners." Mr. Ingram had given Bronson and Fritz some money to invest in other things, which I think they promptly lost. For example, they got into wax coating on milk cartons just at the time that plastic coating on milk cartons was gaining popularity. It was not a whole lot of money, but Bronson was beginning to learn it was best to stick with the things that he knew. Business investments did not always bear fruit.

One business that Mr. Ingram began did not fare well, even though it seemed to fit in the plan of doing what he knew. It was Superglass Corporation, a fiberglass boat-building business in Nashville. John Donnelly explained, "There was tremendous, intense competition in fiberglass boat building, and Bronson decided to shut it down, to liquidate the thing." The company had built runabouts and some cabin cruisers. Again, he learned how difficult and disappointing business could be.

Ingram Corporation was incorporated in Delaware in 1962. Two firms began operation under the umbrella of the corporation in that year. Mr. Ingram acquired Cumberland River Sand and Gravel Company, which he named Ingram Materials Company. Ingram-Armistead, Inc., with offices in New Orleans and Nashville, was engaged in all fields of insurance as agents and brokers, but specialized in petroleum, marine, aviation, land transportation, and construction industries. The next year, 1963, Ingram Corporation purchased Barrett Line, a barge company.

Bronson was learning about his father's business, and I was learning about running a household. I ran it, but I ran it to suit him. We had the menus that I knew he liked, and I saw that the laundry and dry cleaning were done the way he wanted them. He was very good most of the time about staying out of my hair, but sometimes I had to say, "Look, you run your office. I'm running the house." He'd agree:

Above: The M/V Hortense B. Ingram.

Right: Ingram Oil and Refining Company, from terminal to service station.

FROM TERMINAL TO SERVICE STATION

As the Ingram product was produced at the refinery . . . so it is received at the service station. For every member of the Ingram team—the Refiner, the Transporter, the Marketer—has one objective to uphold: "Controlled quality . . . all the way!"

"Okay, I've gone overboard a little bit." He didn't want to deal with the domestic help situation or the challenges there; he just wanted things to be perfect. I do not think he ever went into a drugstore, much less a grocery store, while we were married.

There was no such thing as an unlimited budget for me, but Bronson gave me a very generous allowance for running our first house on Evelyn Avenue in Nashville. Nevertheless I could not understand why I was having such a hard time making ends meet. When my father came to visit, I asked for his help: "Daddy, I feel like such a failure. I can't seem to balance my budget. Look at my bank book. This is what I'm spending my money for each month, and it's equivalent to what you used to give me to travel, buy books, for a whole year in college." He looked over the accounts and said, "Well, honey, you're paying for capital expenditures out of your operating budget. You're paying to have the windows rescreened and the plumbing fixed. You need a capital expenditure budget, too." I had never paid any attention to business terminology at that point. I wasted no time in asking for a capital expenditure budget, and then I was fine. Bronson used to say, "I rue the day your father told you about capital expenditures."

Bronson was not perfect—who is?—but he was the neatest man you could imagine. In all the years that we were married I never picked up a sock or put anything away for him. He had a place for everything and everything was in its place. He really was self-sufficient in the sense of looking after himself and his belongings. He never threw a magazine on the floor that he didn't pick up. That was the way he lived his life, in a very tidy, compartmentalized way, and his neatness made my job very easy in many ways.

When my friends talked about their sloppy husbands, I had to say, "Look, I don't know what you're talking about. I guess I'm just fortunate." We had domestic help from the very beginning of our marriage, but even they said, "There is so little for us to do other than basic cleaning."

He was a conservative dresser. He had all of his business or dress clothes made in New York at Chipp & Company, which for years was right across the street from Brooks Bros. on Thirty-eighth. It was a great point of pride to him as time went along that he could still fit into the same clothes that he had as a much younger person.

The only things he threw away were absolutely in shreds, or sometimes he gave away neckties that were too wide or too skinny because styles changed. But his clothes were made of beautiful fabric, and he never changed his style. Even when the hair styles changed and some people started wearing much longer hair, his children, who were then in their early teens, and I suggested that maybe he might let his hair fluff out or grow longer instead of being so slicked down. His response was, "Don't get me to change too much because I may decide then that I need to change wives." He

Martha and Bronson with Arnie and Winnie Palmer at the President's Ball, Latrobe Country Club, Latrobe, Pennsylvania.

was joking, I'm fairly certain, but I backed off, and the children were horrified at the thought. We said, "Okay, leave it alone." The way he wore his hair then is back in style now, but he never changed and never had long sideburns or fluffy hair.

We sometimes went to social events that required Bronson to wear a tuxedo. He complained about it, but as tux shirts became softer, he complained less. Dressing in tails to go to the balls was something else again. He found that ridiculous, but he did it occasionally and he looked very handsome when he was dressed so beautifully. I always made sure to compliment him repeatedly.

Early on, I let him know how important I felt trust was in a marriage: "The only way I will stick around is with a mutual trust. If that is ever shattered, I'm gone." He told me that he thought I meant it—and he was right. He also frequently told people, "I don't even think about looking at another woman because she would kill me." I said, "That is probably true. I'd probably divorce you first and then kill you."

We saw too many divorces with too much sadness around us. We learned from the experiences of friends, and we realized how fragile a marriage can be. A couple must work at the relationship all the time. One person can't decide to be loyal and trustworthy, and the other not go along with that ethic.

About three months after we were married, Mr. Ingram decided it was in Bronson's and the company's best interests for us to move to New Orleans. I think his father wanted him to get closer to the whole refinery scene so he could have the opportunity to someday run it.

After we first moved there, we saw something of Bronson's brother, Fritz, and his wife, but we were part of a less high-profile group that was somewhat younger. We lived in New Orleans two and a half years, and our first two children, Orrin and John, were born there at Ochsner Clinic.

Fortunately, we made some friends in New Orleans because of friends in Nashville. Eli Tullis had been at the University of Virginia with Jack Bass, who is from Nashville. We had met Eli and his then wife, Molly, at the Basses' at a Steeplechase party. When they learned we would be in New Orleans, they said, "We'll look you up," and they did. Coincidentally, my sister-in-law and her husband, Alice and Henry Hooker, were in the city because he was at Tulane Law School. They had already met some people through their various connections. The two couples introduced us to people, and we were made to feel so at home that it was natural for us to consider living there for the rest of our lives.

With the merging of Ingram Oil and Murphy Oil, we had to decide what we were going to do. Were we going to stay in New Orleans where we had quite a number of friends? Were we going to move to Charleston, where I had come from? Or would we move back to Nashville?

Staying in New Orleans was tempting, but we knew we would be on waiting lists to join most of the clubs that interested us. We weren't really sure we wanted to wait ten years to be members of the Boston Club or the Louisiana Club and some of the groups with which we thought we had a lot in common.

When we talked about Charleston, Bronson did not want to be known as my father's son-in-law for the rest of time, although he had great respect and affection for my father, which were returned. Charleston was out.

We decided on Nashville. We knew everybody, and both of us liked the city. We pulled up stakes and moved into the house on Hillwood, where I still live. We had made several moves in our short years of marriage. We moved into the house on Evelyn Avenue in Nashville. In New Orleans, we lived in a garage apartment until our first child was born. Then we bought a house with twenty-foot ceilings on Third Street in the old Garden District. After it partially burned in a fire caused by some improper wiring we had done on the air-conditioning, we moved onto the boat *Patsea II*—baby, nurse, and boxer dog in tow—that my father-in-law kept in New Orleans instead of an apartment. The crew of four on board had to make many adjustments to us. After the repairs were made on the house, we moved back into it, three wintry months at dockside later. I was more than pleased to be in a house again. Our boxer dog Puncher fell off the dock several times, baby Orrin was often ill with a cold, and our elderly nursemaid was not very steady on the gangplank, making each outing with the baby a scary one. It was not much fun, but it was shelter, and the price was right!

The house on Hillwood is a very family-friendly house. Bronson had been in it many times as a youngster because it belonged to Ed Nelson's family until 1948. Then the James Bass family lived there. Before he seriously considered buying it, Bronson called Ed, who said the conversation went like this: Bronson asked, "Are you ever thinking about moving back into your old house?" Ed said, "Probably not. Why?" Bronson said, "Well, I'd like to buy it, but I didn't want to buy it if you ever had any thoughts of buying it." Ed replied, "I'll let you buy it under one condition." Bronson asked, "What's that?" Ed said, "That you let me come over there anytime I want to." Bronson readily agreed.

When Bronson first suggested that house, I thought it seemed too large for us; there were six bedrooms plus two maids' rooms over

the garage, and there were several bathrooms. After living in a small house with a tiny garden in New Orleans, I felt as though I would be living on a plantation—the house sat on three acres—and I would need to plant cotton or something. But Bronson really didn't want to move again—ever—and he said, "Well, we've moved so many times since we've been married and we've fixed up places. You never get your money out of them. I want to move into a house that they're going to take me out of feet first." (In fact, that was what happened. I, too, hope to be taken feet first from there.)

I commented, "It's awfully big, isn't it?" Bronson said, "Well, let's just fill it up." I said, "Okay, that's fine with me." We had another baby, David, almost right away, and then a little pause and we had Robin. We had four children, aged five and under. We filled it up except for the guest room downstairs. I would have kept

Martha at the helm as Bronson looks on.

Above: Greywalls Inn, Scotland: Dr. Ned Wedlake, Bronson, Martha, Tish Wedlake, and Deborah and Johnny Harris.

Opposite page: Standing behind the Tennessee Cottage, just after it was completed, Hank Ingram, Eldon Stevenson Jr., and Sam M. Fleming, the men who provided the money to build it.

going with more children because we enjoyed them so much, but Bronson thought four were enough. When I talked about having six, he said, "I don't know who the father of the next two is going to be, but it is not going to be me."

Bronson adored all of his children, but he was firm with them, even Robin. He did not want her to grow up to be a spoiled brat, even though to some extent he did spoil her. The boys had good ponies; she had a really fine pony. There were some differences like that. Part of it was probably that she was the youngest; part of it was probably that she was a darling, fragile little girl. He was quite aware that she had a chance at getting really ruined, and he was conscious of not wanting to give her so much or indulge her every whim and then have her impossible for anyone to live with or deal with later.

Above: The Tennessee Cottage at Augusta National (front side).

Right: Hank Ingram and Jay Ward at Augusta.

Opposite page: Hank (Ole Papa) Ingram, Orrin, John, Hortense (Granny) Ingram, and Bronson, Christmas 1962.

All of our friends in Nashville were basically Bronson's friends who were expected to accept me and I, them. That turned out to be the way it has been, which has been a blessing for me. Yet it was a good thing for us to be away for those early years and have a chance to get a sense of ourselves as a couple. We managed to keep our friendships with those in New Orleans and to add many new friends along the way.

A long-lasting friendship with Arnold Palmer and his wife, Winnie, had its start because of golf. Arnie was in New Orleans to film an *All-Star Golf* TV program in 1959 at the New Orleans Country Club. As one of the best golfers in the club, Bronson was

asked to play a warm-up round with Arnie. Winnie was there, too, on vacation; she was following the round, as was I. We were new in town, and we asked them out for dinner at Antoine's Restaurant, then to Pat O'Brian's to drink "hurricanes." We all hit it off, and we started traveling together and seeing each other socially when schedules would allow. (I still hear from Arnie, but unfortunately, my special friend Winnie passed away in 1999.)

In *A Golfer's Life*, Arnie wrote of an incident in which Bronson and I were involved. It occurred in 1961 after what Arnie called "a victorious Ryder Cup match." (If you are unfamiliar with golf, the Ryder Cup is a biennial match between the best players of the

United States and the best players of Britain and Ireland.) Following the match, Arnold and Winnie and Bronson and I were going to take a short trip together. We were to leave the hotel in Lytham before dawn and drive to London. From there we would go on to Rome. But the plans didn't go as smoothly as Arnie had hoped. Someone else usurped our car, so he had to call a cab. I'll let him tell what happened:

Hurrying back inside to the hotel front desk, I arranged for a taxicab, which had to take its bloody time getting to the hotel because of a heavy fog. A short while later, we were informed that all flights to London would be delayed indefinitely because of the peasoup fog, so we decided to sprint for the train station, hoping to catch the same train Joe Jemsek was taking. The fog was so thick we proceeded down the road at about the speed of an elderly caddie. I'll never forget the sight of our taxi driver with his bald head poked out the side window, squinting to see if we were still on the road.

We made it to the train with seconds to spare and discovered Dow and Linda Finsterwald settling into a compartment. We joined them and decided to have a little morning-after-the-victory party, buying up all of the train's grapefruit and orange juice and whatever they had in the way of muffins or snacks. We pulled out our Scotch and Irish whiskey bottles and made a few more toasts to Sam Ryder as the train slowly clanked out of the station, headed for London.

Ten or eleven hours later, we somehow found our way through the even denser fog of London to the Savoy Hotel, where we settled in and had dinner. There we made the unanimous decision to still try to go on to Rome if and when the weather finally cleared.

Wouldn't you know it, the next morning the fog was even thicker! It was like the whole city was wrapped in a thick wool sweater. Winnie looked crushed as we learned that no planes were being allowed to take off from or land at London's major airports. Trying unsuccessfully to keep her grave disappointment from showing, my wife jokingly accused me of arranging the foggy

weather simply to avoid the danger of having to go on a real vacation! Even so, we wandered around London for a couple more days,
seeing the fog-covered sights.

This trip with the Palmers solidified a friendship that greatly
enriched our lives. We traveled with Arnie and Winnie all over the
world to places we might never have gone for golf otherwise.

I particularly remember that first trip with Winnie and Arnie to
Royal Lytham and St. Annes Golf Club for the Ryder Cup in 1961.
I had just had our second son, John, who along with one-year-old
Orrin and a nurse were left in the capable care of my parents in
Charleston. We were the only nonplaying people with the U.S.
Ryder Cup team. Bronson was invited to walk with Arnie inside the
ropes, having been given a special pass, which was a silver and enameled
lapel pin. I had it mounted on a silver money clip for Bronson when
we got home, and it was one of his prized possessions until the day
he died.

On a trip to Wentworth Golf Club in Surrey, England, Bronson
played a practice round with Arnie before a tournament (British
Open, I think). Bronson's nerves overtook him when he saw the
huge gallery lining the first fairway. His snap hook nearly flattened
several people in the gallery, but as he controlled his nerves as he
continued to play, the gallery began cheering him.

Then there was the Turnberry Golf Course in Scotland with the
beautiful old railroad hotel on the hill overlooking the golf course
and sea for several other British Open tournaments. In those years, a
sign on the clubhouse at Royal Troon read WOMEN AND DOGS NOT
ALLOWED. Winnie and I seethed at the hotel across the street while
the men played.

I have such fond memories of several trips to the Muirfield course
in Gullane outside Edinburgh, Scotland. Lovely Greywalls Inn,
formerly a private home, provided cozy lodging for us while we were
there with the Palmers and later with other friends.

We made several trips to Hawaii. I recall the island of Maui the
best, for we met for the first time that "upstart" Jack Nicklaus and his

wife, Barbara. Jack and Arnie were representing the U.S. in the Canada Cup matches. The Nicklauses also became friends as we toured with the Palmers.

One night on the town in London, the Palmers and Nicklauses were joined by Vivienne and Gary Player. They asked Bronson and me

to go with the six of them to a posh Edwardian casino in Mayfair. The doorman recognized the Palmers, the Nicklauses, and the Players, but when Bronson and I filed by him, he said, "And you, sir, I'm sorry, but I don't recognize you." Thinking that I was making light of the situation, I volunteered, "We are the nobodies." After we were admitted as part of the entourage, Bronson whispered to me in great seriousness, "But we are somebody back home!" I learned not to be so flip.

There were many other golf trips, including dozens to the Masters in Augusta, Georgia. When Arnie was winning so often in those early years, we shared his joy. When he lost, we suffered with

Above: Orrin and Bronson at the Iroquois Steeplechase.

Opposite page: John, Martha holding David, Bronson, and Orrin, December 1963.

him and Winnie. I have never known a more loving and supportive wife than Winnie. In fact, Bronson and I thought so much of her that we asked her to be the godmother of our only daughter, Robin. Winnie took that honor seriously as long as she lived.

Bronson and I were in New Orleans on a visit, staying with Eli Tullis, when the call came late one night in April 1963. It was totally unexpected. Mr. Ingram, who would have been fifty-nine in June, had died of an aneurysm. Of

Hank Ingram near the time of his death in April 1963.

the children, only Patricia and her husband, Rodes, were in Nashville then. Alice explained what happened: "Daddy had an aneurysm at home in bed in the early evening. He was gone by the time they got him to the hospital. He and Mother had just been in Florida where they had a house at Hobe Sound. Daddy liked to play golf there, and he loved being out on the water in his boat."

The next day, April 26, newspapers in Nashville and St. Paul carried obituaries. Mr. Ingram had been vice president of the Vanderbilt University Board of Trust and a member of its Executive and Finance Committees; he had been on the Board of Directors of Standard Fruit and Steamship Company; he was a director of St. Paul Fire and Marine Insurance Company, Great Northern Oil Company, and Minnesota Pipe Line Company. He belonged to Belle Meade Country Club and the Cumberland Club in Nashville, the White Bear Yacht Club, the Augusta National Golf Club, the Jupiter Island Club of Hobe Sound, the Seminole Country Club near Hobe Sound, the University Club of Chicago, and the Somerset Country Club.

An editorial in the *Nashville Banner,* April 27, 1963, was a fitting tribute to Mr. Ingram:

> The unexpected death of O. H. Ingram has ended a career whose breadth of accomplishment and constructive influence defies any estimate of the loss sustained by the nation and the community at large.
>
> He was a man whose business interests crossed the broad face of America. They ranged from timber in the Northwest to barge lines

on the central rivers, oil refining in New Orleans, other types of enterprise and varied investments.

All these he directed, not as the driving builder of empire, but as a quiet genius, whose vision and efficiency were matched only by his soundness of judgment, quick concept, a true sense of direction and a deep gratitude that expressed itself in countless benefactions for his fellow man.

Mr. Ingram was not a native of Nashville. His legal residence was in White Bear Lake, Minn., but he had maintained a home here since 1928. And seldom has an "adopted son" done more for any city and its institutions, which have served thousands, of all ages and in all walks of life.

The high principles and fundamental qualities of character that ruled the conduct of his own affairs, he likewise brought to the fulfillment of his obligations as a citizen—all with an easy warmth of understanding and self-effacement. He sought no recognition and shunned even the edge of limelight, but the gloved force of his personality was a dynamic factor in the achievements of any organization in which he had a part. He was not a giver, who signed and walked away. He stood by and saw the project through.

The beneficiaries of his interests were legion, but he is better known, perhaps, for his devotion to Vanderbilt, where he was vice president of the Board of Trust and gave, far beyond the call of duty, both in counsel and financial consideration. He stood firmly with others for the policies that have brought the University international renown for academic excellence and the production of leaders for the days ahead.

There are many who strive for the general good of a community and the extent of their work becomes largely a matter of public record. In the case of Orrin Henry Ingram, the area of his service was so broad and varied, touched so many needs, ranging from the cultural and educational, to those of charity and youth welfare, that the broad spread of his contributions can never be generally known.

In spite of the shock of his sudden death, the full impact of his passing will be long delayed, because he gave both of himself and his means in such a way that many have not been aware of the source of help that came in an hour of necessity.

Truly deep is the void left by one who kept no accounting of the generosity in his own heart, nor paused to measure the ever increasing reach of friendship and concern for others. ·

Mr. and Mrs. Ingram were avid fans of Vanderbilt sports. This commentary by Raymond Johnson in a Nashville paper provided a glimpse into his efforts on the school's behalf:

> Death of O. H. (Hank) Ingram will be felt in many businesses and in many walks of life . . . His passing was a jolt to Vanderbilt University and to Commodore footballers.
>
> Mr. Ingram was a driving force behind Vanderbilt to restore it to football respectability . . . He had suffered with the Commodores in recent years because they were directed by one of his friends, Art Guepe . . . When Jack Green was named to succeed the retiring Guepe, Mr. Ingram gave the new coach his wholehearted support . . . He offered his private plane to Green and Baby Ray in order that they might expedite the recruiting program.
>
> Mr. Ingram's assistance to Vanderbilt football was minute in comparison to the countless beneficiaries of his interest . . . Nashville, the South and the nation lost a topflight citizen in his passing. [The ellipses were in the original; no copy has been left out of this article.]

The *Nashville Banner* on Saturday, May 4, 1963, published a resolution by Vanderbilt in honor of Mr. Ingram:

> The Vanderbilt Board of Trust today adopted a resolution praising the service of O. H. Ingram, former vice president of the board, who died unexpectedly of a heart attack [*sic*] April 25.
>
> The resolution, presented by Chancellor Emeritus Harvie Branscomb, follows in full:
>
> On April 25 Orrin Henry Ingram, a member of this Board and a beloved friend of all of us, died suddenly and unexpectedly. The news was received with a sense of shock and of personal grief. Strong in physique, even tempered and good humored in temperament, moving more and more into a position of leadership amongst us, he was both a personal friend and a pillar of

strength to the University. Vanderbilt University and the members of its Board of Trust have suffered a great loss.

Hank Ingram, as we all knew him, was born in Eau Claire, Wisconsin. He graduated from the Wharton School of Business and Finance of the University of Pennsylvania, and moved to Nashville shortly thereafter. He quickly became an active member of the community, identified himself with many business, philanthropic, and educational activities, and soon became one of Nashville's most influential and beloved citizens.

In 1952 Mr. Ingram was elected to the Vanderbilt Board of Trust to complete the term of his friend, the late Brownlee Currey, and continued on the Board until his untimely death. He served on the Executive Committee of the Board, on the Finance Committee, on Planning and Development. In 1957 he gave much time to the work of a special committee to study the establishment of a graduate school of business in the University. In 1959 he was elected as one of the two vice presidents of the Board of Trust. In 1960 he was appointed as one of the members of the committee for the nomination of the Chancellor, and took an active part in the selection of Chancellor Heard. He was always interested in Vanderbilt athletics, was chairman of an informal committee to advise the officers of the University in this area, and later when this was made an official committee of the Board, was its chairman.

Hank Ingram was a person of great personal warmth, with a genius for friendship. His sincerity and candor won immediate respect. Much of his value in counsel arose from his obvious integrity. Because of the confidence which everyone had in him, he was able to resolve many difficult problems in personal and public relationships with which the University became involved. He was modest and unassuming. He was generous in his judgments, and in his gifts to the University. He was completely loyal to what he felt was right and to the people who he felt were true. He recognized that the University was an institution of unique significance for this region, and he gave it his loyalty and support.

THEREFORE, BE IT RESOLVED, That this Board of Trust does hereby express its deep gratitude for the years in which O. H. Ingram was a member of this Board and one of its officers, and for all of his service to Vanderbilt University;

BE IT RESOLVED, FURTHER, That we record upon the permanent records of the University our abiding appreciation of his life and work, and that we communicate to the members of his family our own sorrow and sense of loss, and our deep sympathy for them at this time of bereavement.

All these years later, in 2001, the Ingram family continues to play a role in the activities of Vanderbilt University, and Bronson certainly carried on the tradition. But I'll save those details for later. (See Chapters 8 and 10.)

Following the death of Mr. Ingram, "Bronson took care of Mother and helped her with Daddy's will and his complicated business affairs," recalled his sister Patricia. Bronson at age thirty-one was faced with the task of running Ingram Corporation. He expected to be in that position someday and had been in training for it, but that day arrived much sooner than he or anyone else could have anticipated.

CHAPTER 4

Ingram Corporation

Hats off to the past; coats off to the future.
—American proverb

At the time of Mr. Ingram's death, Bronson was working with him in Nashville and looking after the barge business, a business that he happened to like very much. His brother, Fritz, was in New Orleans, pursuing some of his own business interests. When Fritz wanted to become more involved with Ingram Corporation, Bronson said, "Why don't you act as chairman? We'll put it all under the same corporate umbrella. There are certain economies of doing that, with staff functions and so on." So Fritz as chairman oversaw the parts in New Orleans, and Bronson as president oversaw the parts in Nashville.

Because they had the two offices, Bronson flew back and forth every week. For a time he flew himself. After we had several children, he had a very close call, and I think he scared himself and I know he scared me enough that I told him I was going to take up flying. He said, "If I've scared you that badly, the notion of your taking up flying scares me worse. We will have a professional pilot from here on." Once he had somebody else to do the flying, he used the time to study or to read.

Maryanne Davidson started working in Bronson's office on January 18, 1965, as his secretary. She described what he was like in those early days: "It was really hard for him to let go of a lot of things. He later on learned how to delegate." On a typical day, she said, "he would come in, in the morning, he would read his mail, and he would immediately sort it out and answer it at once. Mr. Ingram never put off anything. He never had a desk cluttered up. He would read everything that came across his desk. *Wall Street Journal*, trade papers, he was just a voracious reader. He learned so much from the magazines. He really would read everything."

She summed up his relationships with associates in the corporation: "People that worked directly under him had a great deal of respect for his business acumen. He was not easy to work with because he expected so much, but by that I mean they gave more and they respected him. He wasn't just a guy that was going to sit down and let things slide. And they knew that and they had to perform. It was a pleasure to work for him when you lived up to his expectations and when you knew that you did something that you did right and something that helped him, and he was very generous with his compliments. He would tell anybody, 'That's a damn good job you did,' or 'You really found a good company,' or 'I'm proud of the way you did that.' He was quick to compliment, and he was quick to cuss." You might as well know that Bronson's favorite word was *goddamnit*.

Before long, the numbers were getting big as Ingram Corporation diversified and expanded beyond Ingram Barge and Ingram Materials, eventually to international sites. The four primary expansion areas included ocean transportation, petroleum, oil and gas pipeline construction, and service subsidiaries. The brothers were back in the oil business. A book company also entered the corporate picture, a venture that would seem to defy Bronson's dictum to "work with what you know." Later on I'll explain how that endeavor came about.

Fritz and Bronson seriously considered taking the company public. They went so far as to submit an SEC filing in 1970, which summarized the corporation's activities and provided a complete list of subsidiaries. They did not pursue the idea, however, because of the general business climate of that time.

The offshore contracting business needed continuous substantial capital investments in order to effect technical improvements and meet industry requirements. The company had derrick barges in Indonesia, the Gulf of Mexico, the Bahamas, Brunei, and Australia. In 1968, principal offshore platform and pipelaying activities occurred in Brazil and Australia, and in 1969, as many as three of the company's derrick barges were used in Australia. To give you some idea of the diversity in 1969, the offshore contracting revenues were 59 percent, inshore contracting 25 percent, inland waterway opera-tions 8 percent, book operations 7 percent, and other activities 1 percent. As of January 31, 1970, the corporation employed approximately 2,345 people.

The management included the following people: Fritz, director and chairman of the board; Bronson, director and president; W. J. Benton, director and senior vice president; John M. Donnelly, director and vice pres-ident; Bruce K. Brown, director and management consultant; Hortense B. Ingram, director; E. L. Kennedy, director (a partner in Lehman Bros.); Thomas B. Lemann, director (an attorney); J. A. O'Neill Jr., director, president of Trans Ocean Petroleum Inc.; E. L. Hukill, vice president; D. B. Cobb, vice president; E. M. Ornelles, vice president and controller; T. O. Lind, secretary; and G. R. Galloway, treasurer.

Ingram Derrick Barge No. 3 installing a drilling platform in the Gulf of Mexico.

The subsidiaries were Ingram Materials Inc.; Cumberland and Ohio Company, Inc.; Universal Marine Insurance Co., Ltd.; Ingram Book Company; Tennessee Book Company; Ingram Contractors Inc.; Ingram Pipeline Inc.; Little Lake Towing & Dredging Co., Inc.; Ingram Services Inc.; Ingram Marine Inc.; Ingram Industries Inc.; Ingram Overseas S.A.; Ingram International S.A.; Ingram Contractors S.A.; Ingram Contractors Limited; Contratistas Ingram de Mexico S.A. de C.V.; Ingram Contractors Australia Pty., Ltd.; Trans Ocean Petroleum, Inc.; Ingram

The Tennessee Book Company. Management Inc.; Ingram Contractors Indonesia Inc.; Ingram Far East Pte. Ltd.; Ingram Ocean Systems Ltd.; John Paisios & Associates Ltd.; Pipe Line Technologists, Inc.; and Great Plains Construction Company.

Mr. Ingram named towboats after friends and family members, and Bronson continued the practice by naming one after my father, the *M/V John M. Rivers.* My mother christened the 4,000 horsepower towboat, built by the Nashville Bridge Company. After the event, my father wrote Bronson this letter:

> I am enormously flattered to have the useful, and I think most attractive, towboat named after me. I believe you could see Mama's absolute delight at her participation in the happy event, and I cannot completely get over the enthusiasm of our friends in Nashville at the opportunity to participate. First, I think so many of them had no concept of the operation you conduct, and those who did have the concept had really never done anything more than perhaps pass by one of these ships when they were on an outing on the river. To get a close look was a treat to all of them, and I think you will be pleased to note that many people said a year from now if you came back you would see a spick-and-span ship, just as she was on the day of her christening. This, to me, indicates sound management, which I have not always practiced myself, a hand-me-down from your illustrious father.

A tugboat named in my honor rated a write-up in the New Orleans paper, the *States-Item*, on June 7, 1971:

> The assistant secretary of commerce for maritime affairs said today vessels like the ocean-going tug-and-barge system which Ingram Ocean System christened here today likely will rebuild the nation's coastal trade.
>
> Andrew Gibson said maritime unions, which might be expected to complain because of smaller manning scales on tug boats, had "not been heard from at all" because of the increased trade such systems will provide.
>
> He said so much of our coastwise trade is being handled by railroads, trucks and pipelines that increased use of systems such as Ingram's can "do nothing but have a positive impact on sea-going employment."
>
> Gibson was in New Orleans for the christening of the new concept ocean tug and barge at the site of the French Road Containership Terminal this afternoon.
>
> The barge, built by Alabama Dry Dock and Shipbuilding Co. in Mobile, has a U-shaped opening at the stern in which the tug sits, locking with hydraulic rams in a linkage system developed by Breit Engineering Inc. of New Orleans.
>
> The tugboat was built in Slidell by the Southern Shipbuilding Co. and was to be christened the M/V Martha R. Ingram by Mrs. E. Bronson Ingram, wife of the president of Ingram Corporations.
>
> Fritz Ingram, chairman of the board of Ingram Corporations, today hailed the development of the locking system used in the giant tug-barge combination as "another dramatic maritime development to come out of New Orleans," mentioning also the LASH (barge-ship) system and Lykes Seabee Barge-ship system similarly as dramatic New Orleans developments.
>
> Ingram said he has another barge and ship in the building phase, and he hopes to have four to six more units under construction by the end of the year.
>
> Cost of the tugboat-barge combination was put at close to $10 million. "A similar-sized ship," Gibson said, "would have cost $16 million to $18 million."

Gibson, in his speech prepared for delivery at the christening, heralded the new technology "because it brings the low-cost transportation system now available on our inland waterways to our coastal traffic."

The future of that division seemed quite hopeful at a time that the offshore contracting business was causing concern. Bronson and Fritz decided to sell it in 1971. Bronson made periodic reports to shareholders (mostly family members but a few employees), and he summed up the decision in the November 15, 1971, report: "The results of our offshore contracting businesses for 1971 and the outlook for 1972 brought us to the reluctant conclusion that we could much more profitably deploy our assets in the marine transportation field than by continuing in the offshore business. We simply were not big enough to do both and had to make a choice." More than once in his future career, Bronson would revisit the problem of not being "big enough." But instead of selling, he would begin buying.

A major undertaking was the joint partnership of Ingram Corporation and Northeast Petroleum Industries to build a 200,000-barrel-a-day petroleum refinery near New Orleans at San Francisco Plantation, beginning in 1973. Called ECOL (Energy Corporation of Louisiana), it was to be the first of its kind in the nation. It was to be the first built with Mideast and Arab equity participation, and the first designed to refine mostly fuel oil instead of gasoline. The scheduled completion date was late 1975 or early 1976.

Bronson granted a rare interview to discuss the project, which was reported in the *Tennessean*, September 21, 1973:

Ingram said negotiations are under way with the oil-producing Mideast countries for an equity interest in Energy Corp. of Louisiana in exchange for long-term crude supply contracts. They are highly interested in the idea and details will be worked out long before the plant is completed, he said.

Also, he said, Ingram Corp. is interested in the transportation of the crude, and will have an important part in it, but the arrangements are yet to be worked out.

The 1972 christening of the Astraman, part of the Rowbotham fleet: V. D. Thorne, Rowbotham's company secretary; David Cobb, a Rowbotham director; Christopher Rowbotham; P. A. Rowbotham, Rowbotham's managing director; Mrs. V. D. Thorne, vessel sponsor; P. Curtis, director of Drypools Shipyard; Mrs. Christopher Rowbotham; Bronson, Ingram Corporation president; and Martha.

"The value of the transportation during the life of the contracts will be well above the value of the refinery," he said.

Ingram said refineries built in this country in the last 10 to 15 years are designed to produce mostly gasoline, but that the Louisiana plant will produce [mostly fuel oil].

"The gasoline demand and its value has been the leading growth component of crude, and its rate and profit has been higher at the refinery in recent years," he said.

"Now we believe we are facing much higher energy prices, with gasoline prices to rise rapidly as they have in Europe where you don't see big cars any more.

"You can form car pools and turn to smaller cars, but you can't change industrial and heating requirements, so the demand for fuel oil will outgrow that for gasoline as a percentage.

"Since we see no big growth in demand for gasoline, we chose the cheaper fuel oil plant, and since the Mideast has practically the only large crude pool known, we are setting up to refine the high sulphur product from there—something that few in the U.S. are designed for," he added.

He said that on the world market diesel fuel is now selling as high or higher than gasoline.

The Louisiana refinery will be the first of a group of new plants needed in this country to supply future needs, Ingram said.

He pointed out that a study by Shell Oil Co. indicates that if the demand for petroleum could be met by U.S. companies, it would take the output of 70 new refineries by 1980, each with the production of 200,000 barrels a day.

Consider these points he made almost thirty years ago in light of today's energy realities.

Great Plains Construction Company, a subsidiary of Ingram Corporation, was a major joint venture participant in laying the two most northerly sections of the Trans-Alaskan Pipeline. Those sections represented one-third of the line, and weather conditions were brutal. The contract was awarded in 1974.

In 1974, Ingram Corporation participated in large marine construction, refinery construction, and petroleum sales programs, in addition to pipeline construction. Ingram Maritime Company Limited closed a transaction to acquire Richard Dunston Industries, which had two small shipyards near Hull, England. By the end of the year, Bronson reported to stockholders: "The economy is certainly in a recession which will probably be deeper and more prolonged than the politicians will yet admit. Despite the recession and high money costs, we expect to have a satisfactory year and, at this point, still expect 1975 to be our best year ever by a significant margin as some of our major capital programs start to come onstream and earn a return."

As of September 1, 1974, Ingram Corporation had acquired all of the voting stock of Tampimex. Bronson told stockholders, "It is the premier petroleum trading company in Western Europe, with important activities in this country." A more public announcement did not occur until the next year. Then the *Nashville Banner* reported, on February 12, 1975:

> Ingram Corp. of Nashville and New Orleans has acquired Tampimex Holding AG of Switzerland, one of the world's oldest and largest oil trading companies, the *Banner* has learned.
>
> The major financial merger, completed several months ago, is to be announced from New Orleans and London today.
>
> The transaction, shrouded with mystery over the secret identity of the former owners of the trading company and their unexplained reason for selling, may make Ingram Corp. an almost $2 billion a year business by the end of 1976 and is expected to place it in a prime spot in the world oil trading market.
>
> Information about the merger is to be released jointly by Frederic B. (Fritz) Ingram, chairman of the board of Ingram Corp., New Orleans, and M. G. Schubert, managing director of Tampimex Oil Products Ltd., London.
>
> Tampimex Oil Products Ltd. is the foremost of a dozen subsidiaries of Tampimex Holding AG.
>
> Ingram Corp.'s acquisition includes all voting stock of the Zurich-based holding company, which also has major offices in Hamburg, New York and Houston.
>
> Neither Ingram of New Orleans nor Schubert plan to disclose financial terms of the deal in their announcement, but E. Bronson Ingram, Nashville, president of Ingram Corp., confirmed the transaction and said Tampimex, as one of Ingram's holdings, will be "far and away the biggest of our operations in terms of volume."
>
> In 1974, the Tampimex group purchased and resold more than 200,000 barrels per day of crude oil, refined products, and chemicals in their worldwide operation—accounting for gross sales of almost $1 billion.
>
> In a report prepared several months ago, Ingram Corp.—whose subsidiary activities include petroleum and chemical transportation and refining—predicted the Nashville–New Orleans company's sales will be more than $1 billion annually by the end of next year, indicating a combined gross for the two firms possibly as high as $2 billion in 1976.
>
> The merger was transacted between officials of Ingram and the Private Bank and Trust Co., Zurich, with Schubert participating

for management. Owners of Tampimex never have been revealed publicly, even to Ingram Corp., according to Bronson Ingram.

"The former owners are out of the picture completely now," Bronson Ingram said.

"They had good reason to sell and empowered management (headed by Schubert) to choose a new buyer, and management chose us."

Tampico, Mexico, is the origin of the name Tampimex, an Ingram official said, but the owners are not Mexicans. They named the company Tampimex because when they formed it in the 1920s, its principal activity was buying bitumin—used in making asphalt or blacktop—in Tampico and marketing it in Europe, particularly Germany. . . .

Once Tampimex decided to sell, it wasn't surprising it selected Ingram to buy. The two companies, according to officials of Ingram and Schubert, have had a "long, co-operative relationship."

Frederic Ingram said Tampimex will continue to be managed by its present board of directors in London and Schubert will continue as managing director of the Tampimex group.

Ingram's trading operation, Trans Ocean Petroleum of New York, will be melded into Tampimex' operations, adding some of Ingram's management to Tampimex, according to Bronson Ingram.

The merger provides distinct advantages to Ingram and Tampimex—it provides Tampimex the resources of Ingram's petroleum and chemical transportation and refining facilities, and it provides Ingram with the prestige of Tampimex' reputation as an oil trader.

Most Middle East oil-producing countries want to trade exclusively with refiners, Bronson Ingram said. "Tampimex' management feels it will help Tampimex maintain its position as one of the preeminent, if not the most preeminent, traders in the world to be tied to an independent refinery."

Ingram Corp. owns 50 per cent of the $300 million Energy Corp. of Louisiana (ECOL) refinery under construction 35 miles north of New Orleans. The ECOL refinery's capacity will be 200,000 barrels a day—the same number of barrels Tampimex traded per day last year—when it is completed and operating at full production by mid–1976.

Ingram did not say so, but conceivably Tampimex may buy oil from one party, sell it to another, then transport it in Ingram tankers and barges to the Ingram–ECOL refinery from almost any point in the world.

Ingram Corp. benefits additionally, Bronson Ingram said, because it has been trying through its New York trading subsidiary "to break into the world oil trading game for five years. It's very difficult to build the reputation necessary to do that."

Traders are a different breed from brokers. Brokers bring buyers and sellers together, then get out with commissions, but traders actually buy oil, hold it in inventory at times, then sell. Their fraternity is exclusive, made up mostly of old European firms and the largest oil companies in this country.

"The profits are much greater in trading," one Ingram official said, and with the merger of Ingram and Tampimex, Ingram not only gets into the lucrative world oil trading game, it gets in near the top.

In addition to its inland river and ocean petroleum and chemical transportation operations, and its ownership in the ECOL refinery, Ingram Corp. includes subsidiaries involved in pipeline construction, book wholesaling, and insurance.

The corporation's newsletter, *Ingram News*, published a February 1975 interview with Bronson on inflation:

The bulk of revenue required for government programs can come from only one source—people.

Any business, whether marginally or highly successful, needs a continuing infusion of new capital [and there are three sources of capital]: the sale of additional equity shares, the borrowing of money, or the reinvestment in the business of after-tax earnings.

Continuing inflation leads to political instability under which governmental, economic, and social progress becomes difficult to achieve.

If our entire system changes, it will be because we have not demanded that our government eliminate its inefficiencies and adopt a sound economic program. Congress can play politics with our way of life, but when the piper must be paid, he will be paid by us.

> We should stop our throw-away attitude. . . . We must demand that our government become more efficient in the use of the income we as people allocate to it through taxes.

And in management memos to employees, he elaborated on his views of government and politicians:

> Be on the alert for those politicians who would advocate short term panaceas (which bring on long term costs) as opposed to those who would apply short term costs and sacrifices to achieve realistic long term benefits.

> Put those men in office who have the courage to strive for what is truly best for America. Such men do exist and when they run for political office they deserve our full support.

> When society turns increasingly to government for the solution of all of its perceived needs, it feeds upon itself. And as history has taught us, such a society cannot survive.

> A large and growing number of people are becoming aware of the close connection between government actions and inflation, interest rates, business conditions and the like. They have become government watchers! Join them!

The outlook for the firm was promising, despite a weak economy, Bronson told stockholders on April 2, 1976,

> 1975 was a satisfactory year under the prevailing economic conditions with the beginnings of recovery from the deepest recession of modern time. Earnings were $5,005,000, or $0.53 per share, which are approximately equal to 1974, and produced a year-end book value of $3.52 per share.
>
> Energy consumption in this country and Europe was off dramatically from prior year expectations due to effective conservation at all levels caused by the tremendous increase in energy prices as well as another mild winter. Our petroleum barging, shipping, and trading operations were all adversely affected by excess equipment and soft product markets and thus showed lower profitability than we had projected going into 1975. These

markets remain soft today but the latest figures show demand starting to pick up rapidly and we expect all these markets to firm as we get further into 1976.

Our pipeline business had quite a good year in 1975, and expects this year to be better with significant revenues and earnings from the Iranian project. . . .

We continue to expect start up of the ECOL refinery in October. Construction is progressing well within cost tolerance and we continue to work with the Federal Energy Administration to see that their various programs will not adversely affect our economics.

Bronson's hopes for ECOL were soundly dashed, however. Ingram Corporation sold ECOL to Marathon Oil in September 1976. Bronson explained why: "The decision to sell ECOL was made with great reluctance, but was forced upon us by the Federal Energy Administration when they totally reneged on every agreement and guaranty they had made with ECOL. In effect, they threw us to the wolves for what I can only judge to have been short-term political expediencies. It was fortunate for us that Marathon had sufficient long-term interest in a Gulf Coast refinery so that we could put a deal together with them in a week's time after having turned them down cold earlier in the summer."

Roy Claverie, who retired from Ingram Industries as a senior vice president, clarified what happened: "We had been assured by the Federal Energy Administration, which was a new creation in the government, that they supported grassroots refineries [a grassroots refinery is built from scratch, not adding to an existing refinery]. They were very concerned about the shortage of products, and they were promoters of new refineries. They helped promote this particular refinery. When it got time for the refinery to be complete and to come onstream, the government had enacted a new program which put a penalty on residual fuel that would flow into the East Coast and that penalty that the government later enacted would have literally driven the company out of business. So, in the end, before we processed the first barrel of oil, the refinery was sold to Marathon."

But with all of the emphasis on oil and barges and ships, Ingram Corporation was involved in the book business, too. Bronson didn't set out to be in that business. He was an oil man, after all, and he was just helping a friend, he thought, by investing in a portion of a book business in 1964. This "little" business mushroomed into the largest wholesale distributor of trade books in the United States, and it started Bronson into a whole new line of work—distribution.

Jack Stambaugh, a retiring vice chancellor of Vanderbilt University, had been a friend of Bronson's father. Jack was trying to figure out what to do next because he considered himself still a young man, not ready to retire completely. He found Tennessee Book Company, owned by Forrest Reed, which was a textbook depository for Tennessee schools. Jack asked Bronson if he would put up half of the money to buy the company, and Jack would put up the other half. Bronson agreed on one condition: "Sure, Jack. But you will run it."

Phil Pfeffer, who was an executive vice president of Ingram Industries, told the story, as Bronson told it to him, of the negotiations for the book company: "When they were in negotiations with Mr. Reed, they hadn't decided on what the price would be, but they were definitely interested in buying the business. So, what they decided to do was, Mr. Reed would write down a number on a piece of paper, and Bronson [representing Jack Stambaugh and himself] would write down a number on a piece of paper. Then each would turn their pieces of paper over and see where they were. And as it turned out, they both wrote down the same number."

They had a book company, and Jack must have had second thoughts about running it himself. He talked with Bronson about hiring somebody else to oversee the company's operations. John Beasley was then working at Vanderbilt University (and is still there as vice chancellor, emeritus) and had known Jack through the school connection. John had met Bronson during Bronson's freshman year at Vanderbilt, but it was only a casual acquaintance. John said, "Stambaugh approached me, I'm sure on their joint behalf—he wouldn't have done that without Bronson's knowledge—to see if I would be willing to consider coming to work and running the Tennessee Book Company. They sent me away to Chicago to be interviewed by this high-powered shrink [John Paisios] who really was quite wonderful. I made it a condition that I would have to see what this guy said about me because I was as interested as they were, although that is normally not the pattern. This guy correctly spot-lighted where I was, if you will, full of manure. It was really quite revealing to me about myself, so it was worth a whole lot.

"They offered me the job, and I don't know how to say this without this sounding critical and I don't mean for it to sound critical, but I did not want to work for either one of those guys as an employee. I said I would come to work for them if they would sell me a third of the business, but they weren't about to do that."

That left Jack Stambaugh to run the company, and he did for a while. Unfortunately, his wife became ill with emphysema and needed to live in a desert environment to improve her health. After they moved, the book company was rudderless. Bronson came home one day and told me what happened, and he said, "What in the hell am I going to do with this little Tennessee book depository? I know nothing about that. I consider myself an oil man. I guess I better go out there and find somebody to run it."

He found Harry Hoffman, a marketer for the book company. He had been a library wholesaler in Wisconsin, he had worked for Bell and Howell, and for Procter and Gamble, and he had been an FBI agent. Bronson thought he had potential. "I have been talking to Harry and told him if he would step into the chief position, I think I can teach him how to run a business." Bronson spent one day a week teaching Harry about profits and losses and balance sheets.

Harry Hoffman was responsible for the birth of the application of the microfiche, a true innovation in the book business. To expand the business, Harry suggested to Bronson that they make a film, a micro-fiche, of everything in the inventory so that we could sell to libraries. The idea worked, and we sold good quantities of books to libraries because of Lyndon Johnson's Great Society program. Then suddenly as the Vietnam War heated up, the library money was closed off. What could we do next?

Harry and Bronson decided that we would try to get bookstores to buy from us because at that time they were buying solely from the publishers. We soon found that there was a very receptive audience. It took as long as six weeks for them to get books from publishers, and if we could keep some in our warehouses and have the books at the bookstores in a day or two, we had customers who were willing to order just from us. That business grew and grew and grew, and we built ever larger warehouses around the country.

A running company joke had its start with Harry's request to Bronson: he wanted to carry about 500 titles that bookstores would buy. Bronson told him no more than that. Bronson's financial discipline was at work because it would have been easy to overload the inventory and all of that comes to the cost. That could sink the business rapidly. The only thing was, with the growth of the company, Harry had to keep going back to Bronson—asking for 1,000, then 1,500, and on and on. Then Harry's successors had to ask for more, and the number rose to 400,000 by 1998. In 2001, Ingram Book stocked 600,000 titles in warehouses; in addition, the company offered a comprehensive database giving booksellers access to the 1.5 million titles in print.

In 1970, the sales to bookstores were going so well that we created Ingram Book Company for that market, and eventually, Tennessee Book Company became a sister company of Ingram Book Company. Phil Pfeffer commented on the development of Ingram Book: "In 1972, the company began to take orders via the telephone and began to use microfiche as a way of passing on to the customer the catalogue of what Ingram Book Company had in inventory at any point in time. That was one of the big problems in getting a business like this going: your customers needed to know what titles you carried and it was a constantly changing environment.

"As far as the book industry was concerned, Ingram Book Company was responsible for bringing microfiche into play. And it became a standard in the book industry for wholesalers who were selling to library accounts and to bookstore accounts and even some publishers began to use microfiche as well. The Ingram microfiche reader became a basic feature in every bookstore in the country."

Ingram Book Company received its own computer, an IBM Model 40 system, in December 1973. Until then all of the data processing had been done at National Life and Accident Insurance Company. It's hard to believe how dependent on computers businesses have become throughout the world. Before microcomputers, everything was done by hand, on paper. And our family's involvement with the computer industry has come a long way from the purchase of that lonely Model 40.

Another innovation by Ingram Book Company sprang from the on-line order entry system introduced in 1975. The customer could call an 800 number and place an order, which the operator keyed in on a computer terminal at Ingram. Phil Pfeffer explained, "In order to make it go very quickly, we established for each title a five-digit title code, and we communicated the title code on our fiche for our customers. This was an Ingram-assigned number because there was no standard in the industry for numerically identifying new books or any book." The standard now is the ISBN (International Standard Book Number). Ingram didn't establish the ISBN, but Ingram's use of title codes was a catalyst in bringing about the ISBN.

Phil joined Ingram in 1977 as director of financial planning. He noted at that time, "From a financial standpoint, understanding the dynamics of the business, Bronson was very much involved. He did not get involved in publisher relations. He did not get involved in customer relations." He did not go to the meetings of the American Booksellers Association; Harry did all of those things. By 1978, Bronson's involvement with the book company would change dramatically, as would Phil's position.

Throughout the years with Ingram Corporation, Bronson made many personal investments. From the mid–1960s until his death, Bronson communicated regularly with Henry Levy of Goldman-Sachs in Memphis about his portfolio. "Bronson always took the long view," Henry recalled. And Bronson helped him connect with others in Nashville when he was getting started. He said, "Bronson was very helpful to me when the office first opened. He really opened doors for me in the Nashville community. We had a very genuine business relationship."

In the early 1970s, Bronson and Jake Wallace were silent partners in Capitol Chevrolet. The only other business deal between Jake and Bronson was Ingram-Armistead-Wallace, which ended in 1972 when the firm merged with another company.

My brother, John Rivers, had to decline a venture that Bronson brought to him: "Bronson asked me one time if I wanted to buy a TV

Dinnertime at the Ingram home when Bronson was away. Note the riding crop on the floor. Friends Anna and Bobby Morrow from Memphis created this cartoon.

station with him. It was Channel 5 in Nashville. I declined. We owned Channel 5 in Charleston. I was in my late twenties, and I had just taken over. My father had had a heart attack, and I was sort of overwhelmed and wasn't prepared to branch out into another operation at the time. But Bronson had the depth of personnel and the expertise to get into that then."

Business occupied so much of Bronson's time and energy that our son John as a very little boy, maybe four or five years old, asked me, "Mommy, do we still have a daddy?" Bronson spent two or three days a week in New Orleans—leaving on Tuesday and coming back on Thursday evening—and then he sometimes went on pleasure trips, usually to play golf or to fish. I was very quick to tell Bronson that his little children were beginning to wonder if they even had a father. I wanted him to be able to have pleasurable pursuits, but the children needed some of his time and attention. To be fair, I'm sure

Bronson thought that he was spending a lot of time with his children, and he tried to mitigate the situation when he realized that in their eyes it was not really the case.

He subsequently took them at very young ages, life preservers and all, on fishing trips. He wanted to do things he wanted to do, but he didn't want to be a bad father either. We went to the Bahamas during the children's spring break from school and stayed on the *Patsea IV*. We often went to White Bear Lake for the Fourth of July. For years we spent the first two weeks in August at Sea Island, Georgia, with old family friends: the Wallaces, the Tullises, and the Stovalls.

Jake Wallace offered this insight on Bronson's lack of desire to make new friends: "We were having a drink somewhere, and Martha was on his case about something and said, 'Come on, Bronson. You need to do this. After all you'll make some friends.' And Bronson turns and says, 'Martha, I've made all the goddamn friends I want to make in my life.' That's the way he felt. Well, to us, however many there were, that meant a lot because we knew what he meant. And we laughed like hell about it when he said it because it was so typically Bronson. But to us, it meant that he trusted us."

While we were on vacation or even when Bronson was at home on the weekends, he had strict ground rules for employees: "Don't call me unless it's an emergency. If you do call me and it's not an emergency, God help you. But if you don't call me and it's an emergency, God help you."

Bronson tried to keep Saturday and Sunday as family days, after golf. Orrin summed up those days: "The afternoons were family times, and always on Sunday nights we had a Sunday dinner. My grandmother [Hortense Ingram] until she died would come over every Sunday night. I know I can cook a steak a lot better than Dad could. He would only flip it over once. Burned on both ends and pink in the middle. He thought they were supposed to taste like that. Mother used to cook, and she would try to cook fancy stuff that we wouldn't eat. That happened for years and years and years. We were used to more country cooking, and she tried to do heart healthy even back then."

Their father was very much a creature of habit. John offered details: "You could count on Dad waking up between 6:30 and 7:00. He would have breakfast about 7:30, and he was on his way to the office by about 8:00. He was always home by about 6:30. We would have dinner at 7:00. It wasn't 6:59 or 7:01. You better be there or have a damn good excuse. The 6:59 telephone call was not well appreciated [when they were teens and out and about]. You thought about it ahead of time. That was good and quite remarkable. I know I have a hard time doing that in a world where we have cell phones and what not. Business is conducted all the time everywhere now. It wasn't his way."

Orrin, David, and John with Bronson, December 1964.

From the time the children were very young, we had dinner at seven o'clock every night. Dinnertime was frequently lectures—from both parents—that might have seemed a bit severe, and I was often reminded, "Mother, you lecture us too much. You even explain your explanations." But dinner didn't last long. We didn't do dessert. Every now and again we ended up with a good conversation about current events as the children became older.

Bronson was stern enough that there was no food throwing or anything inappropriate at the table. When I was there by myself, sometimes things would get a little out of hand to the extent that I took a riding crop to dinner. I was determined to teach the children table manners, and the riding crop was a great enforcer. I did not use it often, but they all knew that I had used it and would again.

To this day, the children tell tales about how strict dinnertime was, yet all of them wrote at one time or the other when they were off at college, "Thank heavens, you taught us which fork to use. Thank heavens, you taught us how we were to behave because we see so many people that don't know. It wasn't all that much fun then, but we're glad you taught us how to do it." Maybe things had not been so bad at home.

If there was discipline to be meted out, sometimes I was guilty of saying, "Wait till your father comes home." Occasionally, the bad child was being bad to get attention. Sometimes I took one child with me while I ran errands or did some shopping, and the child had full attention all that time. But when I got him or her home, the child didn't want to give it up. Overall, the children were pretty good. Even growing up through the teenage years, they behaved amazingly well.

Part of it was fear of the father. I don't think it was fear of the mother at all. But it was almost like good cop/bad cop. They had me as their friend in court, and I would plead their case when their father clamped down on them. He was definitely the disciplinarian, but if he hadn't been, I would have been because I could not have stood to have bratty children. I felt as though it was too much for both of us at the same time to bear down. I guess we must have done it pretty well because they came out respecting both of us. I think if they had to choose the parent that they respected the most—I don't necessarily mean loved the most, although it may have been that, too—it would have been their father. They always asked, "What does Dad think?" As time went on, they understood more and more not only the effort it took to discipline them but how much he was really teaching them along the way.

Orrin figured out how to take problems to his father: "Dad was very strict. He would usually only tell you once, and then you would suffer the consequences. I learned early on that anytime I had a problem that was going to be a controversial problem, I didn't talk to him about it at home. I would make an appointment and come to the office and talk with him. It would always get resolved at the office. It would have been when I could get on my bike and ride over to the office [early teens]. He wanted to relax at home. He didn't want to deal with our problems, but if you could catch him when he had his problem mode going, it was the difference between night and day. I always appreciated that fact."

Robin commented on her approach to her father: "He'd come in the door, and I'd ask, 'Can I have a new pony?' He'd say, 'No!' Then I'd go, 'Mom!' Mother would talk to him to make him say yes. That was the way everything went. The boys would say, 'You handle your father so poorly. You need to wait at least until he has been in the door thirty minutes. You need to make an appointment.' It was terrifying to me. I didn't want to go to the office and have him sit behind his desk. I'd rather him say no."

Although he didn't display it often, Bronson had a well-developed sense of humor, and when he was amused, he had a hearty laugh. He could tell a good story, but rarely told a joke. He was not a practical joker, either; he didn't like to pull them or have them pulled on him. Some of the children's antics would amuse him, and he got a big kick out of my story of the tippytoe dancers and the legislator.

When I first started working toward establishing the Tennessee Performing Arts Center, a legislator said to me: "Mrs. Ingram, we don't really know why you want this thing. I'm sort of like the old farmer whose wife took him to Atlanta to see the ballet and he saw all of those girls running around on their tippytoes and he said to his wife, 'Honey, if they want those girls to look so tall, why don't they just hire tall girls in the first place?'" I thought, *Oh, dear, this is really going to be hard.* Bronson was not a particularly passionate advocate for the arts, but he had been exposed to enough of it that he understood how silly that statement was. It brought forth his hearty laugh.

Many things were guaranteed to make him explode, and I always worried that he might die of a heart attack because of his temper. Coming home and seeing the front hall strewn with books and coats infuriated him. He wanted to have his home absolutely neat, and with four children, achieving that was not easy. He had no tolerance for one child picking on another one. It didn't mean they never did. They just didn't do it very often around him. Bronson bellowed at the children, but somehow they seemed to think beyond it and not let it worry them too much. Nonfamily members did not fare so well; an outburst terrorized their friends—and sometimes mine!

He was very calm and very measured in dealing with real, honest-to-goodness crises. He exploded primarily over little, almost nitpicking things. His explosion was a way of releasing pressure, like blowing the top off a teakettle. He calmed down once he got it out of his system.

Anyone who was late absolutely drove him to distraction. He thought that it was the most selfish thing to behave as though your time was more important than anybody else's and to hold someone up by not being on time for an appointment. Nor did he have patience with untruths from the children or anyone else.

Both of us encouraged the children in various pursuits. Particularly in sports, Bronson wanted them to work to perfect their skills. He preached integrity in sports, playing by the rules. If you win, that's great. If you lose, you lose with dignity and congratulate your opponent. He didn't talk much about it, but I think that because he considered business a game of sorts, he wanted our youngsters to get the sense of winning, the sense of being able to lose, the sense of hard work that goes into the achievement. That was certainly part of it. Part of it was that they were very high energy, and all of us would have gone berserk if they hadn't had things to do.

Carter Stovall, Bronson, Eli Tullis, and Jake Wallace at the 1968 Belle Meade Classic.

When the children got home from school every day, we wanted them to have a break between school and study time. We did not want them just sitting down in front of the television, however. Our fifteen acres are in the city limits (we had purchased more acres to add to the original three), so we could not have horses on the property. Bronson's sister Alice had a place where we could keep ponies and later horses, and we went into other barn

Bronson reading The Night Before Christmas to our children in 1969.

situations after that. We arranged many riding lessons for the children. Each child had a series of pets: homing pigeons, game chickens, rabbits, dogs, cats, parakeets, owls, and gerbils. At one time or the other we probably had every conceivable domesticated animal.

David was fascinated with snakes. I took him to the library when he was a little boy, and he brought home books about various reptiles and snakes and typed out information on index cards. Of course, he wanted to have one of his own. When we decided that David seemed to be responsible enough for a ball python, he found out about one through Jones Pet Shop in Hillsboro Village.

The snake was to be a surprise for David's birthday, so I called the woman who had the snake, and she said, "I understand that you'd like to buy this snake for your son, but I would have to interview you first." Bronson and I drove to Madison, Tennessee, for our snake ownership interview. Ultimately, the woman decided that we were responsible people, and she would let us buy the ball python for our son.

We could not have asked for a more conscientious snake keeper. He had a series of snakes, and sometimes he had two or three at once. Even when David went to camp one summer, he provided for the snakes by using his BB gun to kill blackbirds, and he left a freezer full of dead blackbirds so that one of his friends, David Tune, could come by once a week and feed the snakes and clean out the cages. His friend would take the bird out of the freezer, defrost it, heat it up just enough to what would feel like body temperature, and feed it to the snakes. It was appalling to me, but that was what went on in our household.

David frequently went to the pet store to buy a white mouse or two to give to his snakes. Orrin thought, *If I raise mice, they multiply so quickly, I'll just go into a little business, and David can pay me, not the pet store, for the mice.*

That seemed to be a fine—and enterprising—idea. The only trouble was, Orrin fell in love with the mice, and he couldn't bear to have the babies fed to the snakes. We ended up with a cage full of mice, and David was still going to the pet store to buy mice to feed his snakes.

One day the cat couldn't stand it any longer. The mice were kept in a large bird cage on the Ping-Pong table. The cat kept pushing and pushing the cage until it fell off the table, and all of the mice spilled out. The cat nearly popped from eating mice. What he didn't eat, he killed and left. It was a mess. We had tears. Oh, dear, we had so many tears.

The snakes were constrictors. It was always horrifying to me to see them constrict a bird in the tree. If a bird made the mistake of landing, the snake would stun it and then constrict it to its death. We had some friends who were so terrified of the snakes that they were reluctant to visit.

Our friend Arnold Palmer came to town with his wife, Winnie, to stay with us for a night or two. The four of us were in the pool house. We were getting ready to have dinner, and the children were hanging around. One rule was that the snakes were never supposed to come into the main house; they were to be in the basement or outdoors. Well, the pool house is quasi-outdoors. David must have thought that he was not supposed to have a snake in the living room part of the pool house, so he tucked it behind a pillow on the sofa, and Arnie happened to sit down there.

I knew something was going on because David looked as though he was about to break out laughing. Well, Arnie moved the pillow, and there was this balled up python. A man I have seen so brave on the golf course nearly came apart. He was so stunned and shocked that he jumped and screamed.

David was totally pleased with himself. We were furious with him and really embarrassed because we never want our guests to be uncomfortable. His father spoke to him rather harshly about that. Arnie has never forgotten this episode, although I hope he has forgiven.

John and Orrin were interested in racing homing pigeons. On Sunday afternoons, Bronson would often drive them and the pigeons maybe thirty miles out of town, and they would see if they could get home before the homing pigeons found their way back. There was a trap door that they had to go through to get to their cages, which were outdoors, I'm glad to say. They would click in, and the boys would see which pigeon was the fastest.

Bronson also introduced them to gamecocks, and I tolerated the game chickens that were being raised in pens in our backyard. Why they fascinated him so, I have never quite understood, but as I said earlier, no one is perfect. I think he was interested in the innate meanness of gamecocks. They did not have to be trained to fight; they simply fought out of instinct.

One night, over my protests, Bronson took John, then age nine or ten, to the country to see a cockfight, which at that time was legal in Tennessee, although betting on the fight was not. Bronson had raised fighting chickens at home as a boy and had fought his chickens with those of his buddies, John Alden Rodgers and John Bransford. He considered cockfighting a sport and had introduced son John to this childhood interest of his.

That night I was already asleep when Bronson crept into our bedroom. To my muttered "How was it?" he said it was fine. The next morning when I asked John about the rooster fight—not really wanting to know many details—his eyes got large and he told me that he and his father had been "'rested." It seems the sheriff raided the fight, and even those only watching—not even betting—had their driver's licenses confiscated briefly and were given a stern

warning. (Their names were in the paper a few days later—not exactly something to be proud of!)

On the way out of the cockfighting area John had said to his father, "Mom is going to be very angry 'cause she told us not to come." Evidently, the sheriff, who was standing in the shadows, overheard this comment, for he stepped out and said, "Little boy, you should have listened to your mother, and your father should have listened to her, too."

Bronson had not told me a word of what happened the night before, nor did he say anything about it the next morning, but he never took John to another chicken fight where there was betting.

The children were totally responsible for their animals, but as parents, we had in the early days to remind them that the animals had to be fed and watered. As they got a little bit older, they had such pride in the pets and such affection for them, they cared for them without being reminded.

John M. Rivers Jr.; Orrin; Martha and John M. Rivers Sr.; John; Elizabeth Rivers Lewine and her husband Richard Lewine; Robin; Bronson; David; and Martha. Thanksgiving 1970, at the Lewines' wedding.

At the same time they pursued athletic endeavors. They had to be responsible for those, too, because I never checked to see whether they had the riding boots or the helmets or the golf clubs and whatever else they might need. If they didn't get it right, that was their problem.

Three of them—Orrin, John, and Robin—rode horses competitively in the hunter-jumper class. In fact, Orrin and John went on to a very high level of showing, and both now play polo. Robin rode in several national shows, including Madison Square Garden in New York City. David had riding lessons but did not care for riding. He preferred golf, partly to get more of his father's attention, I think, because his father was an avid golfer.

I sometimes felt as though we were not the most attentive parents because we were doing our own things. While we did show up occasionally at the horse shows or the golf tournaments, we weren't there regularly. We were in no way stage parents, so to speak, because we had so much going on, on our own. For me, it was to a large extent working to build the Tennessee Performing Arts Center, which took daily effort for eight years, from the concept in 1972 to opening night in 1980.

We certainly tried to minimize their ever blaming each other for something. It's very easy to say, "It wasn't my fault. So and so made me do it or whatever." That just didn't cut any ice with us. We weren't going to coddle them. Nobody makes you fail a test. You fail it because you didn't study. I never got a child up in the morning. If you didn't set your own alarm and get going, you just missed it. If you're late for school, that's your problem. If you miss your ride, then you just miss a day, and that's too bad. We had carpools (called hook-ups in Nashville), and occasionally, Bronson drove them. All they had to do was miss a time or two, and they missed being with their friends at school.

All of these experiences probably helped to make them the strong people that they are today. I'm very pleased with what the sports taught them about their responsibilities, about being competitive, about being an individual out there on your horse or in the golf tournament, and you're responsible for what happens. In the case of a horse, the horse might do something crazy, but you're on its back and you and the horse are the ones who have to say, "Well, we didn't do that very well," or "We did it great, and we won."

Bronson realized that parents don't do a very good job of teaching children things. He was much more likely to hire a pro for them or send them to receive instruction. As David's golf progressed, he and his father talked about it, but in the early levels, Bronson was off doing his own golfing. He was not patient enough to play with children in a sports setting when they were younger.

Winners in March 1970 at the Pro-Am Golf Tourney, Lost Tree Golf Club, Palm Beach, Florida: Bronson, John R. Pepper, Arnold Palmer, and Robert O. Law.

My golf was mediocre at best, so it was in no way offensive to me to have them dribbling the ball down the fairway. I can remember many times taking the three boys out on a golf course, playing six or nine holes, and one of them ending up in tears or mad at the others. It was not exactly the most relaxing thing a

John M. Rivers Jr.;
Martha and John M.
Rivers Sr.; David;
Martha; Orrin; Robin;
Bronson; and John.
Thanksgiving 1975,
Charleston, S.C.

person could do. But then David reached the point that playing golf with his mother was not all that exciting, and he had become so good that his father was delighted to play with him.

Bronson was content to leave religious instruction to the professionals also, and he much preferred to play golf on Sunday morning. We finally reached an agreement when I said, "Look, we don't have to do this forever, but until they're in high school, it's really important that they think that you think that the teachings of the church, the moral issues that are put before young people, are very important. I really need you there to help me keep order with these four squirming children."

I thought we should belong to the same church, and I was willing to become a Presbyterian, but Bronson said that he would join the Episcopal Church, my church, since I went much more than he did. I pointed out that he would have to take classes and then be confirmed. He said, "I'll

do it, but I'm not willing to do that with a whole bunch of other people."
I said, "Oh, dear. All right, let's see what I can work out."

At St. George's we had an assistant rector from England—Rev.
Sidney George Ellis, a charming man who had become interested in
our sons, particularly Orrin who was then going through a spiritual
awakening. I explained to him my difficulty with my husband about
taking the classes. He said, "Would he see me if I come to the house?"
I said, "I don't know. I'll ask him." Bronson agreed to see the rector at
the house and to receive instruction from him. He did receive the full
instruction, and he did join the church and went through the laying
on of hands with the bishop.

Bronson was never one who could be counted on to usher in
church or to do anything like sitting on the vestry, but he went to
church with us, although we took two cars. The minute church was
over, he headed to the golf course, and I stayed on while the children
were in Sunday school to bring them home afterward. He lived up
to the agreement until the children were in high school or
confirmed. I hope we laid the groundwork for moral standards or the
way one should live. I think it was definitely reinforced in church at
St. George's and then at Sunday school. The fact that their father
came for the services, even though he left to play golf, was something
that they duly noted.

Bronson and I traveled extensively even when the children were
fairly young. My parents would come from Charleston to stay with
them anytime we were out of the country. Our being away gave my
parents a chance to bond with our children. We always had domestic
help so that they didn't have to do the bathing and feeding and all that.
They were good at being surrogate parents and reading to them. The
children behaved quite well for them because my father was very like
my husband in that he had a commanding voice, and they didn't mess
around with him.

Although he often had to visit New York, Bronson strongly
disliked the city. He felt as though everybody was hustling him for
money; everyone was pushing and rude. On the other hand, he
adored going to London—the gentility, the manners, the punctuality,
the orderliness—all of that suited him wonderfully. He would go

there at any opportunity, business or otherwise. We went several times a year for business and combined the trip to play golf somewhere or do something pleasurable. I adore London, too, so he could always find me ready to go: have bags, will travel was my motto. After those businesses were sold, we went at least once a year and usually stayed at Claridge's.

We went to Hamburg, Germany, for the testing of a new tug-barge concept because the best tank-testing facility in the world was in Hamburg. We christened a derrick barge in Bordeaux, France, and a number of friends and business associates accompanied us for the celebration. We traveled otherwise to Scotland and Ireland because of golf. We also saw Rome and Venice. We went to South Africa on a bird-shooting safari with friends, and we traveled to Tokyo a couple of times on business with the Weyerhaeuser Board of Directors and slept on tatami mats in ryokans (inns).

I'm going to end this discussion of the family with letters from Bronson. He wrote the first one to Orrin's teacher, and it conveys his interest in seeing that the children did their schoolwork properly. He felt strongly about education—as I did and do—and he wanted to push them as hard as he could so that they would one day go to the best colleges.

March 8, 1967

Dear Miss Elizabeth,

Orrin and I have had a long talk this afternoon about his work and particularly about his paying attention. We have reached a deal between us, based on his future work, which involves both the pony he already has and a fishing trip he is very interested in making.

I would like to ask you to write me a brief note each Friday, covering his work for that week and his effort and attitude as well. Our deal is simply that when he brings home four good weekly reports in a row we will go on a weekend fishing trip that he seems to want very badly, and he can take his mother and/or his brother with us, if he wants to. On the other hand, if he brings home two bad reports in a row he is going to lose the use of his pony.

Since I understand your spring vacation starts next week, I would appreciate it if you would send me the first note then. I would also be glad to have any suggestions or advice you may have from time to time as we go along.

In the meantime, I will keep after him and I am hopeful that his attention problems will be relatively short lived.

Many thanks.
Sincerely,
E. B. Ingram

Bronson wrote these other letters to the boys when they were at camp. They let you see a side of him that may surprise many people. He signed each one, "Love, Dad."

June 20, 1973

Dear Boys,

Mommy just called me and read me several letters from each of you. It sounds as though all of you are doing very well with your various camping endeavors and earning the highest ranks in each of the various activities that each camp gives out.

David called this morning to proudly tell us he had caught a Copperhead with the help of his pal, Tune, and the Counselor. The idea really scared me to death but he told me in detail how careful they were and I have to admit he certainly seems to know what he is doing. On the other hand, even the greatest snake handlers get bit occasionally and I will be much happier if David will leave the poisonous snakes alone.

John seems to be mastering his sailing, even if he did tip over twice, which is all part of learning and kind of fun, and shot 47 for 9 holes of golf, which is spectacular if he counted all the shots. He also beat his Counselor at tennis, which will show you all how lucky you each are to be able to learn under Pro [Bill Lufler].

Orrin is off on his first overnight tonight and went on a long horseback trail ride yesterday and is about to admit, I think, that camp is not so bad after all.

Robin is thrilled with her day camp and was up bounding around the house at the crack of dawn in anticipation of going for her second day.

All the animals are fine and Scott [our yard man] and I are taking reasonably good care of them. We have two baby pigeons born Sunday. Two of the chicks are definitely red roosters. Ducky Jr. is fully feathered and spends most of his time in the pond splashing, and I am sure the snakes will be glad for David to come home and feed them. I have not gotten a gray rooster yet, John, but we will when you come home.

Orrin, Robin and your mother (with her garden gloves) are taking good care of Peter [the parakeet] and Robin lets him fly around your room every day or so to get some exercise. Puncher [the boxer dog] misses you boys and is like a shadow to Robin, or second best to me when I am home.

I am off to New Orleans in the morning but will be back Friday and we are very excited to have David—who is well, finally—coming home on Saturday. I will talk to you all on Sunday.

June 27, 1973

Dear Boys,

I am back in Nashville finally and had a chance last night to read and enjoy your letters.

I am delighted you are both getting along so well and finding an opportunity to do lots of what you each like best.

Things are quiet here with Robin going to day camp and seemingly enjoying every minute of it. David has devoured several more snake books since he got home and has now started on a three-day Pony Club instructional program whereby he has to be at Aunt Alice's at 7:30 each morning for the day. Evidently, he got Mom to take him and his snakes to the vet to see about some skin rash they had developed and it seems they caused consternation when they arrived at Dr. Griffith's. I gather one of them struck at Dr. Griffith, who nearly jumped out of his hospital, and Mom says Rodes Hart's eyes rolled completely around in his head. [The reference was to Rodes Hart Jr.] David was totally unconcerned and explained to everyone that the snakes were perfectly tame and wouldn't hurt anyone. Dr. Griffith gave him some ointment and hustled him out with the snakes in a box, just before the rest of the customers bolted.

Orrin, Timmy got a Fifth and a Seventh on your pony at the State Fair yesterday, which I think speaks very well for the good job you have done in training Foxy, since he obviously had not been schooled for the show and Timmy is hardly a professional campaigner. I suspect you would have done better and you will have your chance in the rest of the shows when you get home. It is lucky you have plenty of chances to practice your riding and handling young horses there at camp.

Johnny, you sound like Daddy talking about the "bleeping" boat that fouled you in the Sunfish race. I am glad you were so close to the front when it happened and know exactly how frustrating it is to get caught dead into the wind with no steerage, since I managed to do that in a big, heavy wind in the next to last race I ever sailed in the inland in the "E" boat when I was leading the race and ahead of Bud Melges, who won the Olympics this year. I finally came in second in the race and was still mad at myself.

Orrin, we won't have a chance to go to White Bear after you boys come home before Granny [Hortense Ingram] goes away on her cruise, since we are going to Charleston for Granddaddy's 70th birthday instead. [Granddaddy was my father, John Rivers.]

June 29, 1973

Dear Boys,

More happy letters from both of you, for which I am delighted. There is not a lot going on here that you are missing. David is still at the Pony Club training session and now has your pony, John, since his pony was lame the first day. He seems to be enjoying it and from his comments getting along well. Robin has her first camp out tonight, which means we will have a basket case on our hands tomorrow.

I have word from Mom that John wants to know all about the animals. The chickens are doing fine and we have two young stags and a pullet. One hen is setting and since the eggs can't possibly hatch I am going to have Scott break up the nest. I have not done anything about a gray rooster since I thought we would go out to Mr. Mayfield's together when you boys get home. The young pigeons are fine. The snakes seem to be getting along fine. Dolly has been eating and shedding at the same time, which David says is a tremendous rarity. My report is that their skin rash is improving. There seems to be more mice than we need or want and I gather some have ended up as snake food. Some others have gotten loose, while the remaining sinks and aquariums are still full. We may have to have a new policy when you boys come home.

I have thoroughly enjoyed John's sailing stories and I am delighted you are doing so well. Now you know why I thought sailboat racing was such fun when I was growing up. Orrin, your letters are so sparse that I don't know much about what you are doing, other than riding, breaking, and feeding the horses, but the reports from your and John's counselors are very good, which makes me know it is all worthwhile.

The fishing in the Gulf is supposed to be very good this year for the first time since I can remember and we are planning to go a week from today with the Tullises. We will come back Sunday night and I will probably ask Elmour [Meriwether, the pilot] to meet you, Orrin, and bring you home. I have found just today that I probably have to go to New York Sunday night to be there for two meetings on Monday, so I will probably not be home to talk to you, Orrin, on Sunday night when you call. I won't be able to write you boys on Monday, but will on Tuesday. We miss you both very much.

July 3, 1973

Dear Boys,

I hope you both have a fine time on the 4th of July, though we will miss you here when we go to see the fireworks. I am sure that each of your camps will have a fine program and that you will have some fireworks and other displays there.

Granny called last night to say that Aunt Patricia and Uncle Rodes had a bad wreck at White Bear in Granny's car but luckily were not hurt badly, just bruised up a little. The people in the other car were not as lucky and were taken off in an ambulance to the hospital, but I don't know anything about their condition today.

John, I laughed myself sick last night when I got home over your letter about the shrimp and hushpuppies in the restaurant in Morehead City. I am sure you were wise not to go out fishing in a small boat if it was really rough and that you had just as good a time in the surf. Uncle Fritz said the fishing in the Gulf last weekend was good and we are going to try it this weekend with the Wallaces and the Tullises. If it stays good I will take you boys.

Orrin, I gather from Mom that she had told you about your birthday present, which is Peter's twin and a new cage. They sing constantly and if they are having half as much fun as they sound like we may have to charge them rent to live around here.

All the other animals are fine, with lots of pigeons on the nest. Mr. Rodgers [John Alden Rodgers] is fixing up a loft and I have told him we will give him some young birds, so I am letting all of ours get at it and only throwing away the eggs on the floor.

Orrin, Elmour will meet you on Sunday and we will see you later Sunday afternoon and be happy to have you home. Then we get John the end of next week and have everyone back together. That I will like.

July 9, 1973

Dear John:

We had a fine fishing trip this weekend with the Wallaces and Tullises and had perfect weather and very calm seas for all three days. There was a pretty rip each day and more dolphin, bonito, and bait fish than you could believe. We caught so many dolphin that we had to start throwing them back the second day, since all the freezers were full including those at the dock at South Pass. The dolphin were big for the most part and Mom caught one that must have weighed 40 pounds. On Friday I hooked a blue marlin and had him through his first run and first jump when somehow or other the leader broke on his first jump. Whether it was bill wrapped or had a kink, I don't know, but so it goes in my quest to catch one. On Saturday we had another one up and as it was striking Bob [the mate] panicked and gunned the boat. I hollered at him that the fish wasn't hooked and to slow down, which he did, but unfortunately stopped whereupon the bait sunk and the fish swam away. We never saw another billfish but late Friday we saw a broad bill sword fish that must have weighed close to 1,000 pounds cruising along and we got him to follow our baits for about 100 yards (we were using big blue runners) but he never tried to strike. I am not sure all of us in the boat could have held him. The only problem with all the fishing was that the blue water was 2–1/2 hours out each way, each day, so that it took an awful lot of running. The Captain [Sweeting] and Bob sent you their best and kept saying it was too bad you weren't there with all the action we had from spinning tackle on up. We will go again when you get home.

Orrin came home yesterday and is really happy to be home. I don't think camp was much fun for him this year, but he has gone to a Pony Club rally today and is all cheered up and in good shape.

David and Timmy Hooker flew to White Bear yesterday commercial and had to change planes by themselves in Chicago. The Delta agent helped them and Granny said they jumped off the plane in Minneapolis as happy as two larks. By last night, they had been sailing, fishing, played tennis, had dinner at the Yacht Club and still weren't wound down. I am sure Granny will enjoy having them there.

We will be delighted to have you home. Unfortunately, I have to go to California this weekend but Mom will meet you and I will see you on Monday. Your letters sound as though you are having a grand time and I am delighted your sailing is doing so well and that you are beating everybody at tennis. I will help you a little with your golf when you get home.

June 27, 1974

Dear Boys,

We are back home, as you know, and pretty well adjusted to the time so that things are close to normal again. Your mother has jumped back into her project [TPAC] and thanks to Mrs. Bush [his secretary, Maryanne] I can write you a decent letter rather than trying to scrawl out any more post cards.

England is in labor turmoil with strikes all over the country, including the mail service. We never heard a word from either of you while we were at Claridge's and from your cards that were here and have come since we got back you obviously didn't hear from us, although both your mother and I wrote you regularly. I am sorry because I know letters are always best when you first get to camp before you have settled into the swing of things.

I am proud of you, John, for getting your Sailfish master certificate—if that's what it is called—and you, David, for getting your first Sailfish license—whatever it is called. I will wait now to hear how you come out in some of your races other than those in the outboards.

The chickens and pigeons all seem to be fine and I have told Orrin to call Timmy today to see that he is going to do exactly what David told him to do about the snake. I had Orrin give the snake fresh water last night. John, your pony is fine and just needs you to ride him.

It is certainly quiet around the house with only Robin and Orrin and I wouldn't like it a bit if I didn't know how much fun you are having with your sailing, golf, tennis, and boating and what a fine opportunity and experience it is for you. Keep us posted on what you are doing and how well you are doing it. I will see that your mother sends you the things that you asked for.

June 28, 1974

Dear Boys,

I have spent the week at home since we got back from London trying to catch up but I am going to New Orleans Monday and Tuesday and will try my best to write you from there as to what's going on. I am going to Chicago Wednesday and then on to Granny's at White Bear Wednesday night with Mom, Orrin, Robin, and probably, Timmy. I don't know whether they are going to have the fireworks this year or not since it has been banned in this country. But perhaps if they had already been bought the authorities will let the Yacht Club set them off.

I am delighted with the news from you both and how well you are doing in your sailing as you work for and get the additional ranks. I am sure you enjoyed sailing the Lightning, John, particularly in a big wind and you have to have a lot of fun with it if you learn how to make it do just what you want it to. I hope they have some good sailing at White Bear next weekend since I enjoy watching it almost as much as doing it.

David, I will get you some golf balls out of my bag at the club tomorrow and ask Mom to send them to you. I am pleased you are playing enough to need them but don't forget to watch where they are going. The scores both of you have reported are excellent and I will look forward to a real challenge match at Sea Island.

I went to your barber today, David, and he asked after you. I told him he would have to get out the sheep shears by the time we got you home.

We miss you both but are glad you are having such a good time and thank you for writing a card or letter every day.

July 8, 1974

Dear Boys,

We got back from White Bear last night after a fun weekend at Granny's with lots of water activities. It was hot and very windy. The sailboat races were quite spectacular particularly on Saturday when many of the big E boats tipped over and then turtle (upside down) and we bounced around in the Volvo and laughed at them. On the reaches the E boats were going so fast we could hardly keep up with them.

Yesterday morning Mom took the boys [Orrin and cousin Timmy Hooker], Patti and Robin water skiing while I played golf. The lake was full of activity with other boats and other skiers and I think your mother drove for three or four hours with sweaty hands. When I got home Orrin and Timmy were skiing fine, while Patti could stay up for a few seconds, but Robin got pulled right out of the skis since her feet weren't big enough to stay in the rubber foot holders. I took Robin skiing with her standing on my feet on the skis and we had a good ride and I think she enjoyed it very much. It didn't scare her in the least and was really her idea.

All told they must have caught 1,000 small fish and Orrin did catch one small Northern Pike while casting with a spinner. He came flying up to the house to get me with his arms spread showing me how big the fish was and I really thought he must have caught a whale until I got down to the dock to see its more proper proportions. Orrin and Timmy did a lot of sailing and overall I think everyone had a wonderful time.

I took Orrin, Mom and the others to Saint Paul on Friday on Orrin's birthday and bought him a .22 rifle at Gokeys. They wouldn't sell it to us under the new federal laws since we were from out of town, so we marched down to the president of the First National Bank and had him fill out the forms as the purchaser so we could take it home with us. Orrin is only slightly excited about it— I think he is still sleeping with it.

The Ensworth report cards came yesterday and you John, David and Robin did very well with all A's and B's, while Orrin managed to pass everything for the year. All in all, a great success. David, they want to put you in Level 2 in math next year and I have told Mom I won't stand for you not being challenged more than that and have told her to write Mr. Fay and tell him that is not acceptable to me and that I want you in Level 3, since I know you can perfectly well do any work you set your mind to.

It was fun getting home last night to find three cards from you, David, and one from you, John. The sailing sounds fun and I am glad that you, David, are working to get your Skipper's rating on the Sunfish as well as crewing on the Lightning and that you, John, are after your Lieutenant (?) rating, or is it Captain? The riflery sounds fun and I know Orrin would be happy to have some competition from you two with his new gun when you get home.

I am off to New Orleans this afternoon and then Weyerhaeuser in Tacoma on Wednesday and Thursday. When I am back in this office Friday it will only be a week until we have you home. We miss you.

July 12, 1974

Dear Boys,

I got back in the middle of the night last night from a Weyerhaeuser meeting in Tacoma and have spent all day wrestling with our bankers trying to arrange the money we need to buy the big English oil trading company that is available to us. You probably don't know anything about it since most of it has come up while you have been at camp but it should make us a much bigger company and that much more for some of you guys to take over and run one of these days.

I enjoyed your cards and letters particularly, David, the letter you wrote me to thank me for the golf balls and tell me about all your sailing activities. I know it is fun and I am delighted you are doing so well. I am also glad, John, that you are spending time working on your Lightning Skipper's rating. The Lightning is a fine and famous sail boat that is raced all over the world, and your mastery of it will be a fine achievement.

I never knew a guy like you though, John, who while away at camp sailing and boating and obviously having a good time could think of almost nothing but chickens and pigeons and, particularly, Gray Thing. You will be happy to know they are all well and ask about you every day. David, I will inspect your snake tonight and see that it has fresh water and has been fed so that it will be in good shape when you get home.

A week from today both you guys will be here and I can hardly wait. Robin and Orrin are fine and good company but it surely is lonesome with only half the flock. Have a good time your last week. We will all be waiting for you next Friday.

July 15, 1974

Dear Boys,

We had a nice quiet weekend at home with a lot of swimming and pretty weather. The Nelsons [Carole and Ed], including their three girls [Carole, Emme, and Ellen], came over to swim and have supper last night (Sunday night), which was very enjoyable. Orrin and Robin did a good job in looking after the girls and making it fun for them. I think they enjoyed it as much as we did.

We had a call yesterday morning from Granny's yard man in Florida to say the house had been broken into and shipwrecked. It seems that a drunk couple got a car on the beach, happened to get stuck in the sand in front of our house, whereupon they broke into the house and got in a fight, tearing up furniture, draperies, and getting blood all over everything. Just one more problem. Granny is on her trip to Tokyo, Japan, and Hong Kong but I won't bother her about any of it until she gets home.

John, Orrin tells me there are four new squabs this morning which should be waiting for you when you get home. David, your snake ate a bird over the weekend and should be well fixed to get along until you get home to give him some tender loving care.

I am sorry you have been having so much rain and wish you would send a little over here. It is awfully dry now and we could use some rain.

By the time you get this letter it will be almost time for you to come home on Friday and we can hardly wait. I know you both have had a good time and we certainly look forward to having you back home.

During the years from Mr. Ingram's death in 1963 until 1978, Bronson's list of civic activities was fairly short. The diverse business interests consumed most of his energies. He became a member of the Board of Trust of Montgomery Bell Academy in 1963 (a position he held until his death) and a member of the Board of Directors of Nashville Boys' Club from 1965 to 1970. His involvement with Vanderbilt University began in 1967 when he became a member of the Board of Trust (see Chapter 8 about Vanderbilt).

As for other board memberships, he briefly served on the board of Northwestern National Life Insurance Company (from 1963 until 1965), and he continued the family's relationship with Weyerhaeuser by serving on the board (from 1967 until his death) and the Executive Committee and the Accounting Policy and Standards Committee.

Bronson's interest in politics was based in his realization of the effects of politics on our daily lives and on the business environment. He never would have had the desire to run for political office. We used to laugh at that idea; he could have governed well, but he was far too outspoken to have been elected to any office. He was content to remain behind the scenes, and even then I would not say he was a major player in political races.

He was very conservative, not quite a Libertarian, but he would certainly feel that he who governs least governs best. He had Yankee roots, and his parents would have been very much of a Republican persuasion. Because he was fortunate to be born into a prosperous family, he wanted to conserve what he had inherited, and at the same time he was thinking about building for the future. He often spoke of wanting to do for his children what his parents had done for him

At home, fall 1972. Photo for Christmas card.

financially. He was very much against any government tax-and-spend approach. He wanted to give everyone a chance, but he preferred letting businesses expand to provide jobs instead of maximizing the giveaway programs. All of that generally would argue for the Republican platform.

Bronson supported Lamar Alexander all along in his political career; he liked Lamar as a person, and he liked his stands. Bronson supported John Jay Hooker once, purely because he was a longtime friend and not because he backed John Jay's Democratic position. He was not so much a Republican, however, that he could not step out and support Ned Ray McWherter, very much a Democrat. Bronson thought he was a fine man who was very conservative in his policies.

In November 1971, Bronson cochaired a fundraising dinner for the national and state GOP at Hillwood Country Club, and approximately four hundred people attended. The GOP was preparing for the 1972

elections on behalf of President Richard Nixon and Senator
Howard Baker, who was on hand along with Senator Bill Brock,
Congressmen Dan Kuykendall and LaMar Baker, and Governor
Winfield Dunn. Television actor Dale Robertson emceed the
program.

The *Nashville Banner*, November 10, reported, "David K. (Pat)
Wilson, co-chairman of the Republican national finance committee,
called the dinner one of the most outstanding events of its kind ever
held in Tennessee." Bronson was quoted as saying that a series of
dinners were held as a "Salute to the President," but he considered the
Nashville event a "real Salute to Republicans in Tennessee as well."
The Republicans won in 1972, and Bronson was pleased to receive
this telegram from President Nixon, dated November 7, 1972, from
the White House:

> All of us have reason to be delighted with the presidential elec-
> tion returns just reported from Tennessee. Certainly, much of the
> credit for our success tonight goes to you and your superb staff.
> As finance chairman for Tennessee, you have made it possible for
> us to take our message to the American voter, and I am deeply
> grateful for your special efforts which have contributed so much
> to this victory.
>
>> Congratulations.
> > Richard Nixon

The following year, 1973, President and Mrs. Nixon invited us to the
White House for a black-tie event on March 17 in honor of Mrs.
Nixon's birthday. At the receiving line, a marine clicked his heels and
announced each person by name with his or her most lofty title. We
were announced as "Mr. and Mrs. E. Bronson Ingram, chairman of
Capitol Chevrolet" (which was in fact one of the titles that Bronson held
because of a loan to a friend there, but he was president of Ingram
Corporation, his bread and butter, where he earned his living). Bronson
was so flustered that he shook hands with President and Mrs. Nixon and
wished her "Happy New Year" instead of "Happy Birthday." You probably have to be an Ingram to fully appreciate the scene. By the time we
reached the end of the receiving line, Bronson had realized his goof and

said in a most deprecating moment to me: "Well, you can take the boy out of the country but not the country out of the boy."

Merle Haggard performed in the East Room for the group including members of Congress and their spouses and many businessmen and their spouses. After the entertainment, we enjoyed a champagne buffet and dancing to a U.S. Marine ensemble.

President Nixon had appointed me to be a member of the Advisory Committee of the Arts for the John F. Kennedy Center in Washington, D.C. From that association I became convinced that Nashville needed a performing arts center to provide a proper venue for all kinds of performing arts. My colleagues and I set out to pursue the building of a center and met quite a bit of resistance from numerous politicians, local and state, but Ned Ray McWherter was on our side. He had been elected to the legislature in 1968, served as Speaker of the House of Representatives from 1973 to 1987, and would become governor from 1987 to 1995.

Ned had met Bronson casually years before, just after Bronson got out of the navy, but they would get to know each other well while working on various projects. Governor Dunn appointed Bronson to be vice chairman of the Tennessee Industrial and Agricultural Development Committee, a position he held from 1972 to 1978. The committee planned ways to encourage economic development and job opportunities across the state. Ned served on the committee as an elected public official and had a chance to see Bronson in action. He said, "Bronson had a vision about how growth should be orderly and organized and build the infrastructure along with the communities as they grow. I was impressed with him at that time because he kept his eye on the future."

The next project was the performing arts center. Ned explained, "I got interested in trying to be of some assistance, and I recall the first time I was aware that Bronson was very supportive of the arts and obviously his wife. He was proud of the leadership role she was taking. Bronson and Martha invited me out to the house one night, and we ate dinner out at the pool house. We were talking about some of the plans for the future, and I said to Bronson, 'I couldn't spell arts when I first got elected up here.' He said, 'You'll damn sure understand it when Martha finishes with you.'

merry christmas

Martha and Bronson Ingram

Orrin, John, David and Robin

Ingram family Christmas cards over the years.

merry christmas

Hope you and you family are well —

Bronson and Martha Ingram
John, Robin, Orrin, David
Ages — 14 - 10 - 15 - 13

"I always knew Bronson was up front and he was blunt as hell, but he had a vision of the future and he believed that people should make some commitment either to public service or from the private sector to make the community and the state and the nation a better place. He really made that contribution. He and Martha carried me up to Ottawa to look at a performing arts center up there. We flew up there and spent the night. It was one of their very cold days in the wintertime [just before Christmas]. The airplane was frozen to the runway and they had to push it off.

"Either Martha or both of them together made plans, and Martha got Mr. Jack Massey involved to help create a foundation. I'd asked the question: 'If we [the state government] participate in building the arts center and state office building combination, then how would the programs be funded?' I felt the state had an obligation, and I requested that the schoolchildren in this area and any other area in the state of Tennessee have an opportunity to come and visit the arts center and learn to get a greater appreciation for the arts. I had more or less been denied that in the hill country I grew up in, in northwest Tennessee. There wasn't a great deal of art in plowing with a mule or a horse.

"The plans were made—between Martha's effort and Bronson's effort and Mr. Jack Massey's [and Pat Wilson's]—and that group created an endowment that has grown over the years and it has been a very successful program. I traveled in the different areas of the state where they were trying to raise funds for the endowment. It amounts to an example of the public-private partnership type interest that made it happen, and it's been wonderful for downtown Nashville. Children from other parts of the state come to Nashville on buses and they have programs for them. I'm very proud of it. I'm proud of her, and I'm proud of the role Bronson played."

The end of the 1970s was shaping up to be good to us and our family. The children were thriving. The business was doing well. I was making some headway with the performing arts center. We were not prepared for the events that hit us like a sledgehammer.

CHAPTER 5

"A Wretched Ordeal"

I hope that I shall possess firmness and virtue enough to maintain what I consider
the most enviable of all titles, the character of an honest man.
—George Washington

From the moment the *Nashville Banner*'s headline proclaimed "E. Bronson Ingram Claims Innocence; 'I Was a Victim'" on Tuesday, June 29, 1976, our lives were in turmoil. This is the article as it appeared that day:

> Maintaining his innocence, Nashvillian E. Bronson Ingram, charged in a multi-count bribery indictment, Monday said he was "victim of a crime rather than the perpetrator of it."
>
> The forty-four-year-old president of Ingram Corp., New Orleans, a large privately held corporation, declared:
>
> "I am not guilty of the charges brought against me by the U.S. Attorney's office in Chicago. I am not guilty of the bribery of any government official or of a conspiracy to bribe any government official."
>
> However, Ingram, of 120 Hillwood Blvd., did not rule out the possibility when contacted by the *Nashville Banner* that Ingram Corp. funds might have been used by a "dishonest" and since-fired company official to make illegal profits.
>
> The Ingram official identified the former employee as [an official] of Ingram Contractors Inc., a major subsidiary involved in offshore oil platform and pipeline construction here and in foreign countries.

[The official], the government's "key" witness in the lengthy probe which resulted in the federal indictments being returned in Chicago, was fired some time ago by Ingram Corp. after a probe had been launched by the U.S. Attorney's staff in Chicago, and by special counsel retained by Bronson Ingram, his brother, Frederic B. (Fritz) Ingram, of New Orleans, board chairman of the corporation, and the Ingram company.

"Since graduation from Princeton University in 1953, I have worked with Ingram Corp. and its predecessors in building up a respectable business.

"I have done this not only for myself and my family, but also for the numerous loyal employees and employee-stockholders.

"Beginning in the mid–1960's with the demand for oil, my company expanded its operation into many countries around the world. This involved an enormous amount of time and required the principal officers of this company to spread their time and attention over multiple activities and in many areas around the globe.

"Needless to say, one man cannot know everything that goes on in an operation like this. The only way a company of this size can be operated on a decentralized basis is to secure the best people available, or at least, those who we think at the time to be the best available, and place them in charge of the operation.

"We did this when we started our operations in several different countries. In 1965, we secured the services of a man [who became an official] of Ingram Contractors Inc. We had no reason to distrust [him], and, indeed, we trusted him very much. We put him in charge of many of the operations of the company, although he worked out of Harvey, La., instead of the corporation's home office in New Orleans.

"Last year we learned that the U.S. Attorney's office in Chicago was investigating circumstances surrounding a contract between Ingram Contractors, Inc. and the Metropolitan Sanitary District of Chicago. The company has a contract to haul sludge by barge out of the city of Chicago and pump it into lagoons about 200 miles away.

"Upon learning of this investigation, I, personally, and the corporation, undertook to determine if there was a problem and the extent of it.

"I've had counsel looking into this matter since the early summer of 1975. I now recognize that our trust in [the official] has been misplaced and there may have been improprieties involved.

"My counsel has advised me that [the official] did indeed obtain corporate funds, and the government contends and alleges that these funds were paid to certain officials in Chicago.

"I do know that I am not guilty of the charges brought against me by the U.S. Attorney's office in Chicago. I do know that I am not guilty of the bribery of any government official or of a conspiracy to bribe any government official.

"I believe the evidence will prove that I was a victim of a crime rather than the perpetrator of it.

"I also know that this may be a long, difficult fight. . . . My family and I have been involved in the Nashville community for many years, and my wife, Martha, and I have been very active in our attempts to help this community. We intend to continue to do so.

"I can only say that in the end, and when I have had an opportunity, in an appropriate setting to explain my knowledge and my lack of knowledge in this matter, my innocence will be established.

"I simply ask the people of this community to recognize that it is easy to charge someone with something. The government, with its power, can take a dishonest employee, give him immunity from prosecution, and then use him to implicate others.

"Thank God, 12 good, decent citizens will pass judgement on my guilt or innocence. I'm satisfied to leave the matter in their hands, confident of the outcome.

"We will continue to investigate the matter. We will continue to fight it. My family and I will continue with the company as it now exists. We will continue with our civic commitments.

"I believe the people of this community and my family will be satisfied with the outcome."

The indictment against Fritz, Bronson, and six officials of the Chicago Sanitary District was returned by the grand jury on January 28, 1976. It charged multiple counts of conspiracy, U.S. wire fraud, interstate travel in aid of racketeering (basically extortion), and tax fraud.

Almost immediately after the news hit the streets, friends called and sent notes of encouragement. They were very helpful, very loyal. Our minister at St. George's, Jimmy Johnson, dropped by the office just to visit regularly. He and Bronson had been on several fishing trips together. We were so glad to have those longtime friends because you can share such times only with a handful of friends. These excerpts from their notes convey the consensus of their opinion: "I've no doubt about the final outcome but what a wretched ordeal"; "I know it is not easy having your privacy invaded"; "Your courage and fortitude will see you through"; "We stand behind you 100%"; "In these days of the sensational press, it is most tragic that good and honorable people find their guilt presumed and their integrity impugned because of what almost without exception prove to be groundless allegations"; and "I hope that it can be resolved quickly."

The last hope was not to be. The trial did not begin until September 5, 1977, and it ended on November 8, 1977. Throughout those weeks, reporters for the *Tennessean* and the *Nashville Banner* covered the trial, and often their articles made the front page. The Chicago and New Orleans papers also had their reporters on the scene. Bronson no longer read any paper, except the *Wall Street Journal*.

It was about as bad as it gets, and it affected all of us. All of a sudden I found myself with sky-high blood pressure. Bronson handled it a good deal better at least as far as his blood pressure went. It was something we couldn't get away from. We had no power over it, no way to change it or mitigate the effect of it, other than to do what Jim Neal, Bronson's lawyer, said we should do. (Fritz had his own attorney, Herbert Miller Jr.) It was a dark chapter, but it was a chapter in our lives.

Nobody had ever called Bronson Ingram into question about anything—his word was his bond. His whole credo was to do it straight by the numbers. The rules are the rules; if you don't like the rules, get them changed, but live by them in the meantime. He was absolutely straight in everything. To have all of this called into question was the worst kind of blow.

The indictments and then the trial occurred at a very crucial time in our children's lives; they were in their early teens. Bronson kept everything bottled up, but I felt that I needed to talk to the children. All I could say was that it underlined even more why it is so important to have integrity because if you have integrity, you will be believed in difficult situations. I said, "Your father has been pulled into something that he was not party to, but he has to deal with it and we all have to deal with it."

I have to commend the children for behaving themselves. They didn't do any foolish things that some teenagers might have done just to act out their frustration or resentment. Part of the reason is that we didn't try to shield them from it. How could we in such a high-profile case covered by papers and discussed by their classmates in school?

Bronson and his attorney, Jim Neal, at the clerk's desk in Chicago for processing and arraignment.

The trial took place in Chicago, and Jim Neal advised us that I should be there every day. I think I helped keep Bronson from spinning out. He was so appalled by the whole thing, and I could reassure him, "This is going to pass. We just have to go through it." That included facing a battery of photographers and reporters as we went to and from the courthouse each day that court was in session.

Before the trial got under way, Jim Neal had asked Henry Hooker, Bronson's brother-in-law and a lawyer, to help Bronson practice being on the witness stand. Henry, who was to be the prosecutor in the exercise, said, "Jim told me to ask the most awful questions I could put to him. The goal was to make sure that Bronson didn't lose his temper on the stand or give a smart-aleck answer. Over the course of doing this, his demeanor changed, and his facility with answering questions improved. The day he testified, he called me afterward and said, 'Henry, you SOB, that federal guy was nowhere near as mean as you were.'"

Jim Neal recalled details of that ordeal for us: "The actual trial. It was a new experience for Bronson—not to be in control of things. I remember, early on, Bronson was suggesting I take one course of action because that was just his nature. It was very new to him to have his life or his destiny or his fortunes in somebody else's hands.

"In the practice of law there are decisions that are purely client decisions. There are decisions that should be purely the lawyer's decisions. And Bronson was attempting to make decisions that I thought were purely lawyer decisions because he was used to making decisions. I said, 'Now, Bronson, you hired me. I know what I'm talking about in this area. I couldn't run a business. I couldn't make your decisions at Ingram Corporation. But I know how to do what I do, and if you're not willing to let me make these type decisions, then you're going to have to get another lawyer.' Bronson looked at me and was very still for a minute or two and said, 'You're right.' We never had a moment's disagreement from that point on.

"He was a perfect client. He would study. He would know what he was supposed to do. He would do it very well. It was a watershed, a life-changing event, this whole episode in Bronson's life and, indeed, in Martha's life."

The trial started early on Fridays so that we could fly back home for the weekends. Jim said of our dash through the airport on those days, "Martha and Bronson and I and Donna Phillips [Jim's assistant] would be rushing through the Chicago airport. One of the trade-offs in letting us off early was that we wouldn't stop for lunch on Fridays. Going through that Chicago airport and grabbing a hot dog. It still, in my mind, is the single best piece of food I've ever had in my life.

"In a trial like that, you will work sixteen hours a day, eighteen hours a day. Many days I'd be up at three o'clock in the morning. On occasion Bronson couldn't sleep. He'd wander into my room, and I'd be sitting up in bed making notes. [All of us stayed at the Palmer House during the trial.] And at three o'clock in the morning we'd talk for a while. But those hot dogs. I'll never forget how good those dogs were."

Character witnesses had to be called, and they were Alexander Heard (chancellor of Vanderbilt University), John Siegenthaler (editor and publisher of the *Tennessean*), Mary Jane Werthan (a longtime family friend), Jimmy Johnson (the rector at St. George's Episcopal Church), and Arnold Palmer (America's favorite golfer). They were to testify as to his character and his civic-mindedness, and they all basically said that he was a man of veracity who could be trusted.

John Siegenthaler volunteered to be a character witness for Bronson, he said, "because I knew him and trusted him and I thought he had great integrity. I'd been through enough little things with him to believe in his character. I knew we came from totally different worlds, totally different backgrounds, totally different ideas and ideals, but I thought that he was basically an honest man."

The night after John testified, all of us went to dinner. John recalled, "The interesting thing was that Bronson never said to me, 'Thanks.' It was not that I didn't know that he appreciated it or was grateful for it. It was that he knew I didn't expect it. What he did do [as we left the restaurant], he walked up by me, reached around my shoulder, and hit me on the right shoulder, standing on my left. I looked around, and he said, 'You're a good man.' And that was thanks. I said, 'You're a good man.' We sort of laughed and then we went on. Afterward [following the trial] he wrote me a letter; it was a couple of sentences that said thank you without saying thanks. We never mentioned it again."

The day that Arnie was there, October 7, the prosecutor almost forgot which side he was on. It was the only light moment in the whole trial. When Jim Neal asked Arnie whether Bronson had a reputation for truth, veracity, and honesty, Arnie replied, "Absolutely, I would say so, yes." When U.S. District Court Judge John Grady asked Assistant U.S. Attorney Gordon Nash whether the government had any questions, Nash answered, "I have some questions, but they don't pertain to this case. They have to do with how to get out of a sand trap." The judge, jury, and spectators burst into laughter.

The jury deliberated thirty-three hours before reaching a decision. The verdict was handed down on November 8. Mrs. Ingram, Bronson and Fritz's mother was there, and so were Alice and Henry Hooker and Patricia Hart. Fritz was first on the list; he was found guilty of all counts. Bronson was second; he was found not guilty of all counts. As Jim Neal said, "It was a terribly bittersweet moment. It was very difficult for Mrs. Ingram." The sentencing was set for a later date.

Shortly after the end of the trial, Bronson and I and friends Jake and Anne Wallace went to Hobe Sound, Florida, where the family had a house. It wasn't a time to celebrate; it was a time to regroup. Jake observed Bronson's overall condition: "He was exhausted, and I think he just needed time to do nothing for a little while." Not long after we arrived, Bronson experienced chest pains, and we took him to a local doctor. The diagnosis: stress.

The sentencing date for Fritz was December 14, and he was to serve four years. His lawyer immediately appealed. While his case was on appeal, Fritz and Bronson discussed the division of Ingram Corporation. A serious consideration was the tax implications if one bought or sold to the other. How could they do it and have something left after paying the high taxes?

Henry Hooker suggested a tax-free split off. Each brother could take some of the businesses, trying to achieve equal worth; no money would exchange hands. If they could get an IRS ruling that there would be no gain, it would be regarded as tax-free.

Fritz and Bronson pursued that idea and issued a joint management memo, printed in the *Ingram News,* March–April 1978: "The proposed division of Ingram Corporation, as announced in early March, will ultimately mean better prospects and greater economic success for all companies within our present worldwide group. We are confident that it is in the best interest of the Corporation, its shareholders and all employees. The decision to proceed was made after extensive considerations of all factors involved."

Bronson's portion included the barges and the books and Ingram Materials, and he created Ingram Industries, Inc., effective November 30, 1978, with the headquarters in Nashville. Fritz's portion encompassed the rest of the divisions and remained as

Ingram Corporation. He continued to direct those businesses during the appeals process. Fritz's appeal failed, however, and he began serving his sentence in January 1980 at Eglin Air Force Base in a federal minimum security prison.

Family and friends went to work to seek a commutation of Fritz's sentence. In the meantime, Bronson and I and his sisters and their husbands made periodic visits to Fritz at Eglin. Anyone who thinks that a minimum security prison is a country club has never been in one. It's a grim place. We went in, we signed in, we were frisked before we saw him, and then we went into a dusty little fenced-in courtyard and sat on concrete benches around a concrete table. Other prisoners and their visitors sat around other concrete tables. We had only thirty minutes or an hour with him. He was then frisked and searched after we left. It was all so degrading, so horrible.

In December 1980, President Carter commuted Fritz's sentence to sixteen months, and he was released in May 1981.

CHAPTER 6

Ingram Industries

When he [Bronson] jumped into something,
he jumped in with both feet.
—Charles Story

With the books and barges as a foundation of Ingram Industries, Bronson set to work to build on them. Dave Sampsell was an Orrin Henry Ingram Scholar at Vanderbilt University in 1967, and Bronson spoke to him about doing an internship with Ingram Corporation while he was in graduate school. Dave described the conversation: "Bronson said, 'You know, Dave, my brother and I inherited this company from our dad. I really don't have to work. I could go out and play golf and do anything we want to do.' But he said, 'Martha and I have several boys and I want to be able to leave something to my children and I intend to build on what I received.' It was an expression of stewardship, and he said, 'I'd like you to help me with that.' I never forgot that comment." Dave completed his internship and then worked as a full-time employee for the corporation and later for Ingram Industries.

Bronson continued to abide by that commitment with Ingram Industries. By the first quarter of 1979, Ingram Industries had acquired Acadian Sand and Limestone, and Bronson was pursuing a 50 percent interest in Gulfco Industries of Oklahoma City, an oil field equipment outfitter. Within another month, he acquired that interest in Gulfco and purchased Maryland Coal and Coke Company.

Less than a year after he became president and CEO of Ingram Industries, Bronson spoke with a reporter for the *Nashville Banner*, who wrote the article "Ingram Has Talent for Profit" (October 18, 1979):

DiMaggio in center field, Landowska on the cello—talent always makes it look easy. With E. Bronson Ingram, it's a deep and silent talent for making money.

Bronson—who with his brother Fritz for a dozen years was one of the most dynamic duos since Orville and Wilbur—chatted easily in his new office across Harding Road from the Belle Meade Theater.

The movie marquee read *Starting Over*. Bronson disclaimed any connection to his present status.

"Fritz is now running Ingram Corp. and I have Ingram Industries—a tax-free spinoff. He is in New Orleans and I'm here."

In his mid–40s, Bronson speaks like someone who was schooled to speak his mind—and who understands the assets of silence. He is built like a middleweight and wears a permanent tan earned on boat decks and fairways.

The walls of Bronson's office, along with the walls of the entire floor of Ingram offices, are filled with color photos and oil paintings of barges and boats.

"My wife, Martha, says she gets seasick here," Bronson says.

Mrs. Ingram herself has been influential in the Nashville community, having served as coordinator for the Tennessee Performing Arts Foundation. She led a successful campaign to raise $4 million for the foundation.

Bronson's barges ply the veins and arteries of America's heartland. About 500 barges, tugs and towboats carry a variety of natural products from Pittsburgh west to Omaha or Tulsa; from St. Paul south to New Orleans and onto the Mexican border through the intracoastal waterways.

They carry coal and oil, sand and gravel—much of it produced by Ingram mines, wells and pits.

The boats are named for family and friends—three towboats now roaming rivers somewhere in the Mississippi watershed carry such bankish names as William Earthman, Sam Fleming, and Andrew Benedict.

The Ingram brothers' affinity for doing business outdoors is probably genetic. They inherited a big block of Weyerhaeuser stock from their great-grandfather, a founder of the north-western timber company. Their multimillionaire father, O. H. Ingram, was a successful oil refiner and marketer. He came to Nashville from Eau Clair [*sic*], Wis., in 1950 [*sic*] to pursue an expansion of his barge business.

The boys grew up spending their summers sailing on the lakes around St. Paul. Ingram made it to the national finals as skipper of a scow. When the time came for secondary schooling, Ingram and his brother were sent to Andover Prep and then on to Princeton. When their father died unexpectedly in 1963 at age 58, the boys took over the business.

Building on a $2 million, money-losing barge business that was part of their inheritance, in 15 years Bronson and Fritz transformed Ingram Corp. into a company with revenues of over $900 million.

Recognizing Bronson Ingram's acute business mind, Edward G. Nelson, president of Commerce Union Bank, said, "He (Bronson) has the highest sense of responsibility and commitment of any man in our city. Any effort he commits himself to he follows through 100 percent and always sees the effort through to success."

Sam Fleming, chairman of the board at Third National Bank, said of Ingram, "Bronson Ingram was born into an atmosphere of great affluence. While many young men under similar circumstances would have taken life easy, he was determined to make his own way. His record is evident of how successful he was in obtaining his objective. Not only has he been highly successful in business, but he has contributed to all facets of Nashville's economy."

When the brothers divided their business holdings in April, Fritz kept the oil refinery business and pipeline operation centered around New Orleans.

Bronson's Ingram Industries includes Ingram Barge Co., Acadian Sand & Limestone, Ingram Materials (sand), Ingram Coal Co., Ingram Book Co., Bluewater Insurance Ltd., an insurance company, and Gulfco Industries, maker of oil well valves.

All are operated under an umbrella of ownership by the Ingrams—with only about 10 percent in the hands of a few of Ingram's 1,500 employees.

It all seems to be working. Early this year *Fortune* magazine placed the Ingram brothers among 62 Americans they termed "the elusive, private rich." Their net worth was estimated at about $100 million.

Ingram values highly his independence and right to privacy. As one of the increasingly exclusive minority of privately owned big companies, Ingram Industries bares its figures for no one and is responsible only to a board of directors of Ingram's choosing.

However, Ingram has been extremely unselfish in many philanthropic endeavors in Nashville including Vanderbilt University.

He is emotionally involved in his companies—not about to "sell short" to capitalize on the expected recession.

The two operations which monopolized his thoughts the other day were the book company and the coal company:

"We got into books to satisfy the need of one of our executives for something more to do. For a while it was great, when we were supplying libraries with funds supplied by President Johnson's Great Society. But when that dried up, we started wholesaling to book shops. We are now the largest book wholesaler in the country. We supply about 10,000 libraries and retail bookstores."

Ingram Book Co. does about $100 million a year.

And about coal:

"America is going to have to return to coal. There is no other way, except a return to darkness. Nuclear energy, because of the environmentalists, is years away and oil production peaked in the fourth quarter of 1978.

"Most people do not realize that—that we will never again see more oil produced than there was in the fourth quarter of 1978.

"Yet, we sit here, with 25 percent excess coal production capacity we're not using. We are being silly. We need to learn to use coal and protect the environment. We need to use our power capability provided by nuclear energy. Nobody ever has been killed by nuclear energy. I'm not willing to see us sacrifice our standard of living because of fear of nuclear energy."

When Bronson Ingram talks about the future, he speaks of coal—and he speaks of his four children. The Ingrams have sons enrolled in Vanderbilt University, Princeton and Montgomery Bell Academy and a daughter in the eighth grade at Ensworth.

Bronson considers himself doubly blessed—"They're great kids—and they all want to come into the business."

To cope with the recession portended by the reporter, Bronson was able to tell shareholders in April 1980: "We have rearranged and added to our credit lines and revolving credit agreement so that we are well financed for the opportunities which the recession may bring and, in any event, to see it through no matter how deep it may turn out to be." He always tried to be prepared for the long term.

I had not been directly a part of the business to that point; I had been rearing our children and working on the development of the Tennessee Performing Arts Center (TPAC). When a professional manager was hired for TPAC in 1979 prior to the 1980 opening, Bronson asked me, "What are you going to do now?" I said, "I'll just go to the beach." He didn't accept that answer: "That won't last but two weeks, and then you're going to be bored." I admitted, "I really don't know what I'm going to do next." He said, "Well, would you consider coming to work for me?" I hesitated before replying, "Oh, Bronson, I don't know how that is going to work." I thought, *Twenty-four hours a day together. This may not be good for us.*

He was very forceful about it: "If something were to happen to me, we have nobody in the family that would be ready." The children were in their late teens, still in college. He said, "We have professional managers, but this is the biggest part of our wherewithal. You have spent so much time raising money. You've really gotten a feel for who's got it and why. I think you could be of some help to me."

I gave in and agreed: "I'll tell you. I'll come maybe one day a week or so." He said, "That's fine. We'll find an office for you." The offices were still in the old Third National Bank Building on Harding Road. I didn't even have a job description, but I came one day and I never left. I kept finding things to do to help him.

People would talk to me about things that they would never talk to him about, such as employee benefits. I sat in on meetings, and someone might ask, "Is my wife covered if we have a baby?" That's very definitely covered by the company's policy, explained in our manuals, but some people weren't aware of it. One long-term associate in the barge company explained to me that those who work with their hands don't read much. It became quite apparent that we needed to have

more Quality Circle–type activities and a stronger Human Resources Department.

Then when we first went to the open office concept with no solid walls, people complained to me about the secondhand smoke. I brought it up to him, and Bronson protested, "We've got to let people smoke. This is a free country." (This was before there was an antismoking movement.) I insisted, "Bronson, you're in an enclosed office, and you don't have to deal with the smoke, but these other people do. Now come with me, and let me show you the haze over these offices." When he realized how bad it was, he said, "Oh, my God, this is terrible." So we put in a smoking ban, other than in heavily ventilated break rooms. Even those are now extinct. That is just an example of something I could do for our associates that they would not bring up to him.

He started getting busier, and he said, "If you would try to organize our giving program, that would save me a huge amount of

Bronson and Martha and Anne and Jake Wallace on the Queen Elizabeth II, *its tenth anniversary, 1979.*

time. And besides I know some of these people who are calling on us for contributions turned you down, and I would like to give you the clout to be able to deal with them. This is a good way to do it." He was putting me front and center and making me feel good, and also I think he felt that I was going to have a huge letdown after working every day for eight years to get TPAC opened.

Before I knew it, I was in the office next door to his, and I was involved more and more with the operations. When he was having a meeting, he would tell me, "Come on in and listen to this."

Finally, I said, "I need to have a title. I think I'd like to be Director of Public Affairs because I'm spending a lot of time dealing with external people." Bronson said, "All right. We'll have some cards printed up." That was how I became Director of Public Affairs.

I never even thought about asking for a salary until sometime during Lamar Alexander's tenure as governor. He sent one of his emissaries, Lewis Lavine, to call on me and ask whether I would consider a job in state government in the educational arena. I thought, *Gee, this would be really nice, but there is no way, dealing with my family and my husband's business and social demands, that I could devote my time to the job,* so I declined the offer. I did say, though, "What would you have paid me if I had taken the job?" He replied, "It would have been a low six-figure number." I was taken aback: "You think I'm worth that!" He said, "Yes, every bit of it, and if you would reconsider. . . ." I still had to decline.

I could not wait, however, to tell Bronson. His reaction was, "I can't believe they were trying to hire my wife away." I said, "I'm not going to accept the job, but I was really flattered." He said, "Would you like to be paid? Why don't you name your price?" (The thought had never occurred to him or to me previously. It was not that he was stingy, for I had a large allowance.) I said, "I just did. It was what they were talking about offering me." He said, "All right." It was nice to have a sense of having my own earned income and pulling my own weight. On the fifth anniversary of that first payment, I was offered a nice award pin like everybody else gets. That was so odd to me because the previous unpaid years at Ingram Industries didn't seem to count because I hadn't received a salary.

A similar story developed around my being asked to serve on a bank board. Several banks tried to get Bronson on their respective boards, but he always turned them down because he borrowed from all of them. Jack Massey had asked me if I would go on the Nashville CityBank board after we had worked together for several years on the TPAC project. I said, "Let me talk to Bronson about it." Bronson dismissed the idea: "I don't think you know enough about business yet to be on a bank board." I had to tell Jack, "Bronson doesn't think it would be a good idea." I was a lot less self-assertive then.

Months later Bronson called on Jack to solicit money for a building at Montgomery Bell Academy. Jack asked, "How much money do you want?" Bronson gave him a figure. Jack replied, "I'll give it to you if you'll let your wife come on my bank board." Bronson

The M/V Robin B. Ingram, a dry cargo tow on the Ohio River.

came home and said rather sheepishly, "Well, I just have to tell you about this conversation." He told me what transpired, and I said, "It sounds to me as though I've been bartered. What did you get for me?" He said, "I got $750,000 from Jack Massey for telling him that I'd encourage you to go on his board." I said, "I would have thought I was worth at least $1 million." It was the first corporate board on which I served.

Bronson was very good at seeing the big picture and understanding the details, but he was not very good at actually doing the details. It wasn't where his mind was. His expertise was in choosing good people, monitoring the financing, and making sure that there was always money to take advantage of an opportunity when it presented itself.

He allowed his people to be entrepreneurial, each master of his own ship, and he was a senior advisor for them. People seemed to grow in his organization. He and they agreed on common goals, and then he turned them loose to figure out how they were going to get there. He never feared expanding to new horizons, but he wanted to know what was going on, particularly if someone wanted to make a capital expenditure. He gave them fair warning: "If you want to try something new, come and tell me about it first. I don't like surprises. If problems develop, they will be our problems. If you haven't told me about it and problems come up, they're damn well your problems."

A staff meeting was held at 9:15 every Thursday morning. (Bronson had a tennis lesson with pro Dave Anderson at 7:30 A.M. each Thursday to stay fit.) The profit center heads and the staff heads told what they and the company had been doing the previous week. Then there were private sessions of people who wanted to expand and make a capital expenditure. Bronson believed that around the table, even though our businesses were disparate, each company ought to know what the other was doing. Then all the staff people who were supporting these operations—human resources, treasury, insurance— talked about what they were doing.

It was about an hour's worth of interchange of information. There weren't necessarily written reports. There were sales numbers from the book company or contracts mentioned for the barge company. I had an opportunity to really see and hear week by week how the busi- nesses developed. Occasionally, if Bronson was to be out of town, he asked me to chair the meeting and report back to him.

Bronson had a proposal for Dave Sampsell in the early 1980s. Dave recalled, "He said, 'We are going to expand this company. We are going to grow like a weed. We are going to grow like mad. And I want you to come to Nashville [from New Orleans] and be in charge of the Corporate Development Department, which you are going to start. And you are going to figure out what it's all about and we are going to start acquiring companies. We are going to grow.' Going back to that original interview, that is perfectly consistent with what Bronson told me that first day that I met him. He had an idea and he stuck by it." In 1982, Dave began work in that department.

Family Christmas cards.

Dave regarded his role as defining the process. "I cannot imagine myself knowing enough, let's say about the book business, to presume what their strategy ought to be. I knew a lot about the barge company and lots of these other companies. So, it seemed to me that the strategic planning ought to be done by the people who run the companies [called profit center heads]. They know what the competitive environment is. They know what the rules of the game are."

Bronson became involved in a few small passive investments as a joint venture partner, but they didn't seem to work out. Dave was in the position to evaluate them, and he said, "It wasn't very long before Bronson and I made a very important strategic decision, and that was, we were not going to dabble in these kinds of affairs. We were going to invest in things we knew about, and we were going to invest in businesses where we could manage them and manage them well." Another important strategic decision was to get deeply involved in the distribution business.

The meetings of the Board of Directors were very structured. Bronson treated our meetings as though we were a public company, even though we were private. We had outsiders on the board, and most of them commented that they received more detailed and better information from our private company than they did from most of the public companies where they had served on boards. He made sure that they received briefing books in advance of each meeting.

He followed the agenda, allocating a certain amount of time to each business. He also was quite good at having our top people report on the subjects they knew the most about. If you were the head of the book company, you would be called on to make the board report. That way the outside board members were exposed to our key people. He conducted the meetings the way he did everything else—with focus, organization, considerable energy, and a fair degree of pride. Bronson sought board members' feedback, and he got it.

I joined the board in 1981, the same year that Dean Samuel B. Richmond of Owen Graduate School of Management joined. Sam said, "Bronson really loved running the companies. That was his joy. He wanted to do it right and better than anybody else—and he did. He knew what he wanted; he was purposive. I was one of the noisier participants on the board, but he never, ever ignored someone who

came with advice. I think he wanted to hear what people had to say. I was very proud that each of us could call the other friend."

Sam noted, "Bronson loved this. The first time we saw a nine-digit number, I stopped the meeting and pointed it out [in the early 1990s]. We had probably set the record for how fast the company went from $1 to $2 to $3 to $11 billion. It was a magnificent achievement." Sam had to retire from the Ingram Board of Directors at age seventy-two. He said it was the saddest day of his life because he loved the board and the businesses: "I remember when we voted in that resolution. I was at that time about sixty-two, and I never thought I would ever get to be seventy-two and have to step down."

Bronson made this report to shareholders in October 1981: "The outlook for the economic environment remains extremely guarded and I expect these difficult times to continue well into next year. I am hopeful that the responsible officials will stick with the basics of their new

Ingram Industries was a sponsor of the Clyde Beatty, Cole Bros. Circus in September 1983 to benefit the Nashville Humane Association. Either Bronson or Martha would ride the elephant.

economic program so that it has time to have a chance to work and not crumple under the shrill screams of shortsighted politicians who think new massive government programs and giveaways will pave their way in the next election and can't see or don't care what happens beyond that."

Two reports in 1982 were fairly grim. Bronson wrote in the first: "Our business, at least for now, is at the lowest ebb I have ever seen it. . . . We have significant financial strength and resiliency for our size and we will ride this out, but a lot of people won't make it." In the second, he wrote, "Our business for the most part continues to be terrible." There was a low demand for coal, and everything was weak except the book and insurance divisions. He offered this opinion: "Long-term rates will have to come down somewhat further and stabilize before I see any sustained economic recovery. Inflation is no longer an immediate problem and I think that subject of the political willingness to face up to the problem of the deficit, we now have at least a chance for a sustained long-term economic recovery which would make some of the current hurt worthwhile."

Our son Orrin had been working in the dispatch office of the barge company while he was taking classes at Vanderbilt. He loved the barge business but felt less loving about his fifth year of college and getting a degree. Bronson in his inimitable and direct way said to Orrin, "Son, you *will* graduate. You will stay at Vanderbilt until you have your degree if it takes ten years. I have enough money to afford it and enough clout there to make them keep you. So put your mind to it and finish up." Orrin took six courses, made all B's, graduated in 1982, and went to work full time. He wanted to stay in the barge business, but Bronson sent him to Ingram Materials Company.

Orrin had first gone out on the towboats when he was eighteen, and he enjoyed the work and the environment. Here is what he said about the barge business: "When I came back into the office and worked during the summers in the office, it was interesting how your word was your bond and you did deals where you made or lost thousands of dollars over the telephone. Whether you were on the good side or the bad side, you honored your deal.

"We've been lucky that we've been buyers of businesses through most of our career. It's hard when you have to regroup and sell

something. It is not fun. It is probably the one part of business that I really hate. We work hard trying not to make mistakes so we don't have to get out.

"The growth in the barge business—it's funny how the government can make good deals bad deals. But during the late seventies, the tax laws were such that barges were very good tax shelters. A lot of investors started building barges as an investment, and supply and demand weren't the reason they were doing it. It was a false, tax-driven thing.

"Then in the early eighties, Jimmy Carter did the grain embargo, and all of a sudden we weren't shipping grain to the Russians and we had overbuilt our fleet. Our export market went away, and about that time the tax laws changed, too. It threw the barge industry into a huge, huge depression. Not recession, depression."

Orrin explained why Bronson sent him to Ingram Materials instead of the barge business: "He thought I'd get depressed because it was so horrible. I was there for two years before I finally convinced him to let me come over to the barge company." That was 1984, a crucial year for decision making about the barge business.

We had to decide to get out of the business or grow the business. The decision: grow the business. A major acquisition was the Ohio Barge Line. Orrin recalled, "It effectively doubled the size of our barge company. We got some really good management with that acquisition. We also got some good contracts and a better mix of barges. Our average age in the fleet got balanced out to where we could ride out the financial storm better."

Jim Neal became a board member of Ingram Industries shortly after its formation, and his recollection of that acquisition is vivid: "I remember the only time Bronson ever got irritated with me during his life and my service on the board was when he came to a board meeting and said, 'I'm proposing that we buy Ohio Barge Line.' And we weren't doing worth a damn in Ingram Barge line. This would double the size of Ingram Barge line.

"I said, 'Bronson, we're not doing worth a damn in Ingram Barge line, and you want to go out and double the size. It reminds me of those two fellows in the watermelon business. They would take a truck, go to Florida, and buy a load of watermelons at a dollar a watermelon. They'd drive those watermelons back to Nashville, and they would sell them at a dollar a watermelon. One day one turned to the other and says, "You know, we don't seem to be making any money in this business." The other one says, "Yeah, you think we ought to buy a bigger truck?"' Everybody broke up—except Bronson.

"He looked at me with such disdain on that but patiently explained to somebody whose whole business experience had been at Ingram Industries: 'Mr. Neal, let me give you a lesson in business. The reason we're not doing well at Ingram Barge line is that we are simply not big enough to have an impact. The way to do business is to get big enough in any field that you can have economies of scale, you can drive the market,' and on and on. I don't remember all he said, but it was a funny event."

Ingram Barge bought other companies. Orrin explained, "We bought ABT [American Barge and Towing]. We bought M/G

Transport Services. We assumed the leases on System Fuel, which was black oil. We bought a little tower down in Florida called Georgia Transporters. We bought some barges from Ohio River Company, some tank barges, about twenty-seven. During that period of time, we bought lots and lots of barge lines. The bankers liked us because we borrowed money, but we paid our bills.

Hortense Ingram, Bronson's mother, in the mid-1970s.

"We had a contract that began in 1976 with Commonwealth Edison in Chicago where we moved residual fuel oil for them. It was a ten-year contract, and it was a take-or-pay contract. We bought forty-eight unit tow barges and six boats for the contract. Then probably three years into the contract, they cut way back on the amount of residual fuel oil that they were burning, and so most of the fleet stayed tied up in Greenville, Mississippi, for the balance of the contract. It was extremely profitable, and it helped us weather the depression in the rest of the barge industry because we were making more with the stuff tied up than we were losing trying to run all the rest of the barge line. We had the benefit of that contract until 1986, and the business wasn't nearly as bloody in the late 1980s as it was in the early 1980s. It wasn't good, but it wasn't nearly as bloody."

The book business had seen management changes in December 1978 when Harry Hoffman resigned to join Waldenbooks. Ingram Book Company was then at Reedwood Drive. Phil Pfeffer, then age thirty-three, explained what happened: "Bronson called me at

Reedwood and said he would like to have lunch with me the next day, which was highly, highly unusual because I had virtually no communication with Bronson whatsoever. That night, I put down on a piece of paper an organization chart of how I would organize the company on an interim basis until we found a president because I thought that's what Bronson would want to ask me about, 'Where do we go from here?'

"I came to his office, and I waited outside his office at Maryanne's desk. He got finished with whatever he was doing and we visited for just a moment and he said, 'What I'd like to do is go to my home for lunch,' which he often did. We went over to his house, and Emma [Guthrie, the housekeeper] had made some sandwiches and soup. We sat down, and he said, 'Before we eat, I have two questions I want to ask you. One, do you want to run Ingram Book Company? Two, can you run Ingram Book Company?'

"I said, 'Well, the answer to the first question is yes. I really would like to have the chance to run Ingram Book Company. And to the second question, I think we can run it. I think we've got the people in the organization who can run this business.' And he said, 'Very well, you are now president and chief executive officer of Ingram Book Company. Let's have lunch,' and that was it."

By 1980, the revenue of the book company was up to $100 million. You must remember that this was long before the inception of the superstores, but chain stores such as B. Dalton and Waldenbooks were branching out into areas other than books, including audiobooks on tape and CD-based classical music. The independent bookstores were much less likely to be selling these or other nonbook products. Phil and his people conducted strategic planning to evaluate the issue because we wanted the independents to thrive. Videos were of special interest.

When they started discussing videos, I made sure that the company's policy was not to sell X-rated videos. They were first-run movies on home video format. Some of the mom-and-pop bookstores thought that all videos were dirty, however, and the cost of each video-tape in the early days—about one hundred dollars—discouraged bookstores from stocking them. When the video rental business took off, we supplied videos to those retailers (or rent-tailers, as some called them). As Phil said, "We certainly had the engine to deliver, the systems to take orders and to get orders into the warehouse and out of the warehouse and customers billed. We had the distribution capabilities." We were able to expand our customer base with Ingram Video, which eventually got into markets that sold videos when the studios reduced the sales price to more reasonable figures.

Not long afterward, in May 1983, Ingram Book Company also started to distribute software to bookstores. The book company had already been selling some computer books.

Phil had to comment on the venture into these businesses: "Particularly in the last couple of years of his life, Bronson would talk about the luck. I think he thought it was by accident that we got into these businesses. That bothered me a great deal, and it bothered a lot of people in the company that had built the business because the strategies that we followed, we didn't end up at year twenty with the same, having executed exactly the strategy that was put together at year zero.

Bronson and Arnie at Bay Hill. (Photo by Harold Kyle.)

"Because we had established a strategy, because we attempted to follow that strategy, the strategy evolved, and the end results, I think, are very evident. Bronson would say something like, 'It was by luck that we got into this or into that,' and for the people who built the business, it wasn't luck at all.

"I think that's one of the things, if I could have a conversation with him today, I wish I could go over that with him again because I think that's a real understatement of the work that a lot of people put together to build these businesses.

"It was a very deliberate strategy to be in video, to be in video games, to be in microcomputer software. Initially, we got into the software business because we thought the bookstores would be centers for education, entertainment, and information, which would include microcomputer software. We didn't know where the microcomputer business was going. Neither did the microcomputer business know where it was going."

E. Bronson Ingram's
Finest Hour
Cypress Point Club
August 24, 1983

Hole	Par	Score
1	4	4
2	5	5
3	3	3
4	4	4
5	5	4
6	5	4
7	3	3
8	4	5
9	4	4
Total out	**37**	**36**

Hole	Par	Score	
10	5	4	
11	4	4	
12	4	5	
13	4	4	
14	4	3	
15	3	3	
16	3	3	
17	4	4	
18	4	5	Three Putts
Total in	**35**	**35**	
Total out	**37**	**36**	
Total 18 Holes	**72**	**71**	

Sam Fleming sent Christmas greetings to Bronson in 1983: "I hope and expect you to do better next year. By all means don't 3 putt the 18th green again."

And we didn't anticipate that we were going to enter the computer hardware business, but I'll save that discussion for the next chapter. Yet Phil knew of Bronson's early consideration of hardware. "I remember in 1973 Bronson was very interested in seeing if he couldn't sell computers for IBM." It just didn't work out then.

Whenever I am out of town, I'll find a bookstore and go in and ask employees or managers without identifying myself, "Do you get any books from Ingram?" They invariably say yes, either a lot or most. Then I'll ask if the company does a good job. Sometimes they'll say something like, "I wish they would arrange the invoice alphabetically instead of numerically." Occasionally, I have been able to take those messages back and have them accommodated. At a bookstore in Nantucket where I was recently, they remembered when I was there a couple of years ago. The manager said, "I couldn't believe it. Within a week of your being here last time the invoices were reversed to the way we wanted them." I have always felt very involved in the business, especially the bookstore part, because I love to read and I love bookstores and libraries.

Sometimes they'll complain that we won't extend enough credit or that our fill rate is not as high as it used to be. At some point I'll identify myself, give them my business card, and tell them to call if anything is going wrong with the service. Phil Pfeffer gets kudos for setting up very trusting relationships with bookstores around the country and for emphasizing a sensitivity to what is important for the bookstore customer.

Bronson was very much front and center in monitoring the operation, but Phil worried the details. Bronson knew the details, but he was not good at dealing with the individual customer. He was into wide brushstroke painting. Phil did an amazing job for years of seeing that there were no unnoticed details. He carried around huge satchels filled with papers and letters. He answered all negative letters and ones that asked for an explanation. He did yeoman's service for the company, and we still tell him on a regular basis how much we have appreciated him.

Even Bronson would acknowledge Phil's efforts. He was not one to give much praise, but he told me frequently that the reason he was able to travel and deal with some of our other businesses and actually have some fun was that Phil Pfeffer was so good at looking after the details.

Economic conditions in 1982 had been bleak, and Bronson wrote to employees in January 1983: "1982 will long be remembered as the year the bottom fell completely out of the United States and world economies. . . . Our company has historically been able to weather economic difficulties reasonably well but we have never faced anything like 1982." Sales were off, and earnings were down 50 percent. Barge and coal divisions were disasters, but books were doing okay: "Nonetheless, we are moving to fight back." Among other things, he wrote, "We have reorganized and significantly increased the sales and marketing staffs of both the Barge and Book Companies reaching toward these new markets [grain barging, microcomputer software] and I believe no one has finer talent than we now have in place."

In January 1984, Bronson wrote to employees in the company newsletter: "Rates [for barges] are simply ridiculous, with too much equipment chasing too little business brought about by the drastic reduction in energy consumption in this country, and reduced exports of both energy and foodstuffs due to the over-valued dollar." Coal and insurance divisions were at the bottom of the cycles. He added, however, "The bright side of our operating companies is consumer products—distribution of books, prerecorded video cassettes and micro-computer software. Here we are having another record year and expect continuing rapid growth for the foreseeable future. Video and micro-computer software will probably constitute increasing percentages of our business in the future, while at the same time I expect we will continue to make dramatic increases in our portion of the total book distribution business."

By the stockholder report of October 1984, Bronson could say that the video segment was "growing by leaps and bounds." Ingram Book Company was renamed Ingram Distribution Group Inc. "to more properly reflect what we do and to give each of the six operating entities within the group, including Ingram Book, Ingram Video and Ingram Software, a separate and stand alone identity." Earlier in the year, he predicted, "There will be a major shake out in software and we are proceeding cautiously while determined to be one of the survivors. We continue to build our organization in the consumer products business in a very dynamic environment."

Two notable bids for businesses were unsuccessful in the period of 1983–84. The first was for Opryland Hotel and theme park. Dave Sampsell helped run the numbers: "We made the strategic decision, with Bronson, that the Nashville Network [part of the Opryland deal] didn't look like a very good proposition. As it turned out, we lost Opryland by about the same number that we discounted the Nashville Network. We were that close. I'm not going to call it a gamble, but it was an expeditionary project that would have framed Ingram Industries very differently and Bronson was prepared to do that."

The other unsuccessful effort was the acquisition of Corroon and Black. Bronson sold Ingram's block of stock because he couldn't negotiate a friendly merger. The *Nashville Banner* editorial page commented on the deal:

> Nashville-based Ingram Industries Inc. has dropped its bid to buy Corroon & Black Corp. but it was a noteworthy endeavor and one that is no less commendable despite the fact it did not succeed.
>
> We commend E. Bronson Ingram, president and chief executive officer of Ingram Industries, for his courageous effort and his willingness to invest $253 million in cash to bring ownership of the New York–based insurance service company—10th largest in the world—to Nashville.
>
> It is the vision and determination of people such as Mr. Ingram that have kept this city squarely in the mainstream of the nation's economic development.
>
> The purchase attempt was a friendly one throughout and it was unfortunate that there were those in C&B who thought the attempted takeover was hostile.
>
> Mr. Ingram issued a statement in which he expressed disappointment that directors of the insurance firm did not present the offer to the company's shareholders, noting that they stood to realize a significant premium on their investment as a result of Ingram's proposal.

Ingram remains one of Nashville's most progressive industries with a diversity of operations that contribute substantially to the city's economy and its business operations and the provision of employment to many of our citizens.

Had the company succeeded in the C&B purchase Nashville's stature as a major insurance center would have risen considerably. Perhaps another effort of similar proportions will be made in the not too distant future.

Meanwhile, the city is indebted to Bronson Ingram for his effort.

Bronson's fondest hope was that the children would one day join Ingram Industries. When they were about fourteen or fifteen, they started asking for extra money. They had an allowance, but they wanted more than he would give them. He said, "I'll tell you what. I'll help you get more money. If you will work for me in one of my companies for one month every summer, I will support your play activity—your horse shows, your golf tournaments—the rest of the year. But I want you to know what I do so that when you grow up, you can decide whether you want to participate or not. And if you can learn it on the ground level, you can do it while you're young in a way that I wasn't able to do."

They all started in the warehouses packing books for a month in the summer. As the boys got older, each went out on the towboats. They cleaned the latrines, they chipped and painted, and they worked on the lowest rung that we have in the company in all areas—in distribution and in the barge business. As a result of doing that, they decided they did not want to stay on the lowest rung, and they became much more aware of the benefits of an education. One graduated from Vanderbilt, one from Princeton, and two from Duke with very nice records. John and David also have MBAs from Vanderbilt's Owen School. And all of the boys eventually worked in the company.

One of my jobs as a mother has been trying to keep the balance, to make them feel competitive with the rest of the world, not with each other, and to help them realize the value of the family. I have done a pretty good job with that, but it's a job that is never finished.

Winnie Palmer, Bronson, Martha, Arnold Palmer, and David at Latrobe Country Club, Pennsylvania, 1983.

There were times, sitting around the dinner table, when the children asked, "Mom, Dad, why do you all work so hard? Don't we have enough money?" We said, "Yes." "Well, then, why do you do this? Why do you go to the office all the time? Why don't you have more fun?" We replied, "This is fun." You do it to generate money, yes, and to generate jobs for people, but then you have money left over to do things for other people and it's another kind of fun.

We talked about it to some extent with the children, but we never said, "You must do things for other people." It was more, "You *will* work. We will have no couch potatoes here." They knew that was a family prerequisite—you find out what you want to do, and we'll support you in doing it. But you will do something. As Robin said, "Dad viewed people who didn't work hard as no-goodniks."

Bronson was more verbal in emphasizing that it was important for them to be prepared and to study, but if they didn't study and they weren't prepared, they better jolly well fail. They were not to cheat to pass a test. In sports they knew that it was fun to win, but only if they won by playing by the rules. Otherwise it was better to lose than to do it dishonestly. He told them, "If you do not play by the rules, you hurt not only yourself but also a lot of other people around you."

David illustrated that he had learned this lesson when he was playing in the Tennessee State Amateur Golf Tournament in Jackson, Tennessee. After starting with rounds of 67, 68, and 74, he was leading the tournament going into the last day, and he called us in Nashville and said, "Come on over and watch. I think I've got a really good chance for winning this." Bronson and I drove to the golf course, and things were going along pretty well for David. He was still leading by a couple of strokes when on the par 3 thirteenth hole, he duck-hooked his ball left into the woods.

When he went into the woods to find his ball—he was twenty feet or so into the woods—he couldn't quite see where the pin was, and he knew he would have to chip a shot out. He came out to see where the pin was, and he realized that he was not only in the woods but there was a red line, which meant he was in a hazard. (David is red/green color blind like my father, which is why he didn't see the red line on the way into the woods.) When a ball is in a hazard, a player is not allowed to touch anything, not the ball or twigs or debris around the ball. It's just tough luck. The player is supposed to hit it out. Unbeknownst to anyone except for himself because he was far enough in, he had moved a twig that was behind his ball.

We saw him roll his eyes and call to an official nearby. He said, "I have to declare a two-stroke penalty on myself because I moved a twig that was near my ball, and I didn't realize I was in the hazard until I came out." The official said, "That's correct. Thank you for telling us. You have two strokes added to your score."

David ended up losing the 1984 Tennessee State Amateur Tournament by two shots. He actually came in third. He was disappointed and we were disappointed for him, but his father said, "Son, I am really more proud of you than if you had won the tournament because you did the honest thing, the right thing. You declared the two strokes. Nobody would have known, but you did it. It proves that you are a person of integrity, and that makes me prouder of you than if you had actually won the tournament."

John started at Princeton in the fall of 1979. Bronson had written a letter to the president of Princeton, William G. Bowen, on John's behalf in January of that year:

Dear Bill:

My second son, John, will graduate from Montgomery Bell Academy here in Nashville this spring and has applied to enter your freshman class next fall. I am sure that all letters from fathers are not guaranteed to be purely objective, but this boy, of my four children, should be able to go to any school in the world he chooses and they would be lucky to have him. His classroom grades are excellent. He has that rare ability to stick to a job until it's done and done well. He is in demand around here among our companies as to which one can land him for summer employment. He is a fine, competitive horseshow rider, like his cousin Bradford Hooker now finishing his junior year with you. He is a steadying influence in our home. All in all, he is a highly satisfactory and thoroughly enjoyable young man you will be lucky to get. The only other school he has applied to is Duke, which took him at first blush, but Princeton is his first choice as it is mine for him.

John has been on campus twice—once with me for a visit to the Admissions Office last spring, and again this past fall with Bradford.

I realize from my own college trustee experience that there is a delicate relationship between the Administration and the Admissions Office, but I also recognize that a relationship does exist and, consequently, I want you to know how terribly interested I am in John's being accepted.

I gather from Bob Cowan and my own observations that things are going well for Princeton now even with the financial squeeze, and I am sure you must be pleased and proud of the status of the University.

On September 10, 1979, Bronson wrote John,

Today should mark your first official day at Princeton and I hope that it is proving to be everything you expected and hoped for. I would certainly have written you sooner to have some mail flowing had you not been gallivanting around the East like a free spirit with your cousins so that it hardly seemed that you needed much cheering up.

I gathered from Mom that your initial meeting with your advisors went well and that first reports on your roommate were good. I hope now that you have met him that he is an attractive guy and that you two can enjoy living with one another. You get along with people so well that I don't worry, but you know you can always change room-mates if there is any reason to. I will be interested to know what courses you are taking this first semester and what you think of your initial exposure to those courses in a college environment.

Your mother is planning to come up on Wednesday to see that you are well settled in before meeting me in New York on Thursday, so I am sure I will get a complete blow-by-blow. I know without asking though that all will be well with you and that you will already have a good start on a great new adventure from which you will benefit the rest of your life.

We miss you very much but I know you are in exactly the right spot doing the best thing you could possibly do to set up the rest of your life. I will hope to talk to you before we go but if not we will call the minute we get back.

Two days later, he wrote again,

Your mother, by the hardest, should be at Princeton with you now and I hope and expect to get a good report from her on every-thing about you when I meet her for lunch tomorrow.

I got back last night from an interesting day in, through, and over the woods of Mississippi and Alabama with the Weyerhaeuser Board. We looked at some of the pine plantations, sawmills, plywood plants, and the site for their huge new papermill complex at Columbus. When the three-mill complex is finished by 1984 and 1985, it will be the biggest thing in that part of the country and perhaps you will enjoy seeing it yourself one day.

As a matter of fact, Orrin and I talked last night about maybe going out West for a short trip next summer and seeing some of the really big trees in the old growth Douglas Fir forests and how they fell them and see them run through the big, old sawmills, before all the huge timber is gone and most everything is smaller—even aged logs. We will talk about it during the year and if you guys want to go I would love to take you.

I have made some reservations for Mom and me to come up there for the Colgate game on October 20 and need you to think and decide whether you would like to go into New York Friday night and meet us or after the game on Saturday, to look around and have an evening on the town. You could bring your roommate or another friend if you want to. It might be nice to spend Friday night at Princeton and go into New York after the game. You think about it while we are gone and we will make the plans to suit you.

With everybody back in school, things are pretty quiet at home and have settled down to the usual routine. Even business is reasonably calm for the moment and I feel pretty comfortable about going away. There is no change in Granny and Dr. [Josh] Billings tells me, after examining her yesterday, that he thinks I am perfectly safe being out of touch for five days but that he will watch her carefully and give me a message on the other end if I need to come home. Really though it looks as though it will be some time yet before anything happens.

I hope you are having a grand time and making lots of new friends. We will write you news of the famous boat trip while we are chugging across and send it when we get to the other side. I miss you and look forward to seeing you in a month.

The reference to Granny (Mrs. O. H. Ingram) concerned a lengthy illness; she had cancer and was under the watchful eyes of doctors. The "chugging across" referred to our trip to England on the *Queen Elizabeth II* with Jake and Anne Wallace, which began on September 13. We would be away only a few days. Jake recalled: "It was a fabulous trip. One of the most fun trips I've ever been on, and it was one of the few times that I've seen Bronson completely relaxed. He was at that time really wrapped up in his business, but we planned it way in advance." We stayed in London a few days and then flew back.

Bronson wrote John a letter on September 26, shortly after our return:

I am enclosing the pictures of your fish which you asked that I send you. I have marked a red "x" on the back of the ones that I would like for you to send back for our scrapbook and am enclosing an envelope for that. I have a letter from Pflueger saying their good friend, Captain Sweeting [captain of the *Patsea V*], had delivered the beast and checking on the wording on the plaque to go with it, which I have taken care of as I said I would.

As we told you on the phone, the trip to England was a great success. The wind blew hard all the way across, but it blew from astern so that the big, old ship was smooth and Uncle Jake never once turned green. London was fun, too. Your mother thoroughly enjoyed working herself up to go before the Committee at Lloyd's, then was—as she acknowledged herself—a great success. The trip home on the Concorde was like riding a bullet again and certainly makes it easy, relative to any other way.

As we agreed, your mother and I will plan to come to Princeton on Friday, the 19th and spend the night and go to the football game on Saturday. We will go into New York after the game and have dinner at the "Frog" [La Grenouille] and see whatever part of town you want to after that. I have reservations at the Princeton Club for Saturday night and we will be glad for you to bring your roommate or any other friend you like, if you want to. The only reasonable flight home leaves New York about 1:10 so that you could go back to school in plenty of time to do any work or riding that you want to do. We will certainly look forward to seeing you in a little over three weeks.

Mom and I are going up to the Greenbrier in White Sulphur Springs on Thursday (tomorrow) for a coal convention. I am not dying to go after the other trip, except that I need to spend some time with our coal people and with the people in the industry and really have to go. David will play golf for me Saturday in the Music City Pro-Celebrity Golf Tournament with whatever player I have drawn, which obviously suits him very well, and I will get home to play Sunday afternoon.

I am glad things are going well for you and we will look forward to hearing from you Sunday night.

As for the appearance before the Committee at Lloyd's of London, Bronson had thought this a good diversification for each of our investment portfolios. I was carefully coached to declare that I understood that I would have "unlimited liability" for the privilege—

and since Bronson had arranged for us to have a backstop for any losses above a certain amount, I felt okay about it. The income was fine for a few years, but then several of our syndicates had wicked asbestos claims, and all of our profits were negated. Thank heavens for Bronson's backstop!

Mrs. Ingram passed away on September 27; she was seventy-three years old. Bronson lost not only his mother but also a trusted advisor on many issues. As I noted earlier, she had an uncanny grasp of numbers and finances, which she had put to use on behalf of numerous boards as treasurer, loving especially the West End Home for Ladies (then called the Old Woman's Home).

A Nashville paper published this tribute to her, "Mrs. Ingram Left Indelible Imprint":

> Friends of Mrs. Hortense Bigelow Ingram, civic and charity leader who died at her home Thursday after a long illness, today praised Mrs. Ingram as a woman who has left an indelible imprint on their own lives and the city of Nashville as well.
>
> Long-time friend J. C. Bradford said Mrs. Ingram was "a wonderful character, very efficient, a fine citizen and a great lady. She helped the city in so many ways."
>
> Mrs. William Waller said, "She was one of the greatest people I've ever known. She had executive ability and was one of the most generous people Nashville has ever had, both with her time and her means."
>
> Waller echoed his wife's sentiments, saying, "She gave a great deal of time and contributed heavily to all worthwhile charitable and educational causes."
>
> Ralph Owen, who said he had known the Ingram family "ever since they moved to Nashville in 1928," described the Ingram family as "one of the greatest assets the city has ever had. They are wonderful people."
>
> Mrs. J. P. Lawrence said Mrs. Ingram "gave more to Nashville than almost anyone I've ever known. She was a great person and very retiring about what she did, very modest."
>
> Former ambassador to Denmark Guilford Dudley said, "She contributed a great deal to the whole area with all of her work and interests in charity.

"She was the type of person who never turned down a call for help from any worthwhile civic, political or charitable organization. She will be missed by her friends and by the city of Nashville."

Vanderbilt University Chancellor Alexander Heard issued a statement saying, "Mrs. Ingram has been an extraordinarily constructive and generous citizen in her interests in a wide range of community activities.

"She will be greatly missed by me personally and by her admirers here at Vanderbilt.

"Mrs. Ingram encouraged significant citizen efforts to make life in Nashville richer. Vanderbilt is especially grateful for her concern for its educational programs.

"The active and generous participation the members of family have taken in Nashville affairs has been a reflection of her own sense of civic involvement."

Mayor Richard Fulton also issued a statement expressing sympathy "to the family of one of Nashville's most prominent citizens. Mrs. Ingram leaves a legacy of commitment to improving our city and an unparalleled record of service to the community. Her actions will long be remembered by those she has helped."

Mrs. Jack Bass Sr. said Mrs. Ingram "made so many contributions to Nashville in so many ways. She was a wonderful board member and had great integrity."

Former Gov. Winfield Dunn said Mrs. Ingram was "a guiding light in this community and a source of great strength to those she came in contact with. Her presence in this community and the impact of her character will be felt indefinitely. She was a great woman and was dearly loved."

Funeral services for Mrs. Ingram were held today at Westminster Presbyterian Church, followed by a private service in Mount Olivet Cemetery.

Her thirteen grandchildren served as pallbearers—the girls as well as the boys. Our children were ages nineteen, eighteen, seventeen, and fourteen and were deeply affected by the loss of Granny, whom they loved and respected.

The family had asked that donations be made to the Old Woman's Home or the Cancer Research and Treatment Center at Vanderbilt University Medical Center. Many people honored Mrs. Ingram by sending donations, and Bronson personally acknowledged the gifts. Pat and Anne Wilson were the recipients of this note that was typical of the ones that Bronson wrote:

> I have just received a nice note from [Dr.] John Chapman [dean of Vanderbilt University Medical School] telling us of your kind contribution in support of cancer research in memory of Mother. All of us appreciate this generous act on your part, on top of everything else you have done, and I simply wanted to say thank you again.
>
> John says that such tangible support for this truly devastating disease process will produce the answer; it simply awaits discovery.

Unfortunately for our family and for many others, the discovery has not come soon enough, but researchers are getting closer.

The family sold Mrs. Ingram's house in White Bear Lake after her death, but the family still had a connection to the area with Mrs. Ingram's sister, Eileen Bigelow. Bronson wrote her in March 1981:

> Thank you for sending me the clipping about the honor bestowed on you by your fellow councilmen of Gem Lake [outside St. Paul, near her home in White Bear]. I certainly think it is well-deserved.
>
> We have had a small horror show this week or I would have answered you sooner. John arrived in Florida Friday night with three of his Princeton roommates for a week and complained of a sore leg after running around on the beach and playing tennis. The pills he had been taking didn't help by Sunday and we found an orthopedic man on Monday morning and they took a picture and found a lesion the size of a silver dollar a couple of inches down from the hip in his left thigh bone which the doctor said could break at any minute and slapped him on crutches immediately. The doctor told him if it wasn't malignant, and the doctor didn't think it was, he would need to have a bone graft and, after some five months on crutches, could expect to be practically good as new.
>
> We flew back here to Vanderbilt where the head of orthopedic surgery [Dr. Paul Griffin] is a friend and outstanding. He put John in the hospital an hour after seeing him that afternoon, did bone

scans Wednesday, and yesterday operated for somewhere better than three or four hours, taking half of his hip and making a bone graft into his leg. He then covered that with a metal plate screwed into the leg and up to and attached to the hip and gave him back to his mother and father who, by then, weren't worth killing. It was not malignant, and John has come through it beautifully and is his usual chipper self except for the few minutes after his morphine shots, and they get him too goofy to think. He is doing much better than we had any reason to hope. They say he can go home sometime next week and perhaps go back to school in about three weeks, if we can make the necessary arrangements there, which I can and will. We were all scared to death, including John, and are thankful that it's over and not worse than it is and was. He has to have another operation in a year to take all the metal back out, but we will worry about that when the time comes. At least it won't be nearly as bad as this one. They have no idea what causes these things and said his leg could have broken at any time which would have made it almost impossible to fix, so I guess, all in all, we are lucky.

On top of all this, today at noon, at a huge luncheon, Martha was chosen the first, annual Century III, 1980, Outstanding Citizen of the Year, by the Nashville Kiwanis Club. I, of course, knew about it but was the only one. John will get to see it on television tonight, and I will hold this letter and mail it after I see if there is a decent newspaper article to send you. Times are never dull around here.

That's certainly true. No one could ever say that times were dull around the Ingram family, and we wouldn't have had it any other way—other than deleting the medical emergencies.

Bronson deepened a dimension in his life following the Chicago trial. The whole event was so stunning that it made him stop in his tracks and reevaluate. I think he became a better citizen because of it, probably a better man because of it, but also in many ways a happier man because of it.

When Albert Schweitzer was practicing medicine in a desperately poor part of Africa, several students reportedly asked him, "Dr. Schweitzer, do you think we will be successful in this chosen career path?" Dr. Schweitzer evidently said, "I don't know who among you will

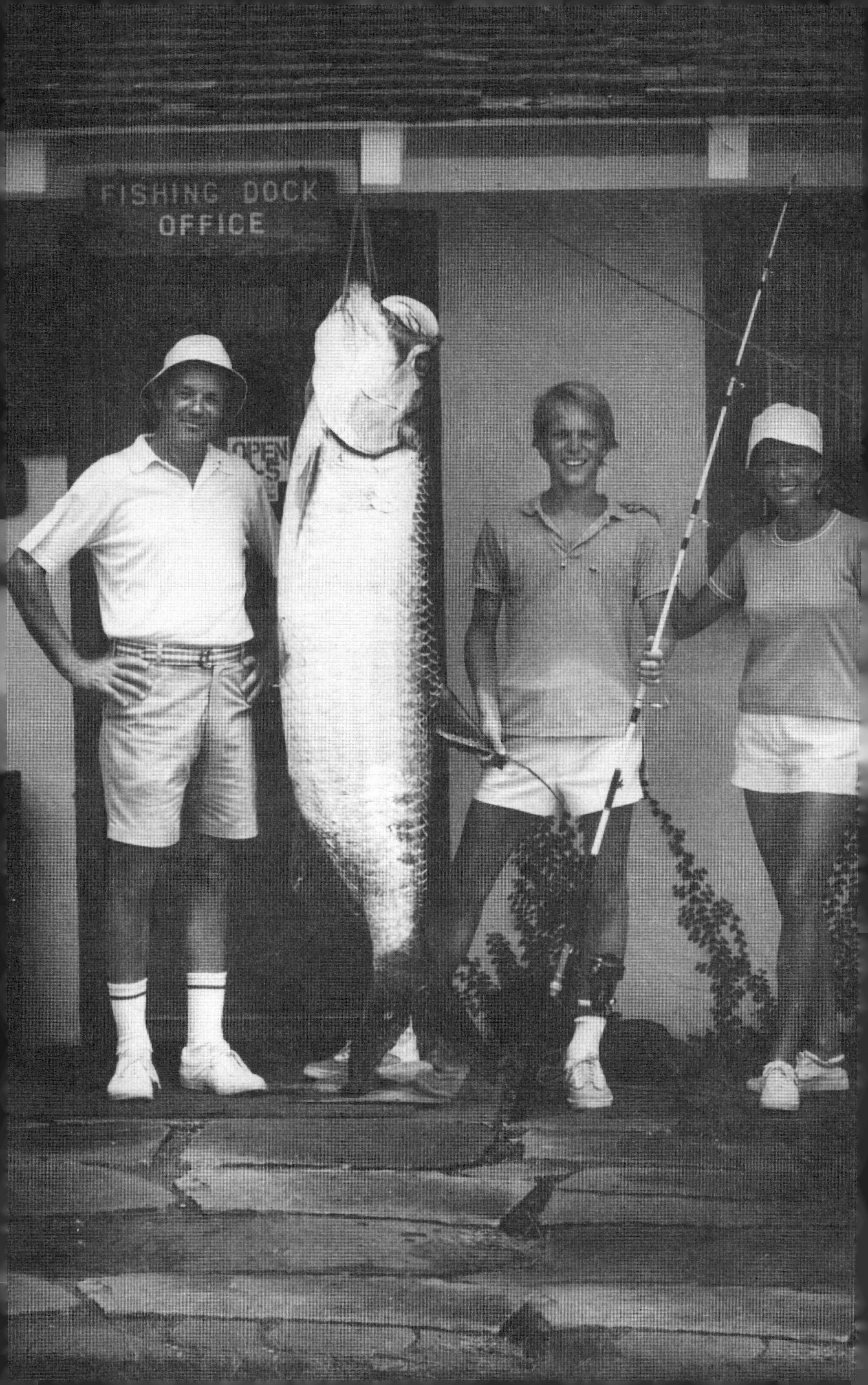
FISHING DOCK
OFFICE
OPEN

be successful, but one thing I do know: The only ones of you who will be really happy are those that have sought and found a way to serve."

In a very strange way Bronson was blessed by the adversities associated with the Chicago event because I think it made him seek and find ways to serve. Part of it was probably for a redemption of sorts for his family, for himself, for his reputation. But I also think that because he was doing this, he was a much happier, more fulfilled person than he had been when he was concentrating only on business and fishing and golf. He still focused on business and fishing and golf, but he developed this other dimension.

I have watched many people and thought often about this quotation from Albert Schweitzer. I really do believe that the happiest people I know are those who are fully engaged in somehow serving their fellow human beings. It can be in any form—a businessman doing volunteer work, a doctor looking after patients—any number of things. The unhappiest people seem to be the ones that observers would have thought would be happy—wealthy people sitting around and playing cards or playing golf or just doing nothing. Their existence seems futile, yet I think most of us, at least in our early years, thought that if you simply had stacks of money and could sit around doing nothing, that would be the ultimate. Well, I would argue that is not the case. I am certainly all in favor of having as much money as possible, but that needs to be coupled with a sense of community and a sense of doing something for one's fellow human beings.

It is not that Bronson was uninvolved in civic duties before the Chicago event, but he was not in any leadership positions. Of course in his younger years, he might not have been asked to assume leadership, or maybe he did not think he had time for it.

His formula for success in business was to believe in it and work hard at it. He was very effective in business, and once those efforts began to translate to having more money and more ability to give money, he brought the same passion to what he was doing civically as he had to his business.

From 1978 to 1984, Bronson held various positions. He served as a member of the Board of Trustees of the Cumberland Museum and Science Center, the

Bronson, John, and Martha with John's catch of the day, Sea Island, Ga.

Governor's Better Schools Program, PASS, and the Board of Directors of the PENCIL Foundation. All had to do with education. He directed most of his energies to INROADS, however; his enthusiasm for the group lasted from the moment he became a member of the board in 1978 until his death in 1995. He was chairman of the board of the Nashville affiliate from 1982 until 1990, and he was chairman of the National Board of Directors from 1987 until 1990. In fact, he was the first inductee to the INROADS/Nashville Hall of Fame in 1995.

INROADS is an international nonprofit organization whose mission is to develop and place talented minority youth in business and industry and prepare them for corporate and community leadership. The Nashville affiliate had its start in 1978. Ken Roberts, then chairman and CEO of First American Corporation, piqued Bronson's interest in the program.

Dave Sampsell heard Bronson say of INROADS, "You know, goddamnit, if there's this sizable group of people who don't have ready access to our economy and have the opportunity to participate fully with equal measure, we will have failed, and capitalism as we know it and love it will fail." Dave added, "He didn't like quotas. But what he did like was to give a helping hand to people who wanted to make better of themselves. This is why he loved INROADS."

Charles Story was director of INROADS/Nashville when Ken Roberts introduced him to Bronson. (Charles is now president and CEO for the entire nation.) He said, "Bronson just developed a passion for INROADS that was really unbelievable. I've been in situations where he would say to big meetings of people: 'You don't have any excuse not to do this. You know you need to diversify your workforce.'

"I think he liked the no-nonsense approach that we took. The fact that students were held accountable. They have to do well academically while they are in college. They had to do well during the internships that they had with the companies. They had to go to the training and advisory sessions that we had scheduled. So, the whole accountability, discipline, no-nonsense approach was what he liked about it. And that was a business proposition. The companies paid us a fee for what we did, and it wasn't to be considered charitable or anything like that."

Charles asked him to host a meeting for publishers, and Bronson honored that request in New York City. Charles said, "I was disappointed with the amount of representation we had gotten in the publishing industry. And so, he hosted a meeting at the Tavern on the Green in New York for INROADS and publishers, to get INROADS involved with them."

Of Bronson's style in a meeting, Charles remarked, "People knew when Bronson spoke, he was going to zoom right to the heart of whatever it was. People might have been pontificating about this, pontificating about that, but if Bronson said something, it was boom! 'What are you going to do about this?' or 'Why is this the way it is?' or whatever. Just the ability to focus relentlessly, I mean, relentlessly he would focus on the issue, and not let people deviate from whatever the issue might have been with a lot of superfluous stuff."

Charles admitted, "I didn't learn how to speak as directly as he did, but I learned how to cut away all the chaff around issues, how to zoom

Ingram Industries Board of Directors: (front row) Bronson, Martha, and Alvin Johnson; (back row) Phil Pfeffer, Neil Diehl, Joe Wyatt, Sam Richmond, and Jim Neal.

Bronson and Bill McDaniel, president of the National Parents Support Group of INROADS.

in and to focus." He considered Bronson a mentor and said, "He was consistently supportive of me."

Mercedes Lytle first met Bronson in the early 1980s when she was applying for the managing director's position at INROADS/Nashville: "I had expected him to be curt and the session to be difficult. It wasn't. It was an easy conversation, and he was direct. But I think my being a Mississippian made me appreciate his directness.

"We could talk about a lot of different things that Bronson did for INROADS, but one of his early contributions was to transform the organization from—and I want to say this with respect—being considered initially as a social service organization to a very well-run business, and I think that's the transformation that occurred under Bronson's leadership. I think that that transformation is not only what he brought to this affiliate, but what he actually brought to the entire organization.

"He was a hard-core businessman and those are the values and that's the mind-set that he brought to us here and to our board nationally. That was all Bronson. That's his legacy to us: that he made us aware of the requirement to be a business in many different ways."

Mercedes pointed out a characteristic of Bronson's leadership in any endeavor: "Part of what made us grow very well was Bronson's active leadership. He was not a board chair on paper or at meetings. He was a board chair, period. If we had difficulty getting into a company or were talking about companies that we wanted to get in to, we'd ask board members to take a list. Bronson always said, 'I'll take this, this, this, this, and this,' and he always had a hefty list. He'd go with us or open the door so we could talk to the CEOs of the companies.

"He knew this community very, very well. He knew when it was a good time to ask some people and when it was not a good time. He also had a good sense of who would be responsive to this idea and who wouldn't be and why.

"It was during Bronson's leadership that we as an organization got a university as a corporate sponsor, and that was Vanderbilt. Vanderbilt was the first university nationwide to sponsor interns."

On the videotape *INROADS: A Partnership of Success*, Bronson declared, "I think that it is recognized in Nashville as a quality program as the source or the primary ongoing source for talented minority youngsters." And he commented on the significance of role models: "Five years from now I think probably the most important change will be the fact we've got a whole lot more alumni out there and consequently we've got something to point to in terms of recruiting new corporate sponsors, but more importantly I think, we've got a whole bunch of role models."

Mercedes noted the effect of INROADS on Bronson: "Bronson and I never had this kind of conversation. I think INROADS added some value to him personally. He gave in extraordinary ways to INROADS in little ways that I can't even enumerate for you, but I think INROADS also did something for Bronson. Because we never talked about it, I can't say what that is. But I think that there was something that INROADS gave to Bronson or that he touched here that he enjoyed that kept him giving at the level that he gave. I'm not talking about money; I'm talking about of himself, just of his person.

"I think Bronson had a passion about the success of Nashville glob-ally. He and I on occasion talked about Martha's involvement with the development of TPAC. I know that we talked very occasionally about his political support and why and how. Not in any particular detail, but enough for me to know that he felt very, very strongly about the success of Nashville as a community and that he felt an obligation to commit to that community as much as he could."

Mercedes also noted Bronson's effect on her: "I come from a teaching background and I do have to say that my parents configured a lot to my just plain, old everyday common sense. But Bronson provided opportunities that I'm not sure that I would have had, were it not for him. He provided experiences that I think empowered me to have some confidence that allows me to be where I am now. I can't imagine having a relationship with anybody else other than Bronson Ingram that would have been better for me at that point and time in my career. I was making this transition from an educator to a quasi businessperson. I'm Mississippian by background and I'm used to people saying, 'I don't like this. I do like that. Move over,' whatever it is, and Bronson's style was just perfect to really challenge and push me to the limit.

"My standard was perfection. You don't ever get there, but Bronson's was the same, and so you got as close as humanly possible. This minority organization happened to be attached to Bronson Ingram, and that meant the standard for this organization was the same as the standard for Ingram Industries. I think that anything less than that would have made me be very different than I am right now today. So, whatever I am today, as far as contributing to INROADS, and my self-confidence and half of the experiences that I've had, I can't help but really thank Bronson Ingram for."

Bronson would be honored to be remembered in this way.

CHAPTER 7

Man in the Arena

It is not the critic who counts; not the man who points out how the strong man
stumbles, or where the doer of deeds could have done them better.
The credit belongs to the man who is actually in the arena.

—Theodore Roosevelt

All of the businesses of Ingram Industries, though they have
grown and changed, have always had one thing in common: we
bring together people who are committed to delivering excellent services and products and providing the highest quality possible.
On a videotape about Ingram Industries, Bronson told viewers,
"We're proud of our well-earned reputation as an industry leader,
and we're proud of the fact that we set an example by which our
competitors try and measure themselves." We have never wavered in
trying to meet that standard.

By the end of 1984, Ingram Industries had purchased substantially
all of the assets of Ohio Barge Line and Mon Valley Transportation
Company from U.S. Steel. With those purchases Ingram Barge became
the third largest river carrier, and Bronson had negotiated with Neil
Diehl to become the new CEO of Ingram Barge. He had begun talks
in the summer of 1984 and needed a decision by December 27. We
invited Neil and his wife, Judith, to our home for the company
Christmas party. Neil recalled, "That was impressive to us. It wasn't
impressive because of the people. I don't remember that much about
the people. I did about the family. I thought if anybody could raise four
kids sanely in an atmosphere of wealth and so forth that they obviously
had and have four children have a lot of sense of values and courtesy,

there had to be something there. And that was one of the reasons that we came down [from Pittsburgh to join the company]. I've often thought about that. They didn't know they were even playing a part because they were pretty young at the time."

Neil commented on Bronson's support: "He was always available. That never changed, by the way, always available to you if you wanted to discuss something with him. Didn't have to wait around for decisions, as most people will tell you. They came pretty quickly."

The barge line business is a chaotic, wild business that changes from day to day, according to Neil, but he and Bronson and Orrin liked it. Neil said, "The good thing about Bronson was, he had a tremendous amount of knowledge, and for me, it was fun to talk barge line business because you never had to start at the first step. I don't know which one of us had the most knowledge in running a barge line. I don't know to this day which one of us had the most knowledge. But I do know that the exchange of information was very rapid. The decision making was easy. The cooperation that I received from him was awfully high." Bronson commented to stockholders in 1985, "We are perceived as the fastest growing and most committed barge company on the river system and intend to use that perception to help insure that we are a survivor."

The barge company always had a positive cash flow, but as Neil acknowledged, "We began to get large enough to become competitive when we coupled the two businesses that put Ingram on the Ohio River." Neil added, "I never asked Bronson to make an investment that he did not make in the years that I worked there. Never. And I know I've told people that before and their eyebrows go up and it just never happened." Once when he was talking about a $3 million investment, he told Bronson, "You may want to think more about this, or you may want to get some more information." Bronson looked up and said, "For that kind of money, I don't think long. Go ahead." Neil said, "That was it. We went ahead and did it. Oh, he always checked up afterward. Always wanted to know if you were successful in doing it. Always wanted to know what happened after you did it."

A dramatic change for the better in barge line rates did not occur until after Bronson became ill. Neil and his associates had positioned the barge line to be ready for the change, and he was able to tell Bronson, "'You know, I believe Orrin was right,' because Orrin had stood up at the previous board meeting and said, 'The rates have changed.' Well, we had seen rate changes before that would be maybe a step toward change, then stop, then maybe retreat, that type of thing." But the positive rate change was going to stay for a while.

Neil described a typical barge line meeting: "Orrin would stand up at the meeting and say, 'We got this contract from GE, and it's a good one!' Then Bronson would say, 'How can a goddamn contract with an eight percent return be a good one?' In truth, it wasn't bad at all, but his stimulus was to say, 'That is simply not any good, Orrin, and you know it is not any good. Don't sit up there and bullshit me.' That's what he would say time and time again with his enthusiasm about the business, but the message was for everybody in the room. I think everybody realized he wasn't just picking on Orrin; that had nothing to do with it. When he felt they were not doing their job, then he would lay hard, even publicly."

To E. Bronson Ingram
With best wishes
Ronald Reagan

Bronson at the White House, meeting Ronald Reagan, 1984.

One meeting about strategic planning stuck in Neil's memory: "We had talked about the estimated profitability for the following year and the years to come but it was the following year particularly and I think we forecasted a loss in that year. Bronson just blew up and left the meeting, and off he went.

"I turned around to the other guys, and I said, 'Well, obviously, he's not happy with the forecast. So, we are going to go back and look at it again. Because if we made a mistake, we want to find it, and if we have to be more optimistic, we'll be optimistic, but I want to know which it is. Whether it's a mistake that we made or whether it is really a thing based on optimism.' I don't believe in saying something that's not going to happen or has a good possibility of happening.

"I sat down in my office, being very contemplative, thinking about the whole affair. It might have been an hour later when the phone rang and it was Bronson. He wanted to know if I would come up and see him. He never forced you to come up. Never. He would say, 'Do you have time to come see me?' Every time we ever had a conversation or if I would ask to see him sometime, he would say, 'Can't see you right now, but how would three o'clock be? How would tomorrow be?' Always set up a date and mainly, he was available to see me about half of the time without any prenotice. And so, I went up to his office and we sat down, and it was the closest I think Bronson ever came to offering an apology in all the time I knew him." Neil observed: "He really wanted to be associated with winners, and that did not necessarily mean that you had to be the ultimate in anything if you tried hard."

In 1994, the barge company marked the end of an era—it would no longer transport heavy oil products. Bronson reluctantly wrote to stockholders about the sale of the long-term charter of black oil equipment, tank barges, and boats: "We got out of this business in which we were the largest player because we simply could not get paid a reasonable return for the environmental risk involved in moving heavy oil products."

Neil came to know Bronson well in his years with the company: "Bronson as an individual always struck me as one who was not understood fully at all. What I saw in Bronson was an absolute shyness despite the fact that he could be so overbearing. You know his favorite situation would be one in which he is in total control." And he saw that "Bronson had a real humanitarianism streak in him. I've never been associated with a company that permitted people to have time off at the workplace to pursue things [community affairs] and at different levels. It wasn't just the chief executive officer. It went right down the troops and still does today."

An article in the *Nashville Banner*, November 12, 1986, titled "Ingram Says People Are Key to Successful Businesses," summarizes much of what was going on in Ingram Industries eight years after its formation but also conveys Bronson's attitude toward his associates:

> Today, Ingram Industries is the largest privately held company in Nashville with sales of $900 million this year, up from about $750 million last year, and 2,600 employees nationwide, 1,200 of whom work in Nashville.
>
> "I've never particularly cared for my business to be public knowledge," Ingram said last week in an interview from his head-quarters, tucked modestly away in the back of a Third National Bank office on Harding Road.
>
> "It's your own business and your own company and you can do with it as you like. You don't have stock, investors, analysts and unhappy shareholders to contend with, and you don't have to report your results on a quarterly basis."
>
> The results that count to Bronson Ingram are kept in the right hand drawer in his desk. Every month, the heads of Ingram Industries diversified companies hand him a report card on their business.
>
> That includes Ingram Barge Co., the third largest carrier in the U.S. inland marine industry, Custom Fuel Services, which refuels barges, Ingram Materials Co., which dredges sand from the Ohio River and sells it, Ingram Coal, which buys and sells coals on both the international and domestic markets.
>
> Ingram Distribution Co. is the nation's largest wholesale book distributor and includes Ingram Book Co., the Tennessee Book Co., which distributes textbooks, Ingram Software Inc., the largest distributor of microcomputer products, Ingram Video, Ingram Audio and Ingram Periodicals, which distribute prerecorded videotapes, audio cassettes and specialty magazines.
>
> Ingram Cactus Co. is a partnership between Ingram and CEO International Corp., which manufactures wellheads and valves for the petroleum industry. Ingram Production Co. owns 5 percent interest in Indonesia's state-owned oil production business.
>
> And when the Ingram companies need insurance, they go to another Ingram subsidiary, the Tennessee Insurance Co., which acts as an agent for them to get reinsurance on the world market. Tennessee Insurance also sells individual automobile insurance.

"Anybody who thinks they are good at start-ups is crazy," Ingram said. "The hardest thing in the world to do is start anything. Most of what we do is start something or build on a small nucleus that we acquired.

"I've always said if you give me enough good people and enough money, we could be successful in anybody's business. People are the key.

"I don't have to know about the details of every business, but I know enough about them to be able to manage them.

"We run the business on a profit center concept. The profit centers have their own management and have a great deal of autonomy.

"I really involve myself in keeping up with the industries we're in so I can be a resource to the profit center heads when they want my advice on something.

"You run any business off the figures because the figures tell you the facts. The advantage we have is we can just flat do it better and cheaper. The big guys never get a chance to step on us."

Ingram Industries' management is thin and extremely able. "Most of the businesses we are involved in are too tough to have anybody we don't need around," Ingram said.

His strategy for attracting and keeping top talents is simple: hire overachievers to begin with, give them the tools to work with and an economic incentive.

"And then you have to give them all the visibility they want and allow them to get recognition. Within very broad bounds, you let them know they are their own boss."

The Ingram family still owns 90 percent of the stock in the company, but its employees hold the rest and top managers are given phantom stock in their subsidiaries that will earn value as the subsidiaries improve.

As for where Ingram Industries will head this year, Ingram said, "I think anybody who tells you they have goals for something is just blowing in the wind.

"I enjoy the business, I enjoy the people we associate with and I want to make it as big and profitable as can be and I don't know what that is.

"It depends on what opportunities come along, but you can't go out and look for opportunities, opportunities come out and find you.

"In the past, we had opportunities that have changed the shape of the company. We had Opryland bought for awhile. We had a commitment that fell through.

"And we wanted to buy Corroon & Black (one of the nation's largest insurance brokers). It was sound but some of the board of directors liked Corroon & Black like it was.

"There's a lot of consolidation going on in the barge and distribution industries. Those are generally opportunities, and we like to take advantage of opportunities.

"As anything becomes available through financial distress or bigger companies deciding this really isn't their cup of tea, we'll try to be adroit enough to take a look at it."

I might add that an element of Bronson's philosophy was this: if we look after our people, our people will look after the company. He wanted to make sure that the facilities were good, we were paying competitive wages with appropriate benefits, and employees felt well respected. That was before the evolution of all these formulas for human resources. He believed the employees should share in the success that they helped to bring about. Part of the rationale of calling employees "associates" was to make them feel that we were all on the same team. It is interesting, though, that the idea of associates was carried out with a CEO who was so authoritarian in so many ways.

Sam Walton's book, *Sam Walton: Made in America*, published in 1992, appealed to Bronson in a way that many other books did not, and he often quoted portions of it to associates in meetings. Sam relied on these ten rules for running a successful company: (1) commit to your business, (2) share your profits with all your associates, and treat them as partners, (3) motivate your partners, (4) communicate everything you possibly can to your partners, (5) appreciate everything your associates do for the business, (6) celebrate your successes, (7) listen to everyone in your company, (8) exceed your customers' expectations, (9) control your expenses better than your competition, and (10) swim upstream. Bronson had been relying on the same rules all the years that he had been in business, long before he read Sam's book, but Sam summed them up nicely.

Roy Claverie believed that Bronson's relationship with associates varied over time: "Bronson was a product of a family that was very entrepreneurial. And I think when he first started into business, his maturity level was such that he was entrepreneurial, but he also had the vision that he knew more things than everyone else and was very controlling in terms of conducting meetings and handling matters with associates. I think his relationship even with profit center heads was probably not as it would have been later in his years.

"I think he came to learn with experience, like most people come to learn with experience, that businesses are made up of many people and that there has to be a table where all those opinions get on the table and where they're shared back and forth equally. I think he really matured in that and I think when he matured, in accepting more advice from the other associates, and being less overbearing in certain circumstances, I think that's when he arrived, from a maturity standpoint, because I think that gave more empowerment to the business leaders that we had and with that empowerment comes development. I think that led to the further development of people like Phil Pfeffer, people like Roy Claverie. All of us would not have grown as much had Bronson's style not changed.

"The greatest strength Bronson Ingram had was knowing how to deal with the financial side of the business and maintaining the capital capacity of the business. He was unique in that; he understood it totally. He always planned to never be in a position to be in a severe capital restraint scenario, and I believe that that forward-looking vision on the financial side is what's really made our business the way it is." He added, "I think in hindsight everyone would say that we knew that the ECOL refinery was a big deal, but I don't think we knew how big the Micro D purchase was going to be."

How right he was! When the computer stores first sprang up, Ingram supplied computer books and software. To better meet that need, we acquired Software Distribution Systems, Inc., which was the fourth or fifth largest micro software distribution business, with emphasis on business software, and next Softeam. Then the small chains became larger chains, and their proliferation was explosive. We started getting calls for hardware, so we bought a little hardware operation. Then at the end of 1985, we had the opportunity to purchase 50 percent of the common stock of Micro D, a California company, and in 1986, we were able to purchase an additional 10 percent of the company's common stock.

David commented on his father's foray into the computer business: "The energy level in the early growth of the distribution business was Phil [Pfeffer], with Dad providing guidelines, experience, and capital. I think Chip [Lacy, who was running Micro D] had a lot of the same energy level as Phil, and Dad and Phil were good balance offs. And they took advantage of very fast-growing markets, and with Phil it was first book distribution, then videos, and then the computer business. They definitely took some risks.

"I can remember asking my dad when he went to buy the rest of Micro D, and I was in the finance area, I said, 'Dad, why are you taking all of this risk? You built the business into a billion or a billion and

Dedication of the new Nashville Metropolitan Airport Terminal, August 1987: (left to right) Gen. William G. Moore Jr., Bobby Mathews, Bronson, and Tom Ervin.

half—and that was total revenues back then, if you can believe how much bigger it is now—why do you keep pushing further?' He said, 'Well, David, it's two things. One is, you have windows where you can do business transactions and buy things right and have them come out successfully.' We were doing lots of things concurrently, and that was my concern. 'Second is, if you have talented executives and you don't give them a chance to enrich themselves, you lose those talented executives.' The point being that Chip, Phil, and others had stakes in the business, and the only way they were going to get rich themselves was if those businesses expanded and became very large and very profitable."

Ingram acquired the remainder of Micro D in 1989. It was a public company, and Bronson took it private. He told stockholders: "The consolidation of Ingram Computer and Micro D has proceeded through the first quarter with substantial success in the face of an extraordinarily complicated set of people, cultural, and systems issues."

The company operated first as Ingram Micro D and later dropped the D. The company's first $100 million sales month was September 1989. The first European acquisition was Softeurop, and other acquisitions followed as we tried to keep up with consumer demand in the United States and in international markets.

While Ingram's computer division continued to grow, the political climate was changing on the world front, and Bronson wrote in the company newsletter at the outset of 1991:

> 1990 continued the watershed events in Eastern Europe ending with Russia, the former "Evil Empire," bankrupt and in ethnic disarray, defeated not by our guns and rockets but by economic muscle produced by the free enterprise system. Had it not been for the madman in Iraq, our economy might have sneaked through a low growth, no growth scenario, but that was not to be. The oil price shock resulting from Iraq's invasion has plunged us into a recession, exacerbated from an overreaction by the federal bank examiners, causing a complete freeze on credit to all but the very largest corporations which will have severe results if it lasts very long. The consumer, reacting to these events, zipped his purse and the retail market is soft to terrible, depending on the area of the country.
>
> Fortunately, your company has not been adversely affected to any serious degree by the economy or other events to date and has finished 1990 with much the best year in its history, significantly above our budget or revised budget expectations. The charge was led by our microcomputer business which ran throughout the year at very high levels.

As Ingram Micro continued its "charge," Bronson spent more of his time on that division.

These excerpts from Bronson's messages to stockholders in 1992 and 1993 briefly tell what was on his mind:

> Heaven only knows what we are doing to our future energy posture in this country with no energy policy and environmentalists in control.

I think the media has finally taken its foot off the neck of the consumer and a better feeling about the economy is at hand.

[After Ingram was assigned an exclusive contract with IBM to distribute a new product to VARs]: We have been working on this breakthrough for seven years and, obviously, we are very pleased.

Europe is our principal trouble spot. Their economy is absolutely in the tank and microcomputer product sales have been affected accordingly.

Clinton and his supporters in Congress will no doubt tax the successful and the successful will no doubt hunker down and figure out how to avoid or mitigate most of it. The government will also spend the lion's share of the proceeds counting on future cuts, not yet specified much less passed, to trim the deficit, which we all know is not very likely to happen.

By 1994, the computer business was so huge that Chip Lacy, who had overseen much of that business, became president of Ingram Industries. Bronson as chairman reported to the associates at the beginning of 1994: "Ingram Micro has become our largest business and will become an even larger percentage over the coming years." There had been record earnings in the United States, but sales in Europe were weak:

Continental Europe . . . is faced with chronic unemployment of about 11% and other problems. They have high government spending with resulting deficits and they have not yet started the corporate downsizing you have seen in this country where microcomputer wide and local area networks are replacing a whole upper level of staff and ancillary management on a permanent basis. . . .

While we fell short of our budgeted profit expectations, we still had a very successful record year with huge volume increase. This growth has put strains on many of you with long hours, many new Associates to train and work with and, in some cases, inadequate space. All this is being addressed as fast as we possibly can because 1994 looks like more of the same. Sales volumes continue to grow at an astounding pace and we expect earnings to grow with it to a new record level. With the downsizing going on all over the country we are fairly unique, but I recognize the enormous and dedicated effort you have all made toward our successful year will continue to make for our success in the new year.

When each of our sons entered the family business, Bronson made certain each son was working for somebody who would be a mentor and teach him. Just as Bronson did not believe in coaching his sons in sports in their early years, he thought there would be too much tension for him to be working directly with them in business.

Our son John considered working elsewhere after he received his MBA from Owen Graduate School, but he admitted, "It certainly wouldn't have made any sense to start at Ingram and then stop and go work for someone else for a while and then come back. I thought long and hard about it, and the fact is, at the end of the day, I had an opportunity to carry my own briefcase." His first job was assistant to the treasurer, Tom Lunn.

Bronson, Martha, and Robin at the Hampton Classic, August 30, 1992. (Photo by "Bruz" [Alonzo P. Boardman].)

Bronson did teach them lessons while they were growing up that they have used in business. John said, "He taught us a deep respect for the people that work for you. They spend an incredible amount of time and energy in their lives helping build your company, and you just don't flick them away. He cared deeply about them—not blindly. If there were people in the businesses that needed to go, he would deal with that. He was always very conscientious about trying to do the right thing for people—whether people who worked for him or people in general. I think that was something we certainly learned and saw. The value of hard work. Being honest. Hiring good people.

"He didn't verbalize a lot. It was really more through his actions. Nor did he compliment a lot. I'd hear about it from Ira, our [former] baby nurse [now housekeeper], who would come up and tell me, 'Boy, your father was singing your praises.' And I had to wonder where that came from. It was something that my mother poked him on all the time: 'Tell them you think they're doing a good job.' Whether it was his children or his employees, he was raised more in an environment where you pointed out the negative and were quietly pleased about the positive."

John was in the monthly meetings with his father and saw him in action: "He understood the business. He was very familiar with the plans, with the directions, and with the budgets that were put together toward reaching those plans. Monthly he was there with the 'attaboys' or the stick, depending on how the company was performing.

"He was not someone who took a very short-term view. That was one reason he didn't want to be a public company. He wasn't situated for it. It wasn't interesting to him. He wasn't interested in how rich he could be. He was interested in building and in enjoying and growing and running the business. He already had the material things that he wanted, and that was that.

"Something else about Dad is, people tended to work hard for him. One reason was, they respected him and they wanted his approval. He had a certain aura about him that was something you wanted. I know it was something I certainly wanted as a child, as an adult. I think that was certainly an important quality because it was part of what made him a great leader. The second reason was, they saw what happened to those who didn't do well. He was not charitable."

Lee Synnott interviewed in 1989 for the job of chairman of the board of Ingram Book. He spoke with Bronson: "'If I come on board, I suppose that one of my roles would be as John's mentor, sort of holding the reins until John could be ready.' Bronson went into a reflective mode and said, 'Yes, I hope that my sons will want to do something with the business over time. I won't always be here. I would like to think that they would have enough energy and gumption to make something out of the business. I hope that happens.' But he said,

'That's not any guarantee. We will be hiring you as a professional manager to run our business. And my children won't be in any slot like you would be in unless they deserve it.'

"I'll always remember how he felt about it, but you could also see a great deal of pride in how he talked about the children, and I quizzed him pretty heavily about each one of them. My interest, as I told him, was, "I'm joining essentially what is a family organization. I want to know a lot about those people and how they are going to influence the way I'm going to be able to do my job." I had him talk about each of the boys at great extent, and I really liked what I saw as a father talking about his children. To me, an outsider, someone that didn't know him at all, I think he was able to do a pretty good job in describing their strengths and what they had to learn. And it gave me some insights." Lee joined the company in February 1990.

The Book Group had not grown as rapidly in 1989 as Ingram Micro and Entertainment had. Lee explained what had happened: "We'd come off of 1989 with a book company that had its first service failure ever. We couldn't ship books in the latter part of December on time because we didn't have the adequate facilities. So, early in 1990, we came back with the recommendation of let's go forward with not just one additional distribution center but let's put two in and why we wanted to do a title expansion at the same time. Bronson bought into it readily.

"It was the shortest discussion of a major capital expenditure in my business career, and I'd been around some heavy-duty players, world-class leaders in my mind like I perceived that Bronson was. I can guarantee you that they took a lot more time going over the numbers and the details. Bronson spent a lot of time studying, but he was also intuitive and understood the markets and was willing to make an investment decision with less information than some would have had to have."

Lee observed other characteristics of Bronson: "He was very capable of growling and doing so where you thought you were going to die. But also because of that, when he passed out compliments, you knew he really meant it. I would say Bronson was a leader's leader. He didn't pick on trivia. He didn't second-guess what you were doing. He was very supportive. If it was a major issue and he thought you were missing some information, he would certainly draw your attention to that. And he would do that in an effective way. He probably organized his thoughts better and was able to deal with high-level numbers incisively better than anybody I've ever seen."

There was a situation where things did not go well, and Lee said, "We had just spent the previous few days really digging to find out how bad the problem was. We'd only said to Bronson, 'There is a problem, and we'll tell you when we get to the meeting how bad it is.' When he got to the building, I was downstairs to greet him coming in the door, took him into a little conference room, apologized, told him how bad the problem was. He didn't even blink. He just said, 'Lee, I know you feel worse about this than anybody else, and I'm sorry it happened. But you've done a lot of other good things with the company, and I know you'll make this one up. Just don't worry about it. Just go fix it.' Couldn't believe it. I'd seen him absolutely eat up people who had done stupid things. He couldn't have been more gracious, and I probably worked harder to fix it because of that."

When Bronson went to the American Booksellers Association meetings, he met all kinds of publishers and customers. He was a well-regarded figure within the industry, and he wanted to make sure that Ingram's service remained exceptional.

The superstore phenomenon was another force in our business, and Phil Pfeffer, by then chairman of Ingram Distribution Group, was integral in seeing that we could meet the demands of that market. We think one reason that Barnes & Noble could grow so quickly and so well was that we opened stores for them. When they built the stores, we came in with all the biographies in alphabetical order, all the fiction in alphabetical order, and so on, and we rolled the books off the trucks and put them onto the shelves.

Michael Lovett, senior vice president of Ingram Book Group, remarked, "We had a very efficient, lean, mean, well-managed, well-financed book company and Book Group." For the Book Group, 1994 was a record year.

Our son David did not immediately find a job at Ingram Industries after he graduated from Duke, where he had been on the golf team. He gave serious thought to becoming a professional

golfer. I thought, *Oh, no! This is not really right for David as a career*, and I expressed my concern to Bronson. But Bronson said, "Let him try it. He's good. I don't think he is probably good enough to make it on the Tour; I don't think he hits the ball far enough. Only he can determine that. Let's give him a chance." Bronson told David to give it a try, then added, "The only thing is, you've got to support yourself." He got an hourly job at Duke in the Development Office.

Bronson and Robin on the Patsea V.

While he had that job, David was also playing in golf tournaments. Bronson asked Arnold Palmer, whom we had known for years, to play a round with David up in Latrobe, Pennsylvania, and help him determine whether he was good enough for the Tour. Arnie was very complimentary when David played with him and told him, "I want you to see my pro down in Bay Hill, at Orlando, Florida." The pro, Dick Tiddy, evaluated him and his swing, and he also got David involved with some of the professional players.

David played a round with Greg Norman at Bay Hill and had played in college against other players that are today big-name professionals, such as Davis Love III, Billy Andrade, and Steve Elkington. Even though David was able to beat these players occasionally, he realized that he didn't have the "pro length," which would probably make life on the Tour very difficult. Thus, he decided to attend Vanderbilt business school for an MBA degree and then pursue a business career.

As he was finishing graduate school, David evaluated his next move: "As a son, you want your father to really be happy about what you choose for an avocation. I guess with both my parents they raised me in the vein that as long as you do the best that you can, it doesn't matter what you do. I thought that was true until I told my father that I was going to go to work for my father-in-law.

"I worked two years for Duke University as a fundraiser/development officer before I went to Vanderbilt to Owen. I guess I'm the only person among my siblings that has worked for somebody else. I would tell anybody that you ought to work for somebody else before you work in a family business because either people are going to be too hard on you and you're never going to live up or people are blowing smoke. You never know how you are—good or bad—when you work for a family business. You can only get that from working outside and understanding and gaining confidence. I think that is one thing that my brothers probably would have benefited from, but I can tell you that my father's pressure to work for the company was significant. His rationale was, 'We do things the right way in business.' Or he felt that we did. He wanted us to have that type of grounding before we got into other endeavors.

"I guess he knew we were going to have access to money because he had given us quite a bit of inheritance, and I think he wanted to make sure that if we were going to apply it to an operating business, we knew or had a model for how a properly run business worked before we got into situations where we were going to blow it.

"Anyway when I told my father that I wanted to move to Baltimore . . . I was engaged at the time to my wife [Sarah LeBrun], who I had known since I was a senior in college and she was a freshman at Duke. I told him that Sarah's dad didn't have any boys; I thought I'd move to Baltimore and see if I might run his business. It was a small insurance and real estate operation. I thought Dad was going to have a conniption fit. He really got upset. He said something to the effect, 'This is as if your mother came home to me and told me she was in love with another man.'

"I was absolutely shocked by that reaction. He went bad, and I was upset. There were some tense moments. We regrouped afterward and talked about it. What I told him was, I had spent summers working at Ingram Book Group. It was a mature business that owned the market-place. For somebody who was wanting to make his mark, it was a giant bureaucracy, and I wasn't interested in being a cog in the wheel in the middle of something that wasn't very energizing. He told me that he wanted me to understand how banks worked and finance. Instead of me starting at Ingram Book, as he had hoped, he said, 'Why don't you work for me for a period of time in our treasury area?'

"In retrospect, now that I'm pushing forty, I realize he really wanted me to see what he had built and what he had spent his time doing before I moved on to do whatever I wanted to do. I agreed to do that. My rationale was (a) he is going to throw me out of the family if I don't do this—that was the implied message—and (b) he had given me an incredible start, an inheritance, what have you, and I owed it to him to try his thing.

"It is very difficult to be born into a family where your father and mother are famous. Maybe *prominent* is a better word. Around the company atmosphere, my father was a god, and people were terrified of him. He put on a pretty good act. He was a hard-ass. It's hard to step out from that shadow and develop your own personality and purpose and be your own man if you're in your old man's shadow. That was my thing."

David worked in the treasury for two years, from 1989 to 1991. He said, "One day I was riding on an airplane with the treasurer, Tom Lunn, and he asked me, 'What do you think you are going to do from here on out? You're not going to get to the top of this company through the finance area like your father did. You need to get out into one of the operating subs.'

"At the time Ingram Micro was the big grower, and you had Ingram Book Company and Ingram Entertainment and Ingram Barge and Ingram Materials and Ingram Cactus and insurance. There was a lot going on. I looked at all that, and I thought, *What would be the best place for me to start?* I felt that my oldest brother was already in the barge

Le Club de Pêche aux Saumons Moisie Inc.

SEASON OF .1985......

SCORE OF ...Mr. E.B. Ingram.........................

```
29 June:  20, 16       Lbs
 1 July:  15, 12, 11    "
 3   "  :  12, 20        "
```

```
Total killed   :   7
Total released:   22
Total lost     :   19
Total weight   :  106
Average weight:   15.1
```

Above: Bronson at the Moisie, Quebec, Canada.

Left: Bronson's scorecard for the Moisie, 1985.

business, and I didn't want to get in his way, on his turf. My middle brother at the time was at Ingram Book. I think maybe he had announced plans to go to Ingram Micro.

"I decided that I would go into the Entertainment Company. My rationale was, here is a business that would do a little over $300 million, relatively small for a distribution company, at least relatively small compared to the other companies. It had relatively inexperienced management. I had just come out of MBA school [Owen School at Vanderbilt]. They make you work pretty hard to get an MBA. They don't just throw it to you when you drive by. I felt like it was a place that I could make an impact, just because it was a business with probably twelve or fifteen competitors and it was a growing-and-blowing industry.

"I went in and I asked the CEO, John Taylor, 'I'd like to come try this thing out.' In my thinking it was, *Okay, I've done the treasury gig, so I'm off the hook on that, I would think. I'm going to go out and go into one of the interesting operating companies. I'm either going to stick it out or not, but I'm going to try it and see if it is something that appeals to me.*" John Taylor agreed for David to join Entertainment.

Bronson's reaction again was not what David expected. He said, "I remember walking into my father's office and telling him, 'Well, Dad, I've decided that I'm going to work in the Entertainment Company.' I thought he was going to fall out of his chair again because he had not dictated or orchestrated my move.

"I think he wanted to have me in something that was more secure, that he knew was going to be a long-term business, so that the business didn't get sold or go bankrupt. I think he very much wanted me in the business. I have often thought about why he wanted me in the business so much. I think Dad was inept at small talk; he was inept at doing things on a casual, chummy basis with his children. Mother used to say, 'Dad is terrible with children. He doesn't want to play with you until you're old enough, until you're eighteen or something.' I think he thought that this would be a way for us to interact.

"Anyway I went to work in his business, and a year later the CEO and Phil Pfeffer and different people agreed to buy COMMTRON, which was our biggest competitor. We went into a merger. That was June of 1992 when the COMMTRON deal was announced. In

September of 1993 Blockbuster decided to go to one distributor. They were using two distributors at the time, and we had last shot at the deal. We were either going to pick up $200 million in additional business or lose $200 million in business. We were going to make less money if we picked up the additional $200 million than we did making the $200. Our sense was (a) you never want to be controlled by one customer and (b) why do we want to build all of this infrastructure for a deal that had a worse return? We figured as they got bigger, they would go to self-distribution, which they did. We were successful in replacing that $200 million in about a year's time. It worked out well."

Our sons chose the areas of the company that they liked, but our daughter, Robin, did not want to work in the company after she graduated from Duke as an art history major. Bronson had told the boys—and she had heard it—that to be Ingrams, they would work. It was just a question of where. He told them that if they did not want to work for him, that was okay. He would help them set up a business of another kind, but they would be doing something. That's just part of what we do. She said, "Dad, I heard you say this to the boys. Will you make the same deal with me?" He said, "Sure, what is it that you want to do?" She replied, "I want to have an art gallery." Bronson nearly fainted. Retailing paintings was not an area of expertise for any of us. So we hired a man, Michael Judge, who had a gallery in Durham that Robin had admired, to be her partner.

Robin operated the Ingram-Judge Gallery on the ground floor of Ingram headquarters on Harding Road for two or three years and then married and moved to Boston. She learned again that her father considered her an equal to her brothers. There was never any question about that. He had already given her the same ownership in the company that her three brothers had so she knew that she was every bit as valued as the sons, which is not always the case in this world.

Since the 1960s, the company headquarters had been at 4304 Harding Road in Nashville. Bronson and his father had built it and then leased a portion to Third National Bank. We were growing so much by the 1980s that Bronson was working with an architect to figure out how to add on a tower to accommodate everyone. When One Belle Meade Place—just up the street—went on the market, a real estate agent contacted Bronson and asked him to take a look.

Bronson told me, "I can buy that building for much less a square foot than adding on the tower to the existing headquarters, and the basic construction is already completed. Doing a build-out will be much quicker and cheaper." That was what we did. The building was just a shell—a see-through, that is, no walls or partitions—on many floors when we bought it, and some floors were already leased. He kept the lessees, added a few more, and moved our associates onto the other floors. We built it out to suit the clients as we went along.

It was such a good business deal that Bronson couldn't turn it down, although the design is not one that he would have commissioned. It was too contemporary for him. He hired Earl Swensson's architectural firm to make it look traditional on the inside with lots of paneling and wood trim. We moved into the building in mid–1987.

The offices of the Distribution Group moved to a new building in La Vergne, where we had a warehouse. Bronson spoke to a group of La Vergne High School students during a Leadership Conference held at the Ingram Distribution Group in 1994. Here are some examples of the questions and answers:

Q: What is your vision for Ingram?
A: We have various visions for our various companies, but basically we just want to be the best we can be and we want to do whatever it takes to be the best. Part of our vision is to be the low-cost service provider in distribution. This makes us competitive and successful.

If you make up your mind to be the best, you'll do very well in life. To share your vision, share your ideas. And tell enough about your ideas so others will accept them.

Q: Some people say, "It's not what you know, it's who you know." Is this true?
A: Who you know is helpful, but you won't know the who-you-knows without knowing the what-you-knows.

Q: Is it important to be on time?
A: It's important to be on time and it's important to be prepared, especially for meetings. Then you can come to a conclusion on what

you're meeting about and go on to the next project. It's terribly impolite to be late. I don't think I'm the only one who is irked by this, but it does irk me.

Q: Does your company interfere with your personal life?
A: It does conflict some, but it also allows me to do countless interesting, fascinating things. But if people want to know if they should call me while I'm home or on vacation, I tell them, "Don't call me just because you're lonely. If you need me, call me. If you don't need me, don't call me. If you don't know what's important, we're in trouble."

Q: Do you feel pressured and stressed a lot?
A: Yes! So I hurry up and get whatever I'm working on done. Don't get distracted—just get it done. Then the pressure goes away.

Q: What is leadership?
A: Leadership is being willing to do it yourself, being willing to help others do it, and not being interested in taking all the credit.

Two new board members in the early 1990s were Denny Bottorff and Clayton McWhorter. They took the places of Sam Richmond and Alvin Johnson, respectively.

Denny regarded Bronson as entrepreneurial: "*Entrepreneurial* is certainly an applicable word to the extent that you think of a trailblazer. The whole hardware/software distribution business is a recent phenomenon in this country. To build those companies was trailblazing."

He commented on the way that Bronson went about these trailblazing efforts: "Bronson really wanted the company to stay private for a lot of reasons. That was clear. Ingram never would have become what it became had it been a public company because Bronson would see where he thought it needed to go and he would stick through a lot of adversity until it got there. If you look at the building of Ingram Micro, where they entered many territories and some of those territories had long periods of operating loss, where he was funding that. That never could have been done as a public company—certainly not in the time period that it was done. This is a testimony to his conviction, to his vision, but it was also intestinal fortitude because it was like he was seeing, 'I have operating losses here, but I'm going to take those losses for many years until we get this territory built.' That is certainly the way they were in Europe."

Clayton was reluctant to accept the board position when Bronson first spoke to him about it: "I said, 'Let me think about it.' He said, 'What do you have to think about?' I said, 'Well, Bronson, let me think about it.' I think that it impressed him—the fact that I didn't just immediately say, 'Oh, yeah, I will.' I called several people to ask their opinions—Tommy Frist and others. They said, 'That is something you ought to seriously consider doing.' I went on the board.

"I was on the board for a year. I kept thinking, *They have all of these businesses—the entertainment business, the book business, the barge business, insurance, and so on. All of a sudden, after being on there for a year, it clicked in that it was the distribution business. It has nothing to do with the segment; they are distributing things.* One day I asked Jim Neal, whom I've known a long time, longer than before I got to know Bronson, 'You know, Jim, I don't understand why Bronson asked me to join his board. I haven't been able to make any kind of contribution as far as advice or counsel. They're smart people. Why do they need me?' Jim Neal said, 'I'll tell you why.' I said, 'Why?' He said, 'Because he trusts you. That's why he asked you.' Well, that not only impressed me but really brought home the responsibility I had to the person.

"He functioned more like a public company as it related to his board—not to the public disclosure. I'm assuming he did this with others, but I know of at least a couple of times when Bronson came to my office to tell me what his plans were, what he had to do with certain management people when he had to make changes, or why a certain person may not be the future or why a certain person had to be replaced because he lied to him, not about necessarily the quality of performance but this person was not truthful to him. I don't remember the details. I just remember being impressed that he would come and explain to me why those things were going to happen or not happen. I was sitting there thinking, *If I was in Bronson Ingram's shoes, I would just pick up the phone and say, 'Clayton, so you won't pick this up on the street, and since you're on my board, let me tell you something.'*

"I've learned a lot from my association with the Ingrams and on that board—I've learned a lot now that I'm involved with my son and involved with a number of private companies how they ought to function as well. Even though we're not public, we do have shareholders."

Clayton remarked on Bronson's colorful language: "Bronson had a unique way of expressing himself that the family understood; sometimes a stranger didn't. It took me a while to be accustomed to that. It just turned out that this is Bronson. Bronson could use profanity, and it was not offensive to the people that knew Bronson. Now it could be if they had never been around him.

"I know one time we were over at the Governor's Residence, and we were talking about education. We were outside under a big tent. Bronson and I were carrying on a conversation, and he had some of his choice words, expressing himself. Well, after dinner we all had to introduce ourselves, and there were eight or ten of us at the table. We had two ministers sitting at our table, which we didn't know. Now being the way I was brought up, with my strict mother, if you used a four-letter word, you got your mouth washed out with soap. I'm saying, 'Oh, gosh,' to myself. It didn't faze Bronson. He didn't realize or think that he did anything out of the ordinary. Again, it was the person. He didn't mean to offend. It was his way of expressing himself, which I grew to admire really."

I had been on the Ingram board since 1981 and had been on other boards, too, but in 1987, I had the opportunity to become a member of the board of Baxter Laboratories. I received a call from the CEO, Vernon Loucks, who had married my roommate at Vassar. I had known him all of those years ago, and Ann, Vern, and their young son Charlie (my godson) had visited us in Nashville, but I lost touch with him after he and Ann divorced. He wanted to add a second woman to his board and happened to mention that fact to a classmate at a reunion of the Harvard Executive Business Program. Oddly enough, the man, Bill O'Neill, was from Nashville and had just met me when I went to his office to ask for his support of the Nashville Symphony. Bill said that this woman might fit the bill. Vern asked, "What is this woman's name?" When Bill told him, Vern had to laugh and relate the story of our acquaintanceship.

So when Vern called me, he said, "You come so highly recommended and I know you from school and the early years of my marriage. Would you consider coming on the board of Baxter? I've got some older gentlemen and they are retiring. I'd like to get some younger people, and I've got one woman. I know you think I only want you because you're a woman, but I've already got one and she is doing a fine job. I understand you are on some other corporate boards, and I'd like for you to at least give it a shot."

I must add that he had called Bronson first to say, "Bronson, would you mind if I were to ask your wife to go on my board?" I happened to be out of the office, and Bronson told me about the call when I came back. I said, "What did you tell him?" He said, "I told him that you were not at all the girl that he remembers. That you have your own mind and you do what you damn well please. But I did tell him that I would give you the message."

When Vern called me back, I told him, "Look, I don't know anything about medicine or anything about what you do." He said, "Would you just let me send the plane for you and at least let me try to sell you on it?" He sent the plane with a couple of pilots just for me. I vividly remember that it was the week after the stock market crash in October 1987.

Vern and others showed me around the company. During a slide presentation, I realized that a major part of the business was distribution of pharmaceutical, hospital, and drug products, getting goods to the right hospital in a cost-effective, speedy manner. I thought, *Oh, my gosh, you're doing exactly what we do. It's the same jargon, the same language, just different stuff that goes in the boxes.* By the time I finished listening to that, I felt totally comfortable and thought, *I think I can help them improve what they were doing if they were only thinking about this or that.* At lunch with Vern I said, "If you still want me, sign me up. I'd love to do it."

They flew me back to Nashville, and Bronson asked, "What did you think?" I said, "Will you believe that Vern sent their Gulfstream to get me? He showed me all around." He said, "Well, what did you say?" I said I told him yes. He said, "You know what, they could have just sent that plane, bigger and fancier than ours, and taxied you around the airport and dumped you out and you would have still said yes." He gave me a hard time about it, but he was pleased that I had been picked and said, "That's a world-class organization. That's quite worth your time. I'm glad you decided to do that. You'll learn a lot from doing it, and you'll probably teach them a thing or two." He was very supportive of my doing it, and I'm still on that board—thirteen years later (at the time of this writing).

I think he missed me when I was away at those board meetings in Deerfield, Illinois, outside Chicago, because it did not quite fit his game plan to be on his own. We had a cook and we had a maid. It was not as though he was left unattended, but he did not like having dinner alone. Even when we worked together, he would say, "Isn't it time for us to go home?" That was my cue. I was supposed to go home first so I'd be there when he arrived; he didn't like to enter an empty house. He always gave me a kiss when he marched in as though I had been at home all day—rather than in an office next to his!

All these years later Robin still bemoans being the only one at home when Bronson hit the door: "After my brothers went to college,

it was just me and them. When my mother started going
in to the office, he used to make her leave five minutes
beforehand so that she would be home when he got
there. When she was doing her arts things, he would

*Entrance of our
cottage in Cashiers,
N.C.*

come in, and I would be doing my homework or watching TV. He
would walk right in the front hall and go, 'Martha! Martha!' If I was
upstairs, I would hear this: 'Robin, where is your goddamned mother?'
I would say, 'She is at work.' He'd go, 'Goddamnit,' then he'd get his
drink." As I've said, Bronson was a creature of habit—two Scotch and
sodas every night.

Robin worked in one of the company's warehouses in the
summers; she had the same deal with her father about working a
month for him and his supporting her activities the rest of the time.
She recalled, "It was very explicit that we should work, that we would
not rest on our laurels, so to speak. He said that often." She was
passionate about riding and was quite good at it. She said, "I think that
riding kept me straight—very straight—because I didn't want to blow
it. I knew that my father would yank that from me in a New York

minute if I gave him any reason to, and I loved it so. It consumed me. I traveled twenty-five weekends out of the year around the country. Even when I got married, I did." Now her three children are learning to ride.

Robin met Richard Patton in Nashville after both were out of school. She had the art gallery, and he and another young man—his Vanderbilt roommate, Robin Delmer—had started two restaurants, San Antonio Taco Company and Granite Falls. When he wanted to marry her, he knew he should speak to Bronson. I'll let Robin tell what happened: "Richard went to ask my father for my hand in marriage, and he made an appointment at the office. He asked my father, and my father said yes. My father said to Mom in the next office, 'Martha, can you come in here? Richard has something he wants to tell you.' Richard said, 'I came in to ask Bronson for Martha's hand in marriage.' My mother said, 'Well, that's very nice, but I'm taken. Robin is available.' My husband nearly died, he was so nervous. He and my father became very close."

Richard had a good relationship with Bronson, and they often talked business. Richard said, "He took a very hands-off approach, never offered advice. When I asked for advice, he would give it, but he never offered it. He was very respectful of that space. I look at that in a positive perspective. I think he didn't think I needed any help, which was a good thing. But I probably didn't ask enough. I know I didn't.

"When I was going back to business school [at Harvard to get an MBA], he did kind of say, 'I don't know why you're doing that. You already know everything they're going to teach you.' On occasion we would talk about things that I was interested in, but it was not specifically to my career or my endeavors, but about something business related, just because that's what I'm most fascinated with, most interested in. With the exception of golf and his family, I would say that that was his interest also.

"I think about him, and I can just think of particular words: *disciplined, exceptionally organized*. I remember one time I was smoking a cigar, and we were in Charleston for Thanksgiving. I said, 'Bronson, would you like a cigar?' [He had quit smoking cold turkey in 1962

in a bet with Arnold Palmer. Arnie lost because he lasted only one week. It was the only time Bronson ever beat Arnie.] He replied, 'I'd smoke your shoe if I could get it lit, but I don't want one.' It was indicative of his discipline. By and large, people who accomplish great things are very disciplined people. Doesn't mean that they're wound as tight maybe, but there is always discipline. Always very organized. He knew where he was going to be and when he was going to be there and why months ahead of time. If you can control that part of your life, you'll go a lot farther than a lot of people do because most people don't control that part of their lives."

Bronson took golf seriously, and he played whenever he had the chance. John pointed out, "Dad had a group—Andy Mizell, David Wiley, Bobby Warner, Jay Ward, Marshall Trammell, and there were others. Apparently, they called him Buddy because they all concluded he was the last guy in the world that anyone would ever call that. I played some golf with him. He always invited me to play in this tournament, a parent-child tournament after Christmas, down in Florida at Seminole. We won it one year. Playing golf with my father was like the crucible of pressure because he was very serious about it, and I wanted to do well. But the more nervous you get, the less well you do in golf. It was a hard thing to do. He was very serious about it. He wanted to win."

Marshall Trammell was among the golfers on Bronson's golf outings. He and Bronson also fell into a routine of playing one year at Indian Creek in Miami and the next year at Seminole in a tournament. Marshall said, "Bronson and I won three times at each place: Indian Creek and Seminole." He added, "We played at Belle Meade Club, the Golf Club of Tennessee, and Shoal Creek [in Birmingham]. He was a member of the Honors and of Castle Pines. He took me and others to Augusta. Jake [Wallace] and Bronson came down to play with me at Key Largo. And we played at Apawamis Club at Rye, New York, and at a club in Greenwich, Connecticut." That is a short list of the places these men played together.

Marshall continued, "Bronson was also a member of U.S. Seniors. Seniors is a very prestigious organization made up mostly of Easterners." The goal of the U.S. National Seniors Open Golf Association is "to unite the professional and amateur golfer in the interest and promotion of seniors golf competition on a national basis and to engender between both groups a close, friendly, and lasting relationship." An individual can join at age fifty after meeting certain requirements.

As I've indicated, son David had aspired to be a professional golfer, and he played with Bronson more than the other children did. David explained his interest in golf: "A lot of people say, 'Your brothers rode horses and your sister rode horses and John did tennis and Orrin did polo. Why did you do golf?' I say, 'Either it is because I was like my father or I wanted to get my father's attention. That was the only way to do it—play his game.'

"Jay Ward was one of Dad's good friends, and they golfed together. Jay died in 2000, and his son Jimmy and I were talking at the wake. Jimmy and I are pretty good friends. He and I used to follow my father and Jay Ward around on Saturday and Sunday mornings at Belle Meade Club because they played every Saturday and every Sunday. We wanted to be around them and spend time with them because they were going to play golf. I even caddied for my father some. If we had a connection, it was definitely on the golf course, and we would practice and hit balls and he would help me with my game from time to time.

"I wanted to putt cross-handed, and he thought no one should putt cross-handed. The only person who putted cross-handed when I went to cross-handed was Bruce Lietzke. Shortly thereafter the whole world went to cross-handed. People started winning major championships, left and right, putting cross-handed. I had my small victory on my father: 'See, I told you it was a better way to do it.' He had his thoughts on how you should play golf. Golf is a solitary sport. You either win or lose. It's you against the course."

David married a golfer, Sarah LeBrun, ranked as the number one amateur woman golfer in the nation in 1993. They dated while both were at Duke. Sarah's first meetings with Bronson were memorable: "I guess it was parents' weekend, so it was probably the first time I met him. We were eating breakfast at a hotel, and they were short on wait staff. He was getting really angry and short-tempered. Then all of a sudden he yelled at one of them, 'Are you going to bring me my damn fruit?' That was one of my first impressions of Bronson Ingram. David and I still joke about that today. We still use that line. I kind of looked at David and he looked at me and we just wanted to sink under the table at that point.

"Another time I was meeting David at the airport in Durham or his family was coming in; maybe they were dropping him off. I walked out onto the tarmac to greet them, and Bronson was mad because they didn't have their rental car in. He was storming off the airplane, and he literally brushed by my shoulder. We touched shoulders. I said, 'Hey, Mr. Ingram.' He didn't say anything. 'Nice to see you, Mr. Ingram.' And he kept going. I knew I was in for it.

"Actually, we did have a special bond. I don't know if it's because I was a daughter-in-law or because I was into golf. He loved the sport. He loved the fact that I worked hard at it, and I was successful. As grumpy as he was and as mean as he could be, he could also be the biggest teddy bear. He was a completely emotional person, and I think as I look back on it, he could come off as being so mean and impatient. He was impatient. He wanted things that he wanted—right now. But he expected perfection from everybody because he was like that. He was a perfectionist. He also had his emotions on his sleeve. He was either yelling at you or he was crying with you.

"On more than one occasion he said, 'I'm so proud of you. You did great.' And he would be crying. I played in the Curtis Cup [a competition for amateur women golfers from the United States and from Britain-Ireland], and I had hurt my neck. It was 1994, about two months before he was diagnosed with cancer. I played two matches and I was in pain, but I did fine. Actually, I had one really great round, and he was there. He and Martha came to two of my Curtis Cup matches. The first one was in England. The second one was in Chattanooga. That was where I hurt my neck. I came off the round, and he just grabbed my shoulders and said how proud he was and that I was the toughest person he ever knew." Bronson rarely displayed that teddy bear side to family or to others, but it was always there.

Sarah and David played at least once at Shoal Creek with Bronson and me before they married. She told the story, "Martha and I were chatting away on a hole, and we were pretty far away from them. But Bronson hit a shot and it went into the trees. As it was going into the trees, he yelled something to us, 'If you all would just shut up, I could hear where my ball went!' Something ludicrous. The two of us from then on every time he hit it in the woods, we'd go, 'Shh! We have to listen to where the ball landed.' He laughed about it."

Richard Patton occasionally played golf at Seminole with David, Bronson, and Sarah, and of one memorable episode he said, "I stood in their shadow. I think Bronson just snapped his first drive, and when that happened, he swatted the golf club at the ground, a g-d-it and a grumbling. It was almost like a big black rain cloud over the foursome. There was a definite pecking order there—Bronson first and the rest of us last.

"We were going along, and nobody was going to have fun until Bronson had fun. That's the way it was. He played like a dog through five or maybe six. Playing like a dog for Bronson was a bogey or par or double bogey. He was well over par by the time we got to six. Then he hit a great shot on six, and he looked around—everybody know I'm the man kind of stuff.

"Then Sarah started playing badly. By the time we got to eight, Sarah was in tears. I'm just scraping it around, trying to get through this. Playing at Seminole is like playing in the desert in a tornado. Right on the water down in Florida, there is all this sand everywhere. Sarah came out of her funk, and then as luck would have it, David got stung with it.

"By that time Bronson was all chipper because he was playing well, Sarah was back, and I was still scraping along. Then David was playing so badly that he got an upset stomach; he pulled into this bathroom between sixteen and seventeen, I think; we left him there. We just kept playing. Then we changed. We had lunch. Still no David. About that time Sarah and I said, 'Do you think we ought to send somebody out for David? Send a cart out for him?' I was the only one who didn't have the rain cloud over my head that day because my expectations were a little bit lower than the others."

Here is David's take on that game: "Richard's story about golf at Seminole is close to accurate—but not totally. I would often get upset playing golf with my father, but in that particular round, I was playing very well and was very happy. I was 2 over par after sixteen holes on this good golf course. My stomach did go out and I did not finish the round (I spent about thirty minutes clearing out my system in a toilet on the course), but it was definitely not because I was golfing badly. In fact, I was badly beating Dad and Sarah! Also remember that this was after I had been working at Ingram for several years and was playing about 50 rounds of golf per year versus 250 when I was in college. Two over par through sixteen was very good for a working man, and I would have definitely been smiling about that—not in a funk. I remember this so clearly because it was the only time I had not finished a round that I started when playing with Dad, and I was badly beating him and the others, which was why it was so frustrating."

A longtime member of Augusta National, Bronson could take friends and family there. To Sarah, it is a favorite course. Bronson took her once with me and David, but he took her again with some businesspeople. Sarah recalled, "It was Bronson and me and these two businesspeople, and it was a really fun weekend. It was probably a year before he died. There was a lot of camaraderie between us, especially because the people that we played with were not good golfers. He was truly happy that I was there. At least he had one good golfer in his group. It was nice to be able to do something like that with him."

Keel Hunt came to know Bronson as they worked together in the Chamber of Commerce (more about that later in this chapter). He knew that Bronson was an avid golfer and had a membership at Augusta, so he asked Bronson about his involvement with the Masters: "Bronson explained, 'Well, if you're a member at Augusta, every member is given a job at the Masters.' I'm thinking, *What kind of job?* so I asked him, 'What is your job?' He said his job was to sit in a chair, just off the ninth green, and keep score. When each player would putt out, [he had to photocopy the card—right there—and then] he would take the score card over to the tent and be sure that it got recorded. I thought, *That is my kind of job.*"

Bronson helped his friend Jake Wallace become a member of Augusta around 1980. Jake had been playing tennis when he saw Bronson on the practice tee at Belle Meade Country Club, and they were talking. Jake said, "I was getting ready to leave and walk back over to the tennis courts, and he stopped me and said, 'Oh, I meant to tell you something.' And I said, 'What's that?' He said, 'In the next day or two you're going to get a letter inviting you to be a member of Augusta National. I just want to make sure you don't wait a long time before you answer.' I said, 'Well, you don't have to worry about that, Bronson. I won't wait to answer.' That was typical of Bronson. He didn't make a big deal out of it. In fact, he almost forgot to mention it to me. It was almost an afterthought as I was walking away from him. Those were the kinds of things you never forget."

Because of his love of golf, Bronson became impatient with having to wait so long to play at the Belle Meade Club, and when he was approached about participating in a new private golf course near Nashville at Kingston Springs, he enthusiastically agreed. It was not his original concept, but he helped bring the idea into reality.

Bronson; Bob Jamieson, head pro of Turnberry; Johnny Harris; and Ed Seay of Arnold Palmer Enterprises, Pro-Am Seniors British Open, 1990.

Jake Wallace knew some details: the founders' meetings took place at Bronson's office, and he solicited many of the founders, who put up a modest amount of money for feasibility studies and preliminary drawings. Jake said, "He really was the guy that pulled it together. He was the guy that got Tom Fazio here. He was the guy that kept it going when it was foundering because the economy was not strong right through that gap, and he was the guy that kept pushing and kept pushing until we were able to get it really to the point of where it could stand on its own feet.

"I don't mean that Bronson forked out an undue amount of his own money, because I don't think he did, but what he did was give it the leadership that it needed and I think gave it the credibility it needed to make it work. Not that others didn't. I don't want this to sound like others [including Toby Wilt] didn't do a hell of a lot of work, because they did. I'm just telling you—you can book it—that it wouldn't have happened if it hadn't been for Bronson." The Golf Club of Tennessee opened in March 1991.

Bronson really wanted his friend Arnold Palmer to be the architect of the course, but Arnie was under contract to do another golf course that was not yet started, and the contract stipulated that the course was to be an exclusive Palmer design in the area. Bronson thought that Tom Fazio might be the answer to the problem—and he turned out to be—so we went to the mountains of North Carolina to see a course that Tom had just finished in Cashiers called Wade Hampton.

As it turned out, Bronson managed to combine golf club business with family business. My brother, John, owned property in Cashiers, and we ended up buying a piece on which to build a house.

John said, "From the time I was a youngster, I always felt very close to Bronson. At Augusta during one Masters—only members were allowed in the stands—I didn't have a green jacket, but he said to the marshal, 'This is my brother.'" In many ways Bronson felt as if John was a brother.

John introduced Bronson to Kathleen, who would become John's wife in 1979, and he was more or less seeking Bronson's approval. Bronson told John, "She's nice enough. Do whatever the hell you want to do." Kathleen recalled, "When I first met Bronson, I didn't know that I should be afraid of him. An inner fear started to build after the initial meeting, or intimidation may be closer to it. But I found that if you refused to be intimidated, he melted, and he was just as charming as any man I've ever known." Kathleen and Bronson developed such a good relationship that if they were at the same dinner, he would set a bottle of red wine between them—just for the two of them. And he loved to dance with her.

Bronson and John had done some business together—investing in a telephone company, Line One, in South Carolina. John said, "We had shared risk. One of Bronson's attributes was that he was extremely focused. On a business deal he knew how to get to the heart of the matter."

He certainly got to the heart of the matter on that property in the mountains of North Carolina. He and I had talked about building a house somewhere in the mountains, but more than likely near the water. Bronson asked John, "Which do you consider the best of all these plots here?" There were about two hundred acres, including a lake at the bottom of the mountain. John said, "I'll show you which I think is the prettiest." He showed us a spot, and Bronson said, "This is a beautiful spot. What would you be asking for it?" John named a price, and Bronson said, "I think we'll take it."

Only then did he turn to me and say, "Martha, that is all right with you, isn't it?" I said, "Bronson, I thought we were going to build on a lake someday and have water skis and motorboats, like on White Bear Lake." He said, "Look, they don't have views like this many places. If you want water, build water into your house plans. Build a damn swimming pool—whatever you want." I said, "May I have waterfalls and pools?" He said, "I don't care what you put into the house. Just build what you want, but this is the most beautiful view I've ever seen. I've been to Switzerland, I've been all over a lot of the world, and I think this is the prettiest spot I've ever seen." Then and there we decided to buy the lot and then build a house.

I turned to my sister-in-law, who is a decorator, and said, "Kathleen, how in the world will I ever get an architect up here from Nashville?" She said, "I know the perfect architect. Jim Meyer is from Charlotte, and Meyer-Greeson is his firm. We can go see him. I happen to know he is in Roaring Gap, North Carolina, right now. He has a house there and is the architect of many others."

Bronson and I went back to Nashville on Monday following that weekend. Then I flew to Asheville to pick up Kathleen, and we went on to Roaring Gap and met Jim Meyer. I told him, "I like your work. I've seen five or six houses that you've built here at Roaring Gap. I like the

David and Martha, the winners of the Parent-Child Tournament at Seminole, Fla., with Bronson and Sarah, 1990.

way you do things—they're traditional but they have a little contemporary kick to them. But you have a reputation for being slow and a procrastinator. You know, I'm married to a man who can be very difficult at times, and he likes things done on time and on the schedule that is laid out."

He said, "I'm used to dealing with difficult men. I can handle it."

I explained, "We're going to be back in Cashiers visiting another friend in about thirty days. Can you be there and meet us with a preliminary plan? Since day before yesterday, I have been sketching out with Bronson's approval the floor plan that I think we would like. We have some inherited furniture and rugs in storage that we would like to incorporate. And we've given some dimensions."

He said, "Sure, that's wonderful. You've given me enough to go on. I'll have at least a preliminary plan in thirty days."

Jim met us thirty days later in Cashiers. He started rolling out the plans. Bronson sat there looking but didn't say anything. Jim kept turning the pages for the house and the floor plan. He got to the last page and said, "I've sketched what I think would be a nice exterior from front and rear. I'll show you these."

Bronson was still silent.

Jim finally asked, "Well, what do you think?"

Bronson looked at it and said, "Just build the damn thing the same way you have sketched it out."

Jim looked at me as though I must be the most wicked woman in the world—or a nut case—to have said all those things about how difficult my husband was, and here he said, "I don't want any changes."

Subsequently, we put in a couple of fireplaces in bedrooms and a few other things that we had not originally planned, but basically, we built the house that he rolled out of those plans. We had never talked about exterior, never suggested that it be one way or the other. Jim just read it right and hit it right. It was a wonderful experience building the house and seeing it go from paper to reality. We· moved in September 1989 as Hurricane Hugo whipped through. It is a happy house, and everybody seems to have a good time there.

There was a tie-in with that house and New Orleans. While the house was under construction, our friends Eli and Deborah Tullis from New Orleans visited us in Nashville, and we brought out the Cashiers house plans to show them. We pointed out the great room that had three arched French doors across the front, and on the other side there were two French doors and a big stone fireplace. Everything radiated from that room. We said, "We're going to have beams in the ceiling, which is about twenty feet high."

Eli piped up and said, "Where are you getting the beams?" Bronson replied, "The architect is getting them somewhere. They're just beams." We wanted to have old beams but didn't know if they could be found. Eli said, "Why don't you use your own beams? You know the San Francisco Plantation near Baton Rouge where you had built the ECOL oil refinery had a sugar mill where the refinery had to go and the sugar mill was torn down. There were beams of old pine that were advertised: anybody who would haul them away could have them for free. Deborah and I went up there with a flatbed truck and had some people help us and we hauled way more than we needed for our kitchen in New Orleans. We have a whole garage full of these beams that we'd like to get rid of."

That was how we had in a company way owned the beams, and we had them put in the house. It is hard to make a new house look as if it's old enough to have charm, but this is one of the things that we were able to do.

There are many people from Charleston and the East Coast—people that I had known in my earlier life—that I am now able to reconnect with on a rather regular basis. I feel very comfortable, very much at home there. And my brother and sister-in-law are nearby on the next ridge. Having a world-class golf course in the vicinity was a clincher for Bronson, and our view from four thousand feet in the Smoky Mountains is breathtaking.

When Bronson told me I could have water, I took him at his word. On the big view side, we have a small wading pool on the terrace. The water emanates from this pool and it cascades over into a stone trough that goes all the way around the terrace and then it drops about twenty feet on one side to a heated swimming pool and it drops about twenty feet on the other side to another smaller pool outside the master bedroom. We have water all the way around, for on the opposite driveway side, we have turned what was going to be a drainage ditch into a Japanese garden with a waterfall that circulates constantly. We have surround sound of water. It was our only complete building project together, and it couldn't have gone more smoothly. I'm fortunate to have the house as a nice memento of something creative that Bronson and I did together.

We had in 1965 built on a room for the house in Nashville and used butternut wood to give it a special feeling. Bronson was so fussy about it that he wouldn't even let me hang pictures on the walls for a long time. With the proceeds that Bronson gained from an investment in Minnie Pearl Fried Chicken, we added the swimming pool and pool house.

Bronson and I celebrated our thirtieth wedding anniversary on the terrace of the Nashville house with a dinner party for sixty of our nearest and dearest. Son John read the following to the assembled group on behalf of himself and his brothers and sister:

To Mom and Dad
On Your Thirtieth Wedding Anniversary

Who's there when things go wrong,
Who's there when things go right,
Who dried our noses and tucked us in most each and every night.
Who spent the time to shape our values
    and steer us past fears and needless plight,
Who made us do those things not then understood
    so we would someday see the light.
You did it for love, yes, unwavering love
    with such determination and might,
Our thanks and love, we re-affirm to you,
    on this very special night.

This touching tribute is framed and still hangs on my bedroom wall.

Before my mother passed away in 1994, she was concerned that I was the only one of her children who did not have a house in Charleston. My brother inherited the larger house on Church Street (built in 1790) that we all grew up in, and then my mother and father (who died in 1988) moved to a somewhat smaller house around the corner on Meeting Street—still four stories and quite old. My sister, whose permanent residence is in New York, has a Charleston house out in the country on the Ashley River and a condominium in town at the Fort Sumter. Mother worried that poor Martha didn't have one. She said, "Martha, I'm going to leave this to you." I said, "Mother, look, the longer you live, the better. I don't really need to have something else to look after." She said, "Someday something is going to happen." So she did arrange it in her will that the house would be mine.

When I inherited it, Bronson commented, "I think that is really nice of your mother, but of course you're going to sell it." I said, "Bronson, I'm not going to sell it." He said, "That is just crazy. You don't need another house." I said, "You didn't grow up in Charleston. You'll never understand why I want to keep that house." He said, "I hope she left you enough money to look after it." I said, "Well, she did." He said, "I guess that is the end of the conversation."

As I evaluated the house, which was built in the 1830s, I realized that behind the plaster, heating, electrical, and plumbing repairs and changes were going to have to be made. It was going to be very expensive, more than I had expected. I had an offer for Bronson one day: "I'll give you ownership of half of this house if you'll help me finance all of this." He said, "What I don't need is half of your house, but I'll help you. Do you want me to do the inside or the outside?" I wanted to change the garden and put in a small swimming pool, and there was a magnolia tree that I knew was going to require a big sheet of steel to hold back the roots from the pool and so forth. I said, "If you'll do the inside, I'll do the outside."

He thought that he had by far the bigger ticket (little did he know). He did step up and help me by paying the bills for updating the interior. Although I think I paid for the decorating, he paid for all the infrastructure, the comfort things, such as new plumbing and heating and air-conditioning. All I can say is, he got off light. Despite saying, "You don't need this house," he did enjoy it during a couple of visits after we had finished everything. We were there the Thanksgiving before he was diagnosed with cancer on December 1, 1994. He finally had to say, "You were right. You really should have kept this house. I can see that you are really enjoying it." He had participated, so I ended up having a very good feeling about that.

Bronson's parents had bought the house in Florida at Hobe Sound, and he obtained the house when he and his mother had swapped some property. His parents had taken good care of the house, built in the 1930s, but the three-car garage with a room for a housekeeper was about to collapse. We were advised that no more could be done to it; it had to be torn down. Bronson wanted to tear it down and redo it. I thought we might as well put a couple of bedrooms on top of the garage because the family had expanded. Well, our little alteration turned out to be considerably more than we were thinking. The little 1930s house could be blown away in the next hurricane or the next big wind, but boy, we've got a garage that will stay forever. The guest rooms are on the second floor above the garage, and you can look right out at the ocean over the main house and have a wonderful view. As it became apparent that the

THE GOLF CLUB OF TENNESSEE
1991

project was going to be expensive, Bronson started calling it the Taj Garage.

Jim Smith, Bob McNeely, Johnny Harris, and Bronson, the Golf Club of Tennessee, 1991.

The main house, built of cypress, is not palatial by any means, but it has a beautiful big paneled room decorated tastefully by my mother-in-law. You would not necessarily think that your mother-in-law's beach house would be one that you would want to leave unchanged, but I have done my best not to change it other than to modify it a bit. She had lovely taste, and I feel privileged to have that house now.

We did not deliberately set out to acquire houses, but I have kept all of them. In addition, I very much treasure the boat that Bronson left me, which is a 75-foot Palmer Johnson Sport Fisherman. There was a time that I thought, *I probably can do without the boat.* But I love the water, and I think because he left it to me, he would expect me to like it and use it. There is a sort of a connectivity to him. When we go out and fish, there are many flashbacks to happy times, and I love it.

My brother John's wife, Kathleen, had a memorable introduction to deep-sea fishing with Bronson. "My first bad experience was at Hobe Sound. We were going deep-sea fishing. I had been on an ocean liner during a hurricane and had bragged about not getting seasick. Well, we weren't even out of the intercoastal waterway, and I was heaving away while Bronson up top was saying, 'Goddamnit, we're not going to turn back.' After I had some crackers, I felt better, but things were grim for a little while.

"About two years later, John and I went deep-sea fishing in Venezuela, and I caught the Venezuelan national record for women's blue marlin on a thirty-pound test line. I was really tired, well, exhausted really. I had wanted a gin and tonic, but they had only gin, so I drank a whole paper cup full. We got to the hotel, and I had to call Bronson to tell him the news.

"David answered. I asked, 'Is Bronson there?' He said, 'Yes.' 'Is he eating dinner?' Again David said, 'Yes.' I said, 'Let me talk to him. Get him up from the table.' David said, 'Are you sure?' I was sure.

"Bronson answered the phone, 'What the hell is it?'

"I said, 'This is your little weakling sister-in-law who just caught a record blue marlin on a thirty-pound-test line.' He just burst out laughing."

David's wife, Sarah, had heard this and other stories about Bronson and the boat, and she knew he wouldn't turn back for anything. She had never been out on the water and had no idea of her seaworthiness. She said, "I took a Dramamine, and it ended up being a pretty rough day. But it was really fun. I did fine, and I caught a sailfish. They had to back the boat up. It was really exciting, and Bronson was happy. He loved seeing other people have fun and do the things that he liked to do as much as he liked to do them himself. That was the only fish we caught that day. That was the only time I went fishing with him."

Bronson started going fly-fishing in northeastern Canada on the Moisie River in the early 1980s. Henry Self, now deceased, and his wife, Virginia, had become friends with us through Nancy and Carter Stovall, people we had known in the Delta. Henry was a member of the Moisie, a club of fishermen, and he invited Bronson as a guest.

The primary fishing is for salmon from canoes. You have a canoe with an indigenous Canadian guide in the stern and another one in the bow, you are towed up the river by a motorboat, and then the force of the river takes you down. It's like having a natural trolling motor.

Tommy and Dathel Coleman, Martha, and Bronson with their catch.

When Bronson first went there, he stayed in the lodge, which is for the men. A few cottages are privately owned and can be rented when men want to bring their wives. It is rustic but not primitive; the men dress for dinner with a coat and tie, and they have French Canadian cooks and people to wait on the tables. He took John a few times because John likes to fish, and it was a good way for them to have father–son time together.

The first time I went I thought, *What is so great about this? It looks ramshackle!* We had to take one hundred or more steps down a cliff to the Moisie River and cross by motorboat to the other side to a fishing camp of weathered wooden buildings. But I soon realized that it's a whole lifestyle of getting away from it all. Because I enjoy fishing, Bronson thought I would enjoy the trip. I spoke enough French to be able to communicate with the help, and Bronson knew he couldn't manage it alone because in Quebec they won't speak English. They don't even pretend to understand a word of it, and he didn't know how to order breakfast, lunch, or dinner. He was very good at including me in many of his adventures. I guess he also had fewer complaints from me about being left if he took me along.

Bronson also enjoyed hunting, although not as much as Orrin does. He was a good wing shot and went quail, duck, and goose hunting. Randy Hooper, now our chief pilot, said that Bronson told him, "I could not care less about killing a deer." Randy sometimes flew Bronson and other family members to Paducah for waterfowl hunting. I accompanied him on some of his hunts, and David and Sarah together hunted at least a couple of times with him. Sarah recalled a hunt at Paducah: "All of the other men that came in said, 'Hey, Bronson! Hey, David! Oh, there is a girl here.' He was great about that. I got my geese [at first light]. We came in, got all cleaned up, and ate our breakfast. The other group came in, and they still had to go back out. We had already limited out. He was fine with taking me out. Of course if I was going to go, I was going to go and not complain about it."

Our son John played tennis with Bronson, Ed Nelson, and Dave Anderson at times. He said of his dad's tennis game: "Dave Anderson asked Brownlee Currey [who would one day be John's father-in-law], 'Brown, Bronson and John are going to take on Ed and me. Who do you think the winner is going to be?' Brownlee said, 'Dave, there can be no winners in that game.'"

Every Thursday morning between 7:30 and 8:30, Bronson would play tennis with pro Dave Anderson, who was a go-between for stories between Bronson and Brownlee. John knew of another story when Dave told Bronson something from Brownlee, and Bronson said, "Goddamnit, Dave, I'm sick of hearing about Currey.

You tell him that." So Dave told Brownlee, who told Dave, "Tell Bronson when he does something important, we'll talk about him."

Bronson's civic activities were recognized as important, and in November 1986, he and I were awarded the first Trevecca Distinguished Service Award by the college. According to Claude Diehl, director of community relations and corporate support at Trevecca Nazarene College, "The reward is to go to someone who gives outstanding service to the city." He added, "We began looking at couples who have meant a lot to the city, and it quickly became apparent that the Ingrams have contributed a lot to Nashville." A newspaper article about the award also noted that Bronson was the president-elect of the Chamber of Commerce.

He would become president in January 1987, succeeding Dortch Oldham. The announcement had been made in November 1985, however, and Bronson had said then, "In today's changing world,

Nashville remains an outstanding place to live and work. The goal of the Nashville Area Chamber of Commerce is to build on our record of past accomplishments to see that our city maintains its highly desirable quality of life as it grows in an orderly and progressive manner.

"The Saturn plant, the American Airlines expansion and other major developments on the horizon will provide Nashville with a full measure of challenges and opportunities during the next several years and, working with the Chamber Board of Governors and staff, I will attempt to maintain a degree of balance between those factors which will most positively influence our city."

As you probably know by now, Bronson's choice of enjoyable tasks would not be giving speeches regularly to people he might or might not know. It's not that he had stage fright. He just didn't like to give speeches, although he was a good communicator and conveyed his message well. Yet he felt that he needed to serve the community and carry out the public responsibilities that accompanied the position.

Bronson's path to the presidency of the Chamber was not the usual one. Keel Hunt, who would become the executive vice president of the Chamber in 1987 (and worked closely with Bronson until his death), observed, "At that time there were still a number of locally directed banks, as we do not have now. There would sometimes be coalitions that would develop, and this would typically be the case when the time came to select who would be the next Chamber president. There would be the First American crowd, then there would be the Third National crowd, and so on. They would sort of take turns.

"Bronson was a new development in that traditional way of doing business. Not only was he not from a bank and didn't fit into that sort of thing, but also he didn't want to fit into it and made a point of saying so. I remember hearing him say in a speech to a large group one evening that he was 'not beholden to any bank.' He was a person who didn't have to be beholden to any bank, of course, but more than that I think he valued his independence and his freedom. He could be above that kind of thing and enjoyed it."

The *Nashville Banner*, January 24, 1987, reported details of the annual Chamber of Commerce dinner at which Bronson discussed his agenda as president:

Despite frigid temperatures, more than 1,200 people gathered at Opryland Hotel for the annual Nashville Area Chamber of Commerce membership dinner.

One of the first orders of business at the mostly social occasion was special recognition for Eddie Jones, who served as executive vice president of the Chamber for 20 years, and who left Jan. 1 to run his campaign for the office of mayor.

Dr. Benjamin F. Byrd, speaking for the Council of Past Presidents of the Chamber, presented Jones with a watch, thanking him for all he had done for the Chamber and for Nashville.

The meeting also included the presentation of the 1986 Business in the Arts Award to Ingram Industries for its accomplishments for the arts in the community.

Honorable mention recipients were Commerce Union Bank, Nissan USA, Third National Bank, Northern Telecom, and Tuck Hinton Everton Architects.

In presenting the award to Ingram, outgoing Chamber president Dortch Oldham noted that nine of the company's top executives, led by Martha Ingram, are personally involved in more than 23 different arts facilities, efforts and programs.

Ingram's contributions include a pledge of $1 million for the Symphony Association capital campaign. Other recipients included: WPLN, the Nashville City Ballet, the Tennessee Repertory Theater, the Nashville Opera Association, the Nashville Institute for the Arts, Cheekwood, WDCN-TV, and the Library of Congress Center for the Book.

Bronson Ingram, the new president of the chamber, said a primary focus for 1987 would be on regional planning.

After crediting Oldham for his efforts in pushing for more unified regional planning process, Ingram said: "I intend to form a broad based ad hoc planning committee as part of the Chamber's structure.

"With their help we will determine exactly what the necessary steps are to maintaining Nashville's quality of life. We will keep the professional planners in Metro, the surrounding counties and the state working together on pooling and coordinating their talents.

"This committee should certainly have full involvement and impact into the consulting group hired by Metro to draw a new general plan for the city. We can't wait for the plan to be drafted, much less completed, before finding out the consultants were on the wrong track."

Ingram said the Chamber will continue to support the Transportation Committee and its efforts to improve traffic problems.

"This planning must be coupled with the financial ability to implement solutions—and these solutions cannot be put in place without substantial commitment from a broad group of community and area leaders and an accompanying commitment of resources dedicated to their success.

"Consequently, I have formed a tax study committee with the specific goal of studying revenue sources, including state distribution formulas which allocate state funds to cities and counties.

"And finally, while lack of growth is not now Nashville's problem, we will market our city to attract high-quality corporate headquarters, technical, research and other jobs to upgrade employment opportunities in what is already a relatively tight job market."

Keel reiterated that Bronson's priority issues were transportation, regional planning, and education: "For example, the issue of transportation and traffic congestion was becoming more and more apparent to Nashvillians. Bill Boner was mayor at the time, and he made that a priority in the early years of his administration. And with the Chamber's leadership, specifically Bronson's active involvement, we were able to get the legislature to pass the Regional Transportation Authority (RTA) legislation." Ned McWherter recalled Bronson telling him more than once that Nashville needed to plan for mass transit because "this city will choke to death in traffic by 2020," and Ned said, "That shows to me the vision that he had, and I think he was right about it."

The RTA is a nine-county regional agency created by state statute in 1988 to plan and develop a regional transit system. The counties include Cheatham, Davidson, Dickson, Maury, Robertson, Rutherford, Sumner, Williamson, and Wilson. Board members are county executives, mayors of county seats, mayors of cities over four thousand in population, the commissioner of the Tennessee Department of Transportation, and six members appointed by the governor. Bronson served as chairman of the RTA from 1988 until his death. To this point,

PATSEA VI

the RTA has established three regional bus routes, the rideshare program (which organizes vanpools and carpools in Middle Tennessee), and the HOV lanes (high occupancy vehicle lanes, reserved for carpools, vanpools, and buses during high-traffic hours each morning and evening). The RTA is also pursuing a commuter rail project for which federal funds have been set aside.

Eli and Deborah Tullis, Boatner Reily, Martha and Bronson, and Kitty and "Bruz" (Alonzo) Boardman, Edgartown, Mass., September 4, 1994.

As for Bronson's leadership style, Keel noted, "There was a private dinner one night at a bank downtown. It involved only nine or ten people, but the guests of honor were the CEO and a second fellow with a company that was just relocating to Nashville. The purpose of this meeting—in which Bronson did most of the talking—was to help them understand that now that they were here, there were certain expectations about their contributions to the United Way and other opportunities that we would like them to consider. It was a very

Awards Ceremony for the National Salespersons of the Year, 1991, by the Sales and Marketing Executives of Nashville.

interesting thing for me to observe because I had not been in one of those sessions before. I said very little because it wasn't necessary. It was very clear, and they understood what they were expected to do."

Bronson was very much in support of the outreach to small businesses and to minority business leaders. Keel explained, "That had not been the case with our Chamber traditionally, and I am very proud of what we were able to accomplish by establishing a formal small business development program as a part of the Chamber of Commerce. Most of our employers are small businesses. I thought that was very interesting that Bronson Ingram, who came from big business (if there was ever a captain of industry, it was him), saw the value of small business and helped other people understand it. He was very clear-minded about the importance of that, and he acted accordingly.

"Likewise with minority business. That had not been a traditional part of our Chamber and now it was. We focused on recruiting minority businesses to become members of the Chamber in a welcoming, open-door way. That showed results. In fact, at that time Nashville was the thirty-second largest market in terms of population in the country, but we had the sixth largest Chamber of Commerce because our membership grew so much in any given year. You always have turnover and there is loss of some businesses or businesses move away, but we had an aggressive membership program. It was a very populist, grassroots sort of organization. I think that continues to be the case today. So Bronson appreciated that, even though he came from a different background."

Advantage Magazine, April 1987, featured the article "Bronson Ingram: The Limelight of Public Concern," by Lindsay Chappell:

> There are, generally speaking, two camps of business people in the world. There are those who enjoy publicity and nearly always accept an opportunity to explain their business and discuss their plans with their community. And then there are those who view media attention in approximately the same vein as table chatter during a serious bridge tournament, as an unnecessary distraction that will, at best, bring brief and fleeting glory, and will more likely tip off competitors and ignite the slow-burning fires of business ruin.
>
> Bronson Ingram falls into the latter camp. Ingram, president of Nashville's diversified Ingram Industries Inc., makes it plain that he has no interest in the light of public exposure. He doesn't need media attention, doesn't particularly like it, certainly doesn't seek it and—no question about it—has managed to do all right without it. Though the privately held company rarely enters into discussions of its size or finances, indications were that annual revenues jumped from about $750 million in 1985 to about $900 million for 1986. The company has quietly positioned itself into one of the largest barging businesses in North America, the largest book wholesaler in the world, the largest microcomputer product distributor in North America, one of the largest video cassette wholesalers in the country, one of the largest audio cassette wholesalers in America, one of the largest computer soft-ware distributors in America, a power in sand dredging, coal

mining, oil drilling, wellhead manufacturing, retail systems, insurance
and now magazine distribution. And it did it all with scant little attention to the fifty-five-year-old man at the top, E. Bronson Ingram.
Though the family business now employs about 1,000 people
locally—more than twice that worldwide—and appears publicly as
key patron of the local arts, Ingram would just as soon say thanks-but-
no-thanks to offers of limelight and the forays of curious interviewers.

Until now, that is.

Until now, life has been business as usual for Ingram—a silent
yearly task of building a corporation with coal deals in Africa and oil
deals in Indonesia and ongoing relationships with 18,000 or so
bookstores and libraries. But something happened a year ago that
drew the executive into the public eye. Ingram became involved
with the Nashville Area Chamber of Commerce. He found himself
addressing issues he had previously considered primarily only in the
confines of Ingram offices or in casual gatherings of business friends.
More important, he found himself growing concerned that something about this city . . . was going awry. The peaceful streets were
growing clogged with traffic. Office buildings were popping up, or
threatening to pop up, where they weren't wanted. A crucial new
airport was being challenged. An air of cynicism and the smell of
antagonism toward growth were rising in a town with a long and
nationally recognized pro-business climate.

Had it been anyone else struck by these visions of a changing
Nashville, the compulsion probably would have been a bid for
political office. But it was Bronson Ingram. Ingram took the private
businessman's approach and accepted the responsibility of serving as
president of the Chamber of Commerce.

Others have served and others have served well, he stresses. And
others will follow and others will serve well in the future. But this is
his obligation. Dramatic challenges are facing Middle Tennessee and
Nashville's chamber is the forum in which to meet them, he says.
Issues of community change have arisen that are larger than the city's
apparatus for handling them. Zoning conflicts have pitted real estate
developers against neighborhood groups. Population growth is
creating a need for intercounty planning. New infrastructure needs
to be developed more rapidly, and the funding mechanism may be
inadequate. The Codes Administration is understaffed during a
period of massive building expansion. The entire planning process

for Nashville's growth must be raised to a new plane to handle the coming generation of change. The Chamber of Commerce is the group to push the solutions to the forefront.

"We haven't used the membership as well as we might," Ingram says. "We haven't been as effective as we could be on these issues. But we're going to do something about that. The Chamber is going to take a position, to say, 'Yes, we want this,' or 'No, we don't want that,' and we're not going to read about it in the back of *The Tennessean* with the obituaries. It's going to be front-page news and six o'clock news and we're going to back up what we say with our actions."

Odds are the issues of Ingram's chamber will gain attention this year as Nashville gears up for a mayoral election that seems to be increasingly oriented to the same issues. However, odds are just as great that Ingram's issues of how Nashville and Middle Tennessee handle their new growth will long outlive this election or the next.

Advantage recently interviewed Ingram and the following is from a transcript of the conversation:

One of your first acts as president of the Chamber was to establish a tax committee to look into the issue of how state funds are allocated to municipalities. What do you have in mind?

It all ties into the prospective growth Nashville now has to deal with. I don't think our growth can be dealt with on the basis of Nashville-Davidson County versus all the surrounding counties. We're all in this damn thing together. Nashville is Middle Tennessee. The surrounding counties are affected by us and what happens here, and we're affected by them and what happens outside Davidson County. To have the kind of growth we're facing, particularly with the new American Airlines hub here, we're going to have to establish some form of regional planning and some multi-county authority with overall control of some parts of that growth—some unified authority that could determine where the growth goes and how it happens and what the infrastructure will be to handle it.

This sort of thing very simply takes money. Planning is one thing. Implementing is something else. The tie between the two is money. What I propose is to try to recognize that now and establish some chamber committees with some real expertise that are involved in more than tourism and country music and determine what it is we need. I'm convinced it's going to take legislative action, but the last thing in the world we ought to do is go to the governor or the Legislature and say we'd like you to do something but we don't know what the hell it is, so you guys figure it out and lay it on us. That would be foolish. If we don't know enough about how to take care of ourselves, how in the world can we expect legislators from all across the state to figure it out for us?

A lot of groups here are thinking and worrying about this same thing and the chamber has some capability to be a leader in the issue. It has a very large membership that encompasses substantially all the business interests in the greater Nashville area. Even people outside Nashville are as concerned as Nashvillians are that you can't get out of your driveway between 7:15 and a quarter to eight in the morning when it used to be if you stood by the road you couldn't hitch a ride because nobody came by.

I'm not a planner, I'm not a traffic consultant and I know very little about zoning. One thing I do know is that when it comes to planning issues we simply can't continue with the practice of councilmanic courtesy here with every Metro Council person effectively having total zoning authority in his little area. But it's still a much bigger problem than that. I took the job as president of the Chamber because I'm not a developer, I'm not a banker, I'm not beholden to anybody and nobody's going to threaten me over any position I take. We need to get a ground swell going and get people talking about the issue of planned growth, get the newspapers concerned and get the concern out of the cocktail parties and off of the golf course. We don't want to be like Atlanta, where nobody knew what it was that they didn't want to be like.

The scariest thing about where we are now, which is each developer on his own trying to see what he can wangle through, is that we could just go on and abuse our area to the extent that the community rises up and says, "Hell, we've had enough of this. We don't want any growth." . . . My god, the last thing in the world Nashville ever wants is to have the people say we've had all the growth we want—you raise your children here, educate them at Vanderbilt, and then tell them to get the hell out because there's not going to be any opportunities for them. We're not going to grow anymore. You already have that syndrome in some cities, and it will eventually happen here if we don't strike some middle ground. . . .

The problem is that any major industrial undertaking today will be fought by a minority in the name of the environment. I have limited sympathy with people who fight progress in the attitude of "I don't want anything to change," or "I don't want more airplanes in the sky." Times are better now than they were in the good ol' days. The problem with the good ol' days is they were so long ago you don't remember all the bad parts. We need controlled progress and controlled growth with broad groups of people, basically the whole citizenry, having some say in how we grow and how fast we grow. . . .

How crucial to Nashville's business growth will easing local traffic congestion be?

More crucial to some businesses than others, obviously. The only way we're going to solve the problem is to change the type of traffic we're creating. The city is growing without any coordinated connection to the arteries that are necessary to handle that traffic.

Metro Planning Commission director Jeff Browning told us the story of one of the major developments in Brentwood that had paid to build a four-lane road right up to the Davidson County line. Brentwood officials wanted Nashville to continue the project into Davidson County. Unfortunately, they never discussed it with us so there was no way Metro could plan for it. Second, by virtue of doing it totally privately, Brentwood had given up the 70 or 80 percent combined state and federal funding that could have been available both to Brentwood and Nashville in continuing the road. As a result, we lost out on funding that would have enabled us to participate.

That's what happens when you don't have intercounty coordination of planning. It's the kind of thing we've got to come to grips with to resolve something like traffic. And really this holds true for issues of codes, water and sewer and schools.

What I find in talking with the few developers I know is that most of them have no real problems dealing with rules and regulations in a development as long as they're clearly spelled out ahead of time, and are consistent and consistently applied. We just haven't had that. Nashville has had what I call government by developer for a long time. Up until now we've had mostly hometown developers. Bobby Mathews, for instance, is a developer here, he was president of the Chamber of Commerce, he lives here, his family has grown up here and he's interested in the city. But now there are 50 or more developers working in Davidson County from out-of-state. Those people don't give a damn about our quality of life. They're interested in building their development, getting it up to speed, selling it, putting the profit in their pocket and going on to the next hot area they can find. The devil take the problems they cause. Yet those people are still perfectly willing to work within whatever infrastructure we have—as long as we have one that is well-defined and well-organized.

You're saying in addition to looking at a several-county planning concept, the Davidson County codes and planning apparatus should be looked at?

Sure. Planning and zoning have to be more centrally controlled. Nobody likes central control, for heaven's sake, but I'll give you the perfect example of what I'm talking about:

This building right over here on White Bridge Road and Harding—One Belle Meade Place. We bought that building. But that thing had no business in the world being built there. That's the tenth busiest intersection in Metropolitan Nashville right there. There's no other high-rise anywhere out here. How in the hell anybody ever got permission to build a high-rise there I can't imagine. My house is two blocks away from it and I never had any conception there was a high-rise going up until I happened to see the picture at the site as it was coming out of the ground. I nearly had a stroke. I and a whole group of other people got together and stopped a bigger one that was going to go up on the other side of the railroad tracks. That's the sort of thing that shouldn't be decided by one person, and that should be built in accordance with a whole area development concept. The Planning Commission should never have allowed something like that in that area. If the Planning Commission had some teeth in it, some oversight or override authority over councilmanic zoning, you wouldn't be seeing it there just because the developer wanted it there. And it was an out-of-state developer, incidentally.

So it's a question of Planning Commission authority?

I don't know what kind of additional authority they ought to have. I'm just saying it doesn't do any good to have a planning authority if it hasn't got any authority over planning. If they can't stop something that doesn't fit into some kind of master plan for the area, we can expect some big problems. At some point, if we continue to build downtown, you won't be able to get there and get back. Eventually we've got to have some kind of moderately priced zoned parking and mass transit distribution downtown or the area is just going to fill up and pop. We've got several places where you could put some rim parking along the inner loop, and then have mass transit from there to five or six stops downtown that put you within a block's walking distance of substantially anything down there. . . .

Your company maintains a very low profile, despite the size of your operations. What's behind your philosophy on public attention?

I'm a relatively private person and I've never gotten any particular kicks from blowing my horn and reading about myself on a regular basis as some people do. Some of them overdo it. They usually have some motive for it and think it's going to get them somewhere. It's never gotten me anywhere I wanted to go. I guess I've just never had any interest in it. My father always believed in being a very quiet person in terms of his accomplishments. He was very active in a lot of things and did a tremendous amount of business. So did my mother. But they did it anonymously. They got their pleasure out of doing it and not out of rubbing anybody's nose in it or taking credit for it. I've been very fortunate. I was born lucky and I've been lucky ever since. I worked very hard at it but I feel like I owe a lot of it back. I try to give financially and with my time. But I don't want any credit for it. It's something I owe.

As far as business is concerned, I know what we do and our people know what we do. We're very open with lenders and with the constituency that needs to know about us. But I don't need to read about what the hell we do and how we do it in a newspaper or a magazine. I don't get any pleasure or any value out of talking about it. The idea of reading that we've got the biggest this or the biggest that is actually a little silly to me. . . . We're doing the best we can and that's all we can do. When we do make an announcement of some kind, I'd rather have the profit center heads who are involved with it making the announcement. They're the ones who are dealing with it. They're the ones our customers know and they're the ones who should be answering the questions. They know the answer and I probably don't. There's just no need for me to be the center of attention.

Both Bronson and I believed—and I still believe—in making Nashville a better and better place to live. In that regard, I guess you could call us salespeople on the city's behalf. At least that is the way the Sales and Marketing Executives of Nashville looked at us. In 1991, the group honored us as the National Salespersons of the Year. Usually, the annual award is given to a man or woman for efforts in selling Nashville to the state, the nation, and the world, but the group selected us as a couple.

A newspaper article reported:

> Both Martha Ingram, director of public affairs for Ingram Industries Inc., and Bronson Ingram, president and chief executive officer of the privately held company, were nominated individually for the award.
>
> "We felt, when we were thinking about either/or as a nominee, that the combination of the two was what we wanted to do," said Shelby Smith, general manager of Superb Motors and chairman of the awards event.
>
> "They have both played such an active role in the community."

I explained earlier that Bronson leaned in the direction of the Republican Party in political ideology, but he also would back a man he believed in. When Ned Ray McWherter considered a run for governor in 1985, he came to our house to discuss it. Ned recalled, "Bronson and Martha and I ate dinner at the pool house. He told me, 'If you want to run for governor, I'll support you.' He was a known Republican, and she was, too. I never had any question about that. At that time he had been a strong supporter of former Governor Dunn. I had respect for him. At that particular time when Bronson told me that, Governor Dunn had never even indicated that he might run. I don't think Governor Dunn, in discussions with him later, had a lot of thought about it early on."

Two or three other Democratic candidates were talking about running. Ned said, "Then all of a sudden after I got out and started running, my friend Jane Eskind decided to run in the primary and Mayor [Dick] Fulton decided to run in the primary, and we had a

very difficult primary. I fortunately was the nominee, and Bronson and Martha fortunately helped me.

The Patsea VI in Cancun, Mexico.

"Then the Republicans elected to talk Governor Dunn into running again. We had a race on our hands. I thought when I heard that, *Ingram will support Governor Dunn*. I just liked Bronson. He was my kind of guy. I thought that he had always been up front with me—again, very blunt. When Governor Dunn decided to run, I called Bronson. I told him I wanted to talk to him.

"Again, I went to the house and had dinner at the pool house. I said, 'I know that you and Martha are friends with Winfield and Betty Dunn. I like him. He is a fine man and his wife and his family. His son and my son are friends. You made a commitment to me, and if you want to withdraw that commitment, I want you to know that we'll always be friends.'

"Bronson stood up and said, 'Hell, I don't want to withdraw my commitment. I told you last year, I was going to be for you, and I'm going to call Winfield and tell him that.' Winfield told me later that he did. He was that kind of man. He supported me and helped me and contributed, and it was nice to know he was right there behind me. The night I got elected he was down at the hotel, among all of the other guests. He was one of the crowd. I saw him and got him up on the stage. I just was very proud of our friendship.

"What I liked about Bronson and what I respected so much about him, if you asked him for some advice, in his own language, he'd give you some advice. If you didn't want to follow it, he'd tell you to go to hell, and it would be just that plain, that quick, that simple. I liked him for that.

"He made it clear back in 1985 when he said, 'We're going to support you, and I'm going to support you. But I want to know one thing: you're going to work like hell, aren't you, and you're going to win this race?' I said, 'Bronson, I'm going to work like hell, and we're going to win this race.' And we did.

"After I was elected governor, I wanted to give a reception at the Governor's Residence for Bronson and Martha, but Bronson asked me to make it a surprise party just for Martha. He didn't want it to be for him, too. We had a black-tie party with a lot of guests, food, and even a band, and Martha's brother [from Charleston] and sister [from New York City] came to the party from out of town. She was *really* surprised. Somehow we all managed to keep it quiet. She thought she was coming to the Residence for a small dinner party with a few people. Bronson cared deeply for his wife, and he wanted to honor her with that event." I was truly surprised by the party and deeply honored by our good friend Ned. Without his stalwart support there would be no TPAC today.

Clayton McWhorter refers to himself as a Ned McWherter Democrat, and Bronson was ready to support him in a bid for governor in the early 1990s. Clayton said, "I was encouraged and I gave a lot of thought to running for governor. I put a campaign staff together and visited about forty of the ninety something counties in Tennessee. The biggest single contributor to the campaign was Bronson. Then when the word was out that I was going to run for governor, we had some unfriendly overtures. At that time I was CEO of HealthTrust, the hospital company. So the board, even though they had sort of agreed that I would take the time to run for governor, they began to say, 'Look, we sure would like for you to reconsider. This is sending the wrong signals [about the company]. We need to send out a signal that we're not for sale.' Then I opted not to go forward, so I had the opportunity to return all of the money.

"But then when Clinton and Gore were elected, it created the vacancy that Governor McWherter was going to have to name a person to fill Gore's seat in the Senate. Bronson said, 'What you need to do, Clayton, is go to Washington. You need to be a senator.' I said, 'Bronson, I don't want to go to Washington.' He said, 'Nah, that is what you need to do. You need to take Gore's place. You'd do a lot better job than he has done,' and on and on. He called Ned McWherter and told him, 'The person you need to appoint is Clayton McWhorter.' Of course, Ned and I are good friends. Ned called and said, 'I got this call from Bronson.' I said, 'Governor, that is not something I would even consider, so please don't put me in that position.' He said, 'Well, I wasn't planning on doing it anyway.'"

Bronson put his energies and his heart into everything I have discussed so far, but I have not yet told you about the endeavor that occupied a great part of the last years of his life—campaigning for Vanderbilt University.

CHAPTER 8

The Campaign for Vanderbilt

You make a living by what you get.
You make a life by what you give.
—**Winston Churchill**

The Ingram family's association with Vanderbilt University now spans more than fifty years. Bronson attended the university for one year, 1949–50, and his father served on the Board of Trust from 1952 to 1963, the year of his untimely death at age fifty-eight.

On November 13, 1964, the *Nashville Banner* ran this front-page headline: "VU Board Approves Ingram Chair." The Vanderbilt University Board of Trust approved the establishment of a distinguished professorship in engineering management, endowed by the Ingram family:

Engineering management scholarships endowed by the Ingram family also were approved as the board opened its annual fall meeting.

The Orrin Henry Ingram Distinguished Professorship is the first such chair at Vanderbilt.

Creation of the new rank, highest in the academic scale, was announced by Chancellor Alexander Heard in a speech to the faculty in September.

Mr. Ingram, vice president of the Board of Trust at the time of his death in April 1963, was active in a wide variety of businesses, including textiles, insurance, lumber, barge lines, and oil refining and distribution. . . .

The professorship and scholarships will make possible a new program in the School of Engineering that will:

- Lead to a bachelor of engineering degree with honors in engineering management after four years of study with at least two summers spent as a management engineering intern with a Nashville area firm.
- Lead to a master of science in engineering management after the fifth year of study.
- Combine education and training in the engineering sciences with courses such as economics, business administration, psychology, English and speech.

Dean Robert S. Rowe of the Engineering School said a person qualified to fill the new chair will be found and appointed as soon as possible.

The new program is expected to start next fall.

The board adopted the following statement in approving the program:

"Orrin Henry Ingram believed deeply in the efficiency of competitive business. He had profound faith in the American free enterprise system, and in its ability to prosper and advance.

"He was convinced that effective university training for business leadership is essential to a dynamic American economy. Over many years he was concerned with improving engineering education and business education at Vanderbilt University.

"He believed that successful management requires training and study that develop skills in communications and human relations along with technical competence—a necessary combination for American economic leadership of the future.

"To further Mr. Ingram's objectives, the perpetuation of the free-enterprise system and the advancement of Vanderbilt University, his family joins with the university in honoring his memory and establishing the Orrin Henry Ingram Distinguished Professorship of Engineering Management in the School of Engineering, and the Orrin Henry Ingram Scholarships in Engineering Management."

The creation of the new academic rank is part of a plan to increase Vanderbilt's ability to attract and hold faculty members of the highest quality.

The following day, November 14, the *Banner's* editorial highlighted the Ingram gift:

> Of the countless benefactions bestowed by the late Orrin Henry Ingram, none exceeded those dedicated to human uplift through education. And Vanderbilt University, which he served as a member of the Board of Trust, was a principal instrument of that generosity.
>
> In the spirit of that devotion, his family is endowing at Vanderbilt a Distinguished Professorship in Engineering Management—appropriate memorial, indeed, honoring the name it wears. For by the substantial gift entailed, blessings of opportunity will flow through the chair it endows, and the scholarships it creates.
>
> As approved and announced by the Board of Trust yesterday, the university's School of Engineering thus acquires facilities for a program broadening its academic scope in special fields of higher education. It opens the door to personal attainment by candidates for such scholarships; and it enhances the stature of the institution. It perpetuates in both respects the concept of service characterizing this benefactor. For O. H. Ingram, eminently successful in the broad field of business his life embraced, made a career of constructive humanitarian enterprise.
>
> He was a giant in steadfast love of his country, and in faith in the principles which are its foundation: integrity and purpose, preserved by individual responsibility. These were incorporated in his own life. More than a mere philosophy, they were to him a creed. . . .
>
> It is the university's gain, but beyond that the region's and the nation's—for from it will flow benefits of individual achievement, far-reaching.
>
> In magnitude and merit, it comprises news fitted to the pattern of a growing university—one salient evidence of which was the authorization yesterday to expand undergraduate enrollment in the College of Arts and Science to a total of 2,600 within three years. To every Vanderbilt graduate assembled for this Homecoming Day, it should serve to remind of that response—in the spirit of willing men—that has built for the present, and still is building for the future.
>
> To a great life, boundless in its usefulness, no memorial could be more fitting. None could better perpetuate the spirit of service that was his.

There is a fitting passage in the Gospel of Mark that says of leadership: "Whoever wants to become great among you must first be your servant, and whoever wants to be first must be slave of all." You don't just grow up and assume leadership. You have to prove first that you know how to serve, then the force of your personality is allowed to emerge.

Vanderbilt proved to be a huge source of challenge but also pleasure to Bronson. Despite having attended the school only one year, he felt a real kinship with Vanderbilt. He became a member of the Board of Trust in 1967 and eventually served on the Executive Committee, the Audit Committee, the Committee for Nominations for Officers of the Board and Membership on Committees, the Committee on University Planning and Development, the Investment Committee, and the Budget Committee. During the Centennial Campaign (1976–81), he cochaired with Gerald Averbuch the building fund for the Owen Graduate School of Management. He took seriously his service on each committee and was faithful in carrying out any assigned duties. Whether he knew it or not, he was working toward a major leadership position in the university.

Pat Wilson believed that Bronson's greatest contribution to the university—and as you will see, they were numerous—occurred when Bronson joined with Pat and one other person on the board to advocate changing the university's investment policies. Before the change was implemented, the university could invest only in bonds, not in equities. Pat said, "I don't think that Vanderbilt University would be where it is today without that move, and Bronson was a fervent supporter of making that change."

Ed Nelson commented, "Bronson was very attentive to the investments that the university made, and I think he felt that he encouraged Vanderbilt to be aggressive, but cautious in what it did. Vanderbilt has a rather forward-looking type of portfolio, and I know he encouraged it. He gave the Treasurer's Office the right environment in which to move forward on that. Vanderbilt has a large endowment partly as a result of giving but partly as a result of investment performance."

In December 1980, Ike Robinson, M.D., first met Bronson. Ike was being considered for the job of vice chancellor for medical affairs

Mrs. T. A. Clarkson, T. A. Clarkson, Martha, Bronson, Mrs. O. H. Ingram, and Chancellor Heard gathered to award Mr. Clarkson the 1970 O. H. Ingram Scholarship.

at Vanderbilt, and Emmett Fields, then president of the university (the only time Vanderbilt had anyone with that title), held a party to introduce Ike and his wife, Ann, to trustees and others. Ike recalled: "I don't remember who all was there. But I remember Jack Massey. I remember Don McNaughton. I remember Harvie Branscomb. But the person that really made an impression on me was Bronson. Bronson was standing apart from everyone else, alone. And I don't remember but I guess he made some beckoning gesture to me, and I went over there and I think he must have—I don't remember—introduced himself. But what I do remember is what he said. I've never forgotten it. This is the gist of it: 'You're going to hear a lot of recruitment talk here tonight, and a lot of people are going to promise you that if you come, they'll be supportive and help you. Some people will mean it, and some won't. But if you decide to come—and I hope you will—I'll help you, and I mean it!' And he did. He really did. He was tremendously supportive."

Ike took the job and began his duties in 1981. Over the years, Ike and Bronson became friends and even went deep-sea fishing together in addition to working on behalf of Vanderbilt.

Sam Fleming had been president of the Board of Trust from 1975 until 1981, and Pat Wilson succeeded him in that position. One of Pat's first duties was to join in the search for a new chancellor to succeed Alexander Heard, who was to retire in mid–1982. Bronson was a member of the Search Committee that had to sift through more than three hundred names presented as possible candidates, and Chancellor Heard appointed John Beasley as secretary to the committee. (John recalled, "Mr. Heard said, 'You must not be only neutral; you must be neuter.' Which I thought was asking quite a lot for them to say I must be neuter." His was a staff position with no ties to the board.)

Lewis Branscomb, son of former chancellor Harvie Branscomb and a board member, recommended that the group call on a man at Harvard who taught computer science and was vice president for administration. According to John, Lewis had told the committee: "There is a guy at Harvard that is in terms of credentials an unlikely candidate, but he is going to make a great president somewhere, in my opinion." They followed Lewis's advice and arranged to meet Joe B. Wyatt while they were in his area of the country.

They first had to overcome Joe's reluctance to discuss the position, however. When John called Joe to tell him that there was some interest in his coming to Vanderbilt, Joe replied, "I'm flattered, but I'm just too involved. I couldn't get free from Harvard in any short period of time."

Then Pat called Joe: "I know you said you have other commitments. But two or three of us are coming up to Boston anyway, and would you mind if we stopped by to see you?" Joe said, "I couldn't refuse an offer like that." Pat, Sam, Bronson, and John visited with Joe for about an hour. Joe added, "At that time they didn't realize this and I didn't mention it when we talked, but our son was already a student at Vanderbilt. He had come to the university as a premed student. He wanted to get five hundred miles away from home. He had gone around and looked at schools and settled on Vanderbilt. Then we did our due diligence and learned that Vanderbilt had an outstanding reputation for premed students. So he was already here.

My wife and I came down for parents' weekend, and by that time they had come up one other time and Don McNaughton had come with them."

Joe described Bronson in those meetings: "Bronson was a great listener, and he didn't dominate a conversation or the meeting at all. He was a very direct but a very stylish businessperson who wasn't out to impress you. He was out to accomplish something and therefore was a very, very good listener. Bronson was better than most people realize on the input side—good listener, good reader, could understand and assimilate an enormous amount of information. He did that on anything that he undertook. He really studied it and thought about it carefully.

"It is fair to say that when I began to discuss with them what their goals were at Vanderbilt, why they thought I might be able to help them, it was very clear that Bronson had a thought in mind that made sense about the predecessors, Harvie and Alex, and what the issues were here in terms of building and innovating, not necessarily traditional academic development. Development of a lot of different dimensions of the institution. It was a very comfortable relationship with Bronson and with Pat Wilson."

Bronson and I hosted an event for Joe and his wife, Faye, at our home to give them a chance to meet people associated with Vanderbilt. It was held while talks were still ongoing about the position. That was the first time I met him—a tall, easygoing Texan with Harvard polish—but it was certainly not the last. The board made its decision, Joe accepted, and he started work as the sixth chancellor of Vanderbilt University in July 1982.

In 1988, Bronson became the vice president of the Board of Trust, and the next year, he assumed the role of chairman of the Campaign for Vanderbilt, which had a goal of raising $300 million. Joe Wyatt recommended him to the board for the position but not before speaking to Bronson about it: "Pat Wilson and I talked about who would chair it. We said, 'There is only one person to chair it.' And I said, 'Let me ask him. It is going to be something that he and I will spend time doing, and I'd just like to do that.'

"The way I approached it was, I went to see him and said, 'Bronson, you know we're going to do a capital campaign. It's time.

We need to. We have a case for what we want to do. You know, there were three people who came to recruit me from Harvard—you and Pat and Sam. And you're the only one of those three that hasn't done a capital campaign, so I want you to do this one with me.'

"I didn't know whether he would say, 'Gee, I'd love to do it, but, Joe, you know that I've got too much on the table.' Or whether he would say, which would be very typical, 'I'm very flattered that you've asked. Let me think about it for a while.' He sat there for what seemed like a long minute, and he looked at me and said, 'I'll do it if you'll stay with me and finish it.' I said, 'I'll certainly do that.'

"We basically shook hands, and that was it. We covered that ground. He made the commitment. He knew he would stay and see it through, and I had promised to stay with him."

I have never seen anyone spend so much concentrated time on such an extensive effort while running a major business, too. I think one reason that Bronson was so involved with Vanderbilt—and he more or less told me this—was that he had seen me have so much fun (most of the time) establishing TPAC. Yes, it was hard, and sometimes it almost got away from us because of political maneuverings or one thing or the other, but it was a great challenge, a great source of pride, and very energizing. He found much the same in the Vanderbilt Campaign.

Over the years Bronson and I refined our philosophy in regard to philanthropy. We wanted to give not only of our resources but also of our time. We did not want to be people who just lobbed money at causes—even very good causes. We wanted to have the chance to roll up our sleeves and be full, passionate participants in actualizing projects or taking leadership roles rather than standing to one side and giving money for somebody else to decide what to do with it. And when you have this sort of philanthropy going, you usually get more out of it than you could possibly put into it. You could say it involves money, passion, and elbow grease.

Nelson Andrews, a Board of Trust member, said about the Campaign: "To really do that kind of thing, you need somebody who can set a tone in and of themselves. The epitome would be somebody who can lead from a giving standpoint, somebody who can open almost any door, who commands respect, who's got enough time. You got to have somebody that is energetic. You got to have somebody who is committed. Got to have somebody who is dependable, who gets a job done, who sees it through. And all those things were Bronson.

"You'd like to have maybe someone who is extremely personable who could schmooze people out of their wealth, and that was not Bronson. That's not the way he could do it. Bronson was not the Mr. Chips, warm and fuzzy academician of any sorts. He did it by deed, not by personality or persuasiveness, because that just wasn't him. But he sure did it." Bronson gave the lead gift for the Campaign.

John Beasley described how the planning progressed in the Campaign Office within the Office of Alumni Development under his direction: "Every two weeks at 8:30 in the morning Bronson, Pat Wilson, Joe Wyatt, I, and about five of my key staff met. [The Campaign lasted six years, and Bronson attended those meetings every two weeks. The staff included approximately 160 people.] We had a good time. I think Bronson genuinely enjoyed the staff people that he was working with. He got instant information. We'd know exactly what it was he was going to want to know because it was the things we wanted to know, too. Not all the calls panned out, but many of them did. He didn't expect all of them to pan out."

Bronson personally called on some potential donors, accompanied at various times by John Beasley, Joe Wyatt, or staff persons from the Campaign Office. The first call was significant in setting the tone and moving the Campaign in the right direction, and Bronson was successful in his goal on that call. He didn't have to make too many personal calls. Often, John said, Campaign staffers only had to say, "Bronson is going to ask you this, and they'd say, 'Oh, well, uh, look, uh, listen . . . I'll just give it to you now.'"

Joe Wyatt described the reactions of a few potential donors: "We had a lot of people that we both knew had substantial resources, owed a good deal of their success to Vanderbilt. Bronson was very stylish but also very relentless with those folks. I can't name names. But I have seen people after having a meeting with us where perspiration was dripping off their chins. Their shirts were wet. Bronson used to say, 'You can run, but you can't hide. I know you. I know your net worth. I know what you ought to do, and one way or another you're going to do it.' With some people it was clear that he was serious but enjoying doing this—and successful at it, I might add. Some people never did come forward, even though they should have. They just didn't."

Bronson spoke out on his decision to accept the leadership of the Campaign in the *Campaign Courier.*

> **Courier:** Why do you think the Campaign is needed at this point in the life of the University?
>
> **Ingram:** Every university can profitably use more money and Vanderbilt is no exception. We are in a competitive business; all schools are seeking the best faculty and the brightest students. Though we like to think that we are one of the top universities in the country, relatively speaking, we have less endowment than many and fewer scholarships, professorships, and chairs.

> **Courier:** What are the overall goals?
>
> **Ingram:** The Campaign needs to raise a minimum of $300 million in gifts, pledges, and irrevocable trusts, although the final goal must be approved and set by the Board of Trust. We have a separate goal of $50 million for new planned bequests. Besides support for faculty and students, we need to have several building projects funded. During the Campaign counting period—from July 1, 1989, to June 30, 1994—we will count all restricted or unrestricted funds that the University receives, everything!
>
> But the most important thing that can come out of this Campaign is an increase in total private giving to the University each year. I would like to see us raise our ongoing annual support by 100 percent. In the long run, I believe that will be a good deal more important to Vanderbilt than raising $150 million or $200 million in new, one-time dollars.

> **Courier:** How will volunteers be involved in the different phases of the Campaign?
>
> **Ingram:** We will certainly involve as many people as we possibly can in the Campaign. I think one of our objectives is to solicit on a more intensive and much broader geographical basis than we have done in prior campaigns, where a very significant portion of the

money was raised in the greater Nashville area. We will raise a lot of money in the greater Nashville area this time as well, I hope, but we now have more graduates and more dispersed alumni than we have had in the past. Vanderbilt is more national in scope, and I hope that we can reach out into a much broader arena than we have before. That takes more volunteers, it takes more organization, and it takes more people. We will have a national campaign organization, a national business organization, and a national parents organization.

Courier: How do you view your role as chairman of the Campaign?

Ingram: The Campaign is a big people business, and I am a manager. I have spent my life managing people. I think that my basic functions as chairman are to help attract good people to work in the Campaign; to make some key calls, which the head of any campaign is expected to participate in; to be generous myself, in order to set an example; and to help the very fine professional organization that we have at Vanderbilt. I am here to help the development office organize and run what will be, for the next four years, a large business in and of itself. My responsibility is to see that we stay on track and on schedule, that we make the right choices as we go along, and most of all, that we stay focused on what it is we're doing.

Courier: What have you emphasized in your first year as chairman?

Ingram: During the first year of the Campaign, I have begun to learn something about what it really entails. I have been getting to know the people in the development office that I will be working with daily. With the help of the Chancellor and the development staff, we have recruited the vice-chairmen that we need to be successful. Obviously, you have to arrange to solicit the Board of Trust and a small number of other prospects early. This sets the tone of the Campaign and gives you the basis on which to set the goal of the Campaign. Also, I have supervised the overall design and organization of the Campaign. We've tried to organize and set it up so that it is as nearly foolproof as it can be.

Courier: Why did you agree to chair the Campaign? Why were you willing to make this kind of commitment of your time to Vanderbilt?

Ingram: I've been very much involved with Vanderbilt for a long time, and I've been interested in and involved in education as a principal charitable endeavor for quite some time too. I think education is absolutely critical to the future of this country and our leadership position in the world.

On a much more selfish basis, I am keenly interested in the success of Nashville. Vanderbilt is an extraordinarily important piece of what Nashville has going for it, and the better Vanderbilt can be, the better off Nashville will be.

But I guess it really boils down to the fact that the Chancellor, speaking for himself and some of the other Board members that I have particular respect for, said that they wanted me to do it. The Chancellor said that he was prepared to commit whatever time necessary to the effort, because he was convinced that it was that important to Vanderbilt. With that sort of commitment and considering the time that I have spent over the years on the Board of Trust and on the various committees of the Board, it just sort of seemed like it was my turn.

Courier: Is there any message you would like to leave with our readers?

Ingram: The people who are critical to the success of the Campaign are the prospective donors, and they know who they are. No matter how persuasive we may or may not be during our calls, in the final analysis, they are going to set the tone of the Campaign. They are going to determine whether it is successful or not. We have to raise money from people who can afford to give it. And, really, charitable giving is that simple.

I hope that we can instill in those people who can give the understanding of the pleasure that goes with doing something that I think is as worthwhile as supporting this University. We are now witnessing remarkable quality gains in Vanderbilt as a national and world-class university. I hope that our donors will enjoy feeling that they are contributing to that as much as I am.

For the Campaign, kickoff dinners were held in more than twenty major cities across the country. They were lavish, black-tie affairs that Bronson emceed. Three or four hometown people talked about what Vanderbilt meant to them, Joe Wyatt spoke briefly, and then a spectacular slide show about the university was presented. The Campaign staff made sure that each event ran smoothly and all details were handled, right down to the black ties of Bronson and Joe.

Joe recalled, "Neither of us could tie a bow tie. And neither of us planned to learn. It is a simple enough skill, but we just didn't want to bother with it. We always had to find someone to tie our bow ties. Or I think what the staff ended up doing was to make sure they had one of those clip-ons if they couldn't tie a bow tie."

At the Houston dinner, for example, Bronson opened the event by praising the city's alumni for student recruitment. He continued, "Those of us here tonight come from a variety of backgrounds and ages, but together we share Vanderbilt. Together we share many qualities that make up the strength of Vanderbilt—intellect, character, conviction, integrity, talent, and commitment to service.

"Those of us who went to Vanderbilt are part of its past. As alumni and parents, we are part of its present. In the Campaign for Vanderbilt we all have the opportunity to be part of its future." The Campaign was increasingly successful.

In April 1991, the Board of Trust elected Bronson board president at its spring meeting. He succeeded Pat Wilson, who had to step down because of an age limitation. Bronson was fifty-nine years old.

The *Register*, May 6, 1991, reported Bronson's comments on the honor: "'I appreciate this honor,' Ingram said. 'I appreciate the confidence that the Board has shown in me. The University is in good stead because of the leadership of Pat Wilson. I am fortunate to have been preceded by Pat and Sam (Fleming). It would be presumptuous of me to say I can follow in their footsteps, but I'll do my best.'"

Several old friends with Vanderbilt ties who read about it wrote Bronson letters of congratulation; they included Merrimon Cuninggim, Margaret Branscomb, Delbert Mann, and Madison Wigginton. To Madison, Bronson responded, "Thank you for your nice letter about my recent election as president of the Vanderbilt Board of Trust. I especially appreciate your confidence in my leadership, but then you taught me so I ought to know how. I have to follow some awfully good examples in Pat and Sam, but thank

goodness for Joe Wyatt who certainly makes the job a lot easier."

Joe and Bronson had a solid working relationship, and they got things done. Joe said, "We never wasted each other's time. Ever. I always respected his time; he always respected mine. He never reached in, in the sense of reaching around me as the chairman of the board, which is always a temptation for chairs of universities particularly. He had ideas. We consulted about them. I always felt free to present any new ideas to him, whether they were academic or whether they were very businesslike.

"He was encyclopedic in terms of what he remembered out of all that [board minutes and other reports]. He was the best partner that a chancellor could possibly have in terms of dealing with a whole set of complicated issues that ranged from the political to the business to the full academic spectrum. He was always there to play a role in dealing with student issues. Some college students take on this antibusiness attitude. You might not expect that Bronson would be patient enough to—in fact many people who knew him well would not believe that he would be patient enough to—sit and listen to a collection of students, most of them privileged, never having had to work a day in their lives, complaining about corporate America ruining the world and so forth.

Vanderbilt University Board of Trust members, November 1968; Bronson is on the last row, third from right.

"But Bronson was absolutely terrific. He may have exercised his frustration by hitting golf balls. I don't know. I never saw him frustrated. He would just sort of go through patiently. Once he decided that he was committed to helping Vanderbilt, it was an amazing commitment, the level and depth of that commitment."

Joe added, "When Bronson bought Micro D, that was their first venture into the computer business, and that was when he asked me to join that board [Ingram Industries] because he didn't know about the computer business, although I must say that he certainly did learn quickly. I was on the Ingram Industries Board, and then when we spun off Ingram Micro [and took it public on the New York Stock Exchange], it made all the sense for me to go on that board, which I did and still am. I'd say he was very different in the Ingram Industries meetings than he was at the Vanderbilt meetings because he was also the CEO of Ingram Industries. I was the CEO of Vanderbilt, and he was very respectful of the role of the chairman as opposed to the role of the CEO. On the Ingram Industries Board he was both.

"Bronson had all the characteristics of a great leader—he was decisive, he was a terrific listener, he was terrific at interacting, probing in a skillful way, not in an abusive way, just seeking information and seeking consistency in response. And he was willing to do the work. Everyone knew that Bronson was willing to burrow into something in as much detail as it took to understand it and decide. He would ask others to do that. He was just a natural leader in every respect. He never abused people. He would chastise people for not doing something they said they would do or for being incomplete in something they knew how to do but just didn't do it when they and he both knew they could have done better. He didn't dwell on it. He pointed it out and moved on. He had all the characteristics of leaders that I have known in government and industry, and I've known quite a few."

Rosalind Smith interviewed Bronson for the *Vanderbilt Hustler*, September 20, 1991:

> Bronson Ingram is not afraid to talk about the power of money.
> Ingram, who replaced David K. Wilson as Board of Trust president this spring, sees from the top of University administration how financial concerns can pervade every aspect of a community's life.

The growing expenses of higher education in the face of drastic cutbacks in governmental support define the most difficult area of concern Board members will confront over the next few years, Ingram said in an interview this week.

"One of the biggest areas the Board of Trust is going to have to deal with over time is the continuing financial liability of private education, in competition with public education at a much higher price," Ingram said.

He said private universities must carry the burden of proof in convincing students that a Vanderbilt education is worth its cost.

"We'll have to be able to demonstrate that Vanderbilt is worth a $15,000 tuition, opposed to the University of Tennessee at five or six," Ingram said.

"That's a big investment. If you are going to get a return on that investment over the rest of your life, then it is good enough so that you're glad to make the investment," he said.

Ingram faults legislators for not taking steps to ensure the governmental funding that universities rely upon.

"Basically I think that the government's whole thrust is being unwilling to limit its own spending, and instead of having the guts to go out and raise taxes, they're trying to cut reimbursement of all kinds," Ingram said. "One of the major areas of reimbursement is in higher education."

Government cutbacks in scholarship funding can hinder a university's efforts to recruit minority students, he said.

"Some of the primary areas the thrust of diversity is for is toward those certain economic backgrounds who generally need higher financial support," Ingram said.

"This is one of the big reasons we're in a big financial campaign right now. People say, 'Gee, what in the world could Vanderbilt need money for—they're rich as Croesus.' In fact we are not rich as Croesus, in relation to a budget of $600 and some odd million this University represents," he said.

Ingram said donors in the capital campaign, aspiring to raise $300 million over the next five years, generally give money to a specific University goal.

"We'll take it any way we can get it," he said. "Most of the bigger gifts are earmarked for a more or less specific purpose, and that's probably the most important way that you can raise money.

"Two-thirds of the money we're trying to raise is for endowed scholarships and endowed professorships," he said.

Ingram said although gifts are made to designated areas of the University, donors do not exercise any control over specific decisions about expenditure.

"There is very little, I don't want to say none, very little money given to Vanderbilt that has total, ongoing, complicated strings attached, because that just doesn't really work," he said.

Members of the faculty have been critical of the Board of Trust for granting Chancellor Joe B. Wyatt a 17.6 percent pay increase two consecutive years when the average faculty pay increase has been 5.5 percent.

Ingram said faculty pay and pay increases should not be compared to those of the Chancellor because of the contrasting nature of their jobs.

He said Vanderbilt must offer competitive compensations to both faculty and administrators in order to attract top talent, but the competitions occur on different levels.

Ingram said faculty have a "great deal more leeway" than people who choose careers in the business world.

"Amongst the faculty members, (those who are) tenured, they can stay there the rest of their lives, do relatively as much or as little as they please.

"None of that goes on in the business profession. The management of a university is extraordinarily complex, at least as complex as the management of a major corporation, or a major section of government. It happens that the best university leaders today are subject to being lured away competitively to places like that," Ingram said.

"The fact of the matter is Joe Wyatt could make three times that much any time he wanted to in the private sector. He's that good. I happen to think that he is the very best university administrator and leader that I have ever had any contact with at all," he said.

Money spent to keep Wyatt at Vanderbilt constitutes a worthy investment for the University, Ingram said.

"He has done an exceptional job, and if we look at the difference between what you might pay a Joe Wyatt and what you might pay a much more faculty-oriented or faculty-type of administrator, we've gotten the money back a hundred times over," Ingram said.

He said Wyatt has worked to raise faculty pay drastically during his tenure.

"One of the major thrusts of Wyatt's assets has been his raising the level of faculty salaries to an absolutely competitive level amongst the best universities, adjusted for cost of living in the area, from where Vanderbilt was 10 years ago, at the bottom," Ingram said.

"I think that if that weren't so, we wouldn't have been able to attract the outstanding faculty that we've attracted in the last several years. They came to Vanderbilt because they liked the idea of Vanderbilt, and they wouldn't have come here if their compensation hadn't been sufficiently competitive so that it wasn't an issue with them," he said.

Ingram said Trustees enjoy the benefits of being able to visualize progress in the University over a long period of time, whereas students may grow frustrated when changes are realized slowly.

"I've spent enough time with Vanderbilt, with the Board and what goes on . . . you get to the point where you have a pretty good feel for how it works, what happens, why it happens and start to understand that student perspective is much, much shorter than a trustee's perspective," he said.

"The student is only going to be there for a few years, wants to see whatever change they want right now, so it happens, whereas the trustee sees what can be involved with major issues, they're looking at a much longer time frame," Ingram said.

Ingram began his undergraduate career at Vanderbilt but transferred to Princeton University after his freshman year at the advice of Madison Sarratt, former dean of students.

"Vanderbilt accepted me, and Princeton put me on the waiting list and let me sit there all summer. That aggravated me, and I decided I was cured of going to Princeton," Ingram said.

"But I didn't like the fact that they wouldn't take me, so I made a good record my freshman year, and I applied as a transfer student. They took me in about a week," he said.

"Then I couldn't bring myself to go. I went down to see Madison Sarratt, and he sat me down and said, 'Bronson, Princeton is a better school today than Vanderbilt. I could cut out my tongue for saying that, for telling you that is where you ought to go to school, but that is where you ought to go to school.'

"And he said, 'I'll make a deal with you. If you go to Princeton and you don't like it, send a telegram. By the time you can get back here, I'll have you enrolled at Vanderbilt,'" Ingram said.

"I don't believe I would have gone to Princeton if he hadn't said that," he said.

Ingram earned his bachelor's degree in English at Princeton and played on the University's varsity golf team.

"I probably wasn't the greatest student in the world, but I worked hard to stay there. I made reasonably good grades, but I worked hard to do it," Ingram said.

By the time that the university was about two-thirds of the way through the Campaign and it was clear that the goal was within reach, the board made the decision to extend the goal and set it higher—to $500 million. Joe Wyatt explained what happened before that board meeting: "We talked about extending the capital campaign, and at the point of the discussion when just Bronson and I were talking about it, he said, 'Let's discuss one other thing. I know you've gotten offers from other places to do other things.' I said, 'Yes, I have, but I told you I was going to finish this Campaign, and I'm gonna do it.' He said, 'I understand that, but we're talking about extending this Campaign. And I don't want to assume that you're committed to do that automatically. I want to know, is that something that you want to do?'

"That was what triggered the discussion of what we might do next, and that was when he started talking about retiring in a couple of years, beginning to hand off his businesses to other members of the family or other people. I told him I had thought in terms of staying here [at Vanderbilt] ten years, and obviously, we were past that point. But I think that when I turn sixty-five, if I stay that long, I would want to do something else. He said, 'We ought to set it up that way.' We actually wrote down on a piece of paper that that was what I would do. I would retire in July 2000, which is when I turned sixty-five. This was 1991. That was agreed, and we kept on going.

"Once Bronson took on a task, he would finish it. The Campaign was six intensive years. He just added it to his workload."

To me, the legacy of Bronson and Joe Wyatt is that they got the university on a sound business footing, all the while raising the level of academics. The university is now in a position of not having to worry so much about the buildings and their maintenance, and five or six new ones are under construction as a result of the Campaign.

Bronson's efforts did not go unrecognized by others who worked closely with him on the Campaign. John Beasley wrote him this letter on October 5, 1992:

A dinner for Vanderbilt University Board of Trust members and spouses, held May 1, 1971, at the Hillwood Country Club: Pat and Anne Wilson, Francis Robinson, Martha, Bronson, and Brownlee Currey.

I've been wanting to write you this for better than a year, and somehow the right words didn't seem to come and so I'd put it off. Wednesday night, coming back from Lexington, I was musing on your plane and thinking that—here you were, having made a key call at lunch, then flown us up and handled a cocktail party and dinner before doing your stuff at the microphone, and flying us back—a full day all without a complaint, just as equable and even as you could be, volunteering the time and the money and everything else. And I was terribly grateful, and decided then that I must write. The words eluded me Thursday and Friday, as they may now.

When our staff discusses you, as we do not infrequently, we do so with great admiration and gratitude, and substantial affection. You treat us thoughtfully and with respect, and it is a respect we work very hard to deserve. You don't shoot from the hip, at least you don't appear to, and we remark often on the balance and care you give to one of our viewpoints. You may not agree, but you certainly listen. None of this is lost on any of us. I remember the difference between "leadership" and "command" from my Navy days. You give us outstanding leadership.

It is a privilege to be in the trenches with you. We work extra hard because you work so hard. And what you are doing individually is paying such extraordinary dividends. I honestly don't know of anyone else who could do what you do for Vanderbilt, and it thrills me that you put yourself over and over on the line for this institution.

You're probably as uncomfortable reading this as I am trying to get it out. It won't happen again, at least from me. But for this time, it is sincere and fervently felt. We all, every one of us, know the measure of your contribution to institution, and to a person we are grateful.

You must remember that Bronson was still running his business and fulfilling other civic responsibilities at the same time. And he was playing golf and fishing. He took Joe Wyatt with him on one golfing adventure, and Joe remarked, "He invited me to play golf at Augusta for several days. We played with two relatively young people, well, everybody who works for Microsoft is young.

"Bronson played very well. He was a serious golfer. He could just stand and hit balls. I like to play. I was pretty good at it at one time. I don't play enough to stay all that good. But I played really badly that first day. These young guys were good golfers, and they beat us pretty soundly. I was really embarrassed. Bronson never, never threw a golf club. Never lost his cool in any way whatsoever on the golf course. You could tell he was frustrated sometimes, but he wasn't a club thrower.

L. Jay Tenebaum, Mr. and Mrs. Charles Buck, Bronson, Martha, and Chancellor Heard at a dinner, May 22, 1971, held at the Heard home in honor of members of the Chancellor's Council (individuals who annually give a major unrestricted gift to Vanderbilt University or one of the eight schools).

"The second day I knew I had to do better. The second day we played the par three course. My game was coming back, and I was playing well. Then we played the regular course, and we beat them that second day. I could tell without Bronson ever saying a word that he was very pleased about the fact that I had come from being a terrible partner to one that was at least playing at a level that wasn't disgraceful. It was the kind of communication and approval that never found its way into words."

Bronson regularly attended the meetings of the Medical Center Board after he became president of the Board of Trust, although his attendance was not a requirement. Ike Robinson had made it a practice to talk with Bronson even before that: "Bronson had been on my list of key trustees who I did one-on-ones with frequently. First of all, I wanted to know what they thought. And I'd go over the Medical Center financials with them and get their advice about this or that: 'Do you think it's appropriate for us to borrow this amount of money?' Those kinds of issues. 'Here's where we stand. Here's how much money we have. Here's what's in reserve, etc. Here are my plans. What do you think?'

"Bronson was on that list, always helpful, always encouraging. Right across from the main entrance to Vanderbilt Hospital is a big building, and we call that building Medical Center East. On the top floor is ophthalmology, what have you. Anyway, I wasn't sure that I had enough money to build that whole building, so I was going to build a couple of floors and finish them out and maybe just shell the rest or add on to it as I could. Bronson said, 'Goddamnit, Robinson, build the whole thing. You've got more money than Ben Gump.' That was the kind of encouragement you got from Bronson, and that was significant. So I did. I built the whole thing. We didn't finish it all out at once, but we did build the whole thing."

Ed Nelson, chairman of the Medical Center Board, commented, "The Medical Center was a financially big part of that balance sheet and income statement, and he [Bronson] was very attentive. He accepted my reports and my discussions, but at the same time, he had a good, strong relationship with Ike Robinson. He was very up to date about what went on there.

"Bronson could carefully listen to whatever you wanted to say and then sort of sit back with maybe a half frown of concentration and then move on to what he thought ought to be done. If he didn't know, he would say he didn't know. But he would find out more about what the situation was and he had great follow-through."

In 1994, when Ike was giving thought to retirement in the coming years, he spoke to Bronson about it, and Bronson and Joe Wyatt encouraged him to find someone to replace him, preferably someone inside the Medical Center. Ike agreed to do that. (He found Harry Jacobson, M.D., who took Ike's place in 1997 after being approved by the Board of Trust.) But in discussions with Bronson,

Ike told him, "You know, Bronson, I could give you a list of at least fifty things that need to be done that will not have been done or addressed after I'm gone. The job is just never done in a university. There is always a program that needs to be revised or strengthened. There is another building that needs to be built or a children's hospital to get under way. Whoever follows me is going to come in and say, 'My God, I wonder why this wasn't done. An idiot could see this needed to be done. Why didn't old Dr. Robinson do that?' Bronson said, 'By God, they better never say that around me.' He was very loyal to people. I felt that he was very loyal to me and very supportive and a good friend."

Bronson also took time to read letters sent to the board and often personally responded to them. This excerpt is from a letter he sent to someone who was unhappy about a policy regarding Vanderbilt athletics:

> I am writing in response to your recent letter to the Vanderbilt Board of Trustees in my capacity as President, but also because I do care what our friends think about the University and I do read their letters.
>
> When the administration and the Board first undertook in depth discussions about the rising cost of athletics at Vanderbilt and all other universities, and its potential serious problems for the educational mission of the University, we realized the probable answers would not be universally popular. . . .
>
> We looked seriously at whether we could continue in major intercollegiate athletics, the pros and cons to the University between establishing significant new athletic fund raising activities and going out of athletics entirely, and the consequences of each. Are we just in the public entertainment business or is there an academic purpose and/or learning experience in intercollegiate athletics?
>
> We determined that our best course of action for the overall mission of the University and its alumni was to remain in athletics on as competitive a basis as possible consistent with our resolve to be a world-class university. . . .
>
> I hope you will understand our decision in a somewhat more sympathetic light with this background. We do, as a Board, care very much about how our acts are viewed by Vanderbilt's alumni and friends.

Joe Wyatt had an idea for a unique scholarship program with a specific donor in mind, he wrote up the proposal, and then he asked Bronson to read it from the standpoint of that donor. Joe said, "As usual, Bronson did a very thorough job of that, made some important suggestions to it. One was to emphasize the fact that the students who would be scholars would have goals of being a professional—a lawyer, a physician, a businessperson particularly, not necessarily just a social worker or a teacher. But a person who was going to pursue a professional career and also was committed to a philanthropic or constructive social side. I made those changes to the proposal."

But the person for whom Joe wrote the proposal declined to participate in the program. Joe explained how the program found its supporter: "I came back to Bronson and said, 'Is there any way you would be interested in doing this?' That was when we started talking about his willingness to do it on a scale that would start out at a level and grow. Right from the beginning the concept was comfortable to him. He was committed to it. He identified with it. He spent a lot of time with the program, always participated in all the interviews for the Ingram Scholars. He did things to facilitate their work. He was very much a part of that proposal. I don't know what was going through his mind. I can tell you that I'm delighted that it bears the Ingram name. He followed his beliefs. He wasn't the kind of fellow to embellish his ideas with words. He embellished ideas with deeds."

Thus, the Ingram Scholarship Program was established. We set up the funding so that as it grows, we can have more and more students. The original plan was to grow to twenty Scholars by 2003, but in the academic year 2000–2001 alone, there were twenty-eight—a total of fifty, counting graduates.

Ann Neely, associate professor of the practice of education, has been the faculty director for the program since its beginning. The first class of Ingram Scholars was in 1993, and Bronson, Joe Wyatt, Tom Burish, John Siegfried, Neil Sanders, and Ann evaluated them. Criteria include volunteer community service, strength of personal character, and outstanding academic achievements. Ann observed that although she had seen Bronson be pretty tough in some situations in

the university, "he became almost like putty when the high school seniors came to be interviewed. He thought the Scholars were wonderful, and I saw him kind of sparkle. He was really interested in what they were about."

Pat Wilson, Joe Wyatt, and Bronson at the Campaign kickoff dinner in Nashville. (Photo © 1992, Harry Butler, Nashville.)

Basically, the program sponsors students who want to take an active social role in addition to their academic studies and then carry that commitment forward into their professional lives. They are to devote twenty hours per month during the school year and at least one of their summers to a service project. The program provides half tuition and funds to make it possible for the students to have transportation to locations throughout the world and have enough money to live modestly while they carry out their summer projects. To date, they have undertaken projects from New Delhi, India, to work in an orphanage, to a peace and reconciliation group in Londonderry, Northern Ireland, to a sports camp in Tupelo, Mississippi, to a community services project in Washington, D.C., to a UNICEF Read and Lead Project in Lithuania, just to name a few.

Ann Neely explained, "Bronson didn't put any expectations on them about the summer projects. It didn't matter what they did as long as it was something useful. It could be handing out sheets of music at the symphony. He never raised the issue of whether it was conserva-

tive or liberal or whether it agreed with his agenda. He just thought it was important for them to get hands-on experience during the summer. One summer is manda-tory, but they can do more."

I made arrangements so that the Scholars can be my guests at TPAC for a symphony, a ballet, a theater piece, or the opera. All they have to do is call my assistant, and she will take care of the tickets. I have told them that I don't want them to be educated in the ways of philosophy, history, or medicine and not have an understanding of the arts, too.

Here is a list of the students by year: for 1994–95, Micah Dailey, Michael MacHarg, Brad Robinson, Ann Tseng, Zac Willette, Suzanne Wirth; for 1995–96, Nicole Alvino,

Bronson standing in front of Kirkland Tower at Vanderbilt University, 1993. (Photo courtesy of Vanderbilt University.)

Micah Dailey, Jason Dinger, Joy Dyer, Michael MacHarg, Brad Robinson, Ann Tseng, Maryanna Turner, Zac Willette, Spring Williams, Suzanne Wirth; for 1996–97, Patrick Alexander, Nicole Alvino, Ginger Baker, Micah Dailey, Jason Dinger, Joy Dyer, Alan Linch, Karen Lovelace, Rachel McDonald, Patricia Myers, Brad Robinson, Ann Tseng, Maryanna Turner, Spring Williams, Suzanne Wirth, Jon Zeiders; for 1997–98, Patrick Alexander, Nicole Alvino, Ginger Baker, Christina Barnes, Micah Dailey Douthit, Joy Dyer, Lyndi Hewitt, Alan

Linch, Karen Lovelace, Rachel McDonald, Patricia Myers, Jamaal Nelson, Brad Robinson, Jeff Robinson, Gayle Rogers, Roger Sahni, Spring Williams Barnickle, Jon Zeiders; for 1998–99, Patrick Alexander, Ginger Baker, Christina Barnes, Jennifer Chang, Bradley Cordes, Micah Dailey Douthit, Joy Dyer, Rasheedat Fetuga, Melissa Garrity, Lyndi Hewitt, Alan Linch, Rachel McDonald, Margaret Murphy, Patricia Myers, Jamaal Nelson, Jeff Robinson, Gayle Rogers, Roger Sahni, Fred Valizadeh, Preethi Venepalli, Spring Williams Barnickle; for 1999–2000, Patrick Alexander, Ginger Baker, Christina Barnes, Jennifer Chang, Bradley Cordes, Brian Deignan, Rasheedat Fetuga, Melissa Garrity, Abbey Goldstein, Katherine Hurst, Alan Linch, Margaret Murphy, Patricia Myers, Lee Ann O'Neal, Rusty Phillips, Katherine Randall, Jim Reynolds, Jeff Robinson, Gayle Rogers, Roger Sahni, Fred Valizadeh, Preethi Venepalli, Monica Wattana; for 2000–2001, Christina Barnes, Robert Clothier, Bradley Cordes, Brian Deignan, Melissa Garrity, Abbey Goldstein, Sarah Hams, Katherine Hurst, Jill Johnson, Nana Koram, Ross Lucas, Michelle Martin, Millie Mast, Justin Memmott, Margaret Murphy, Lee Ann O'Neal, Erin O'Neil, Soha Patel, Rusty Phillips, Erin Quinn, Katherine Randall, Jim Reynolds, Gayle Rogers, Roger Sahni, Joe Stephens, Fred Valizadeh, Amber Wallin, and Monica Wattana.

Micah Dailey (now Douthit) interviewed for the scholarship in February 1994 as one of twelve finalists. The question that she remembered from the process was, "What is the most important thing you've been able to accomplish so far?"

She followed two other people in responding: "The first two people talked about fundraising. They had managed to raise a lot of money for their organizations through bake sales and what not. I was thinking, *Oh, gosh, what do I say?* The answer I gave was, during high school for two years, I got to mentor my sister, who is three years younger, and two other young women in a Bible study. We met on a weekly basis for a couple of hours. I guess my greatest accomplishment as I explained it to them was that my sister and I had an opportunity to move beyond being siblings to being very intimate friends, to be very close. That was the answer I shared, and it seemed to resonate with Mr. Ingram. He responded very warmly to that. It was nice for me because my fear was, 'That's not big enough.'" She was awarded a scholarship before the end of the weekend.

Bronson and I attended a picnic for the Scholars before they started in the fall, and Micah recalled, "My impression was that Mr. Ingram enjoyed life. He ate corn on the cob with two hands and it was all in his teeth and all over his cheeks, and Mrs. Ingram was constantly giving him napkins. He ate ribs bare-handed and got sauce everywhere. We were terrified. We had come to an Ingram picnic and saw those ribs and corn on the cob. How could we possibly stay neat and somewhat civil with that kind of food? He just dove right in, could not care less, really enjoyed the meal and the time with other people."

We also invited them to our home for a Christmas party before they left for the holidays—a custom that continues. Micah observed, "Mr. Ingram was very relaxed and joking and having fun. The Christmas party was not business; it wasn't even the Ingram Scholars program. It was just friends."

Micah regarded Zac and Mike, the first two Scholars to graduate, as the "foundation of the program in terms of student participation. They were very intelligent, very passionate men. They were very wise in service. From a freshman's perspective, they had a lot to offer, and they put a lot into writing about what we hoped to accomplish with the program and what should be a student's initiative within the program." The students continue to work together and with advisors to refine the program.

Jason Dinger initially was not accepted into the program after his interview, and other scholarships did not materialize in the spring of 1995. He was a premed student and knew that his parents, both schoolteachers, could not meet the financial requirement. He said, "There was no way I could stay. I was going to go back to the University of Washington [in Washington State]. I went to Ann Neely, who had been great throughout the whole process and had to kind of shepherd me through it. I said, 'Now you know me better than anybody else at this university. Can you write me a recommendation to go back to the University of Washington? I'm applying for some programs there.' She was more than happy to do it. But at the same time, Ann Neely, bless her heart, took it upon

herself and actually went to Bronson and said, 'Here is the story. He is going back home. There is nothing he can do.' Bronson gave me the scholarship then and there."

Ingram Scholars Picnic, 1994: Mike MacHarg, Martha, Bronson, and Micah Dailey.

Jason noted, "There are several visionary things about the scholarship that were unique. One was that it would produce responsible business leaders. That was its original intent. Unfortunately when you're eighteen to nineteen, few people really know that they want to go into business, and if they do, they probably aren't coming out of the socially responsible side of things—myself included. When I joined the program, I was going to medical school. I had absolutely no intention of going into business. I might go so far as to say, when you live in the nonprofit side, you always feel that you're the have-not. If you head up organizations, you're in the business of asking for money—usually it's not you executing on it. Throughout my career, I had been in that situation and had harbored . . . disdain would be too strong of a word, but close, around these hyper-wealthy individuals and this glass wall.

"I was going to medical school and was really excited most about the fact that not only was it a tuition stipend but there was also a summer program, which for me was just the coolest thing in the world. Up until then I had been working since I was around fourteen. You work twelve, thirteen hours in the summer and never even fathom the ability to do what you like to do. That summer I went to Norfolk, Nebraska, to live with my grandparents and translate for an immunization clinic up there. Kind of staying in the medical vein. And I also taught English as a second language."

Jason graduated from Vanderbilt but did not continue in medicine. He has become a businessman and formed the company Weberize, which employs people in Nashville, New York, and Cairo, Egypt. The firm specializes in building digital companies from the ground up and launching Internet initiatives for established businesses and institutions.

He expressed his appreciation to Bronson: "I really do feel a profound indebtedness to him. Who knows where I'd be now and what I'd be doing and what kind of contribution I'd be making now? Thinking about where I was and what I was doing and thinking about where I am now and what I am doing now, it's nice to be able to say, 'We're doing what you wanted us to do. We're making this vision a reality, working very, very hard to be responsible and to give back and to do all of those sorts of things.'

"Now we're here, we're in this community, and we've got fifty-eight people who love coming to work, who have a new vision of what it means to be a responsible company and giving back, having that value system. We'll grow and they'll leave, but they're going to go somewhere else and they're going to espouse those same values. I always wondered about the real value of a scholarship program. I thought it was hit and miss. You don't know what you're going to get. Upon reflection, you can really make a world of difference in a short period of time. I'm just glad that I was given the opportunity.

"I am consistently thankful for that, to the point where I got married—I've been married about a year—a year ago I wish Bronson Ingram could have been there. My dad in his toast at the wedding

reception literally had Ann Neely stand up and Mike Schoenfeld [vice chancellor of Vanderbilt], because he has been instrumental, and said, 'This is my son's wedding, but I want to acknowledge Ann Neely because if she hadn't done what she did and Bronson Ingram hadn't done what he did, none of this would have happened.' I wouldn't have

Ingram Scholars, First Reunion, January 2001. (Photo by Jonathan Rodgers.)

been here. We wouldn't have had this company. It had reached so deep into the psyche of my family at that point in my life and at that type of event that it was so important that she be recognized and the program in so doing being recognized for making all the difference. That is right in the front of my brain. Every day that is really, really clear."

The first reunion dinner of the Scholars was held January 19, 2001. Most of the Scholars were present; the missing ones were abroad for the semester. Joe Wyatt spoke to the group and said, "This gathering is the final piece of the vision. The graduates are returning; they are making a difference. The Scholars benefit not only from the generosity of the Ingram family but also from the example of seeing them live their beliefs and values. It is a privilege to be associated with this program. Government can do a lot, should do a lot, but can't do what individuals can do—from personal hands-on efforts to financial gifts."

Gayle Rogers, a Scholar who had just returned from Australia, said, "The beautiful thing about the program is that it now has a history. What the scholarship has meant to me: I've learned how to think about service. We are fifty different Scholars, with fifty different dreams. And there are some very lofty dreams. We have covered every inhabited continent."

I must say that I am impressed not only with their accomplishments so far but also with how much the Scholars genuinely like each other. They are already doing what Bronson desired for them.

Bronson and I founded the Ingram Charitable Fund in 1995, which must distribute at least 40 percent of its income and assets for support of Vanderbilt University. Bronson also made the final gift to the Campaign to push it over the goal of $500 million, and he designated the money to be used for cancer research. I like to think of his gifts at the beginning and the end as bookends for the Campaign. The Campaign concluded on June 30, 1995, having reached a total of almost $560 million, but Bronson did not live to see that final total.

CHAPTER 9

Adieu

Life is a great big canvas,
and you should throw all the paint on it you can.
—Danny Kaye

I f it is true that life is a great big canvas—and I believe it is—Bronson
was always working on that canvas with several large brushes dipped
in paint of various colors. But something happened to him in 1994
that abruptly took away the brushes and the colors.

By the fall of 1994, attaining the goal for the Vanderbilt Campaign
seemed a certainty. The various parts of Ingram Industries were doing
exceptionally well. Bronson started thinking seriously about retiring
from active participation in the company when he reached age sixty-
five in November 1996.

To take a little break, Bronson and I decided to go fishing in
Venezuela, and we invited Dr. Ike and Ann Robinson to accompany us.
We flew to Caracas where the *Patsea VI* was docked, and we planned to
stay a week. We were catching white marlin and sailfish, then the captain,
Jim Garrity, asked Bronson if he would like to try for swordfish.

Ike described the process: "Bronson had never caught a swordfish,
never been swordfish fishing. Lord knows, I didn't know anything
about it. We must have been 25 miles out at sea at night, and it is like
fishing in a pond. At least that's the way we did it on this trip. You have
a big bobber, a great big red thing, and a big hook that goes down 300
feet and a halibut at 300 feet and one at 150 feet, and then you sit there
with a searchlight on the bobber. If you see it move, you've got a strike.

"Darned if we didn't catch a swordfish, a nice big swordfish, which Bronson would have released. He was a sport fisherman. He didn't keep anything he caught. That swordfish had come under the ship. The motor was at idle, but I guess that the rudder or the prop had kind of slashed him, so when we brought him on board, he really had been wounded, getting caught up underneath the boat. We couldn't toss him back in, so we kept the fish. It had taken Bronson a while to get him in, and it had been a lot of work. The next morning after he caught that swordfish, Bronson got up and said, 'Damn, my back, Ike. It is just bugging me.'"

Back home, Bronson's back was still bothering him, and he underwent therapy to relieve what seemed to be a strain from his fishing expedition. He tried not to let it slow him down, however.

Not long after we had returned, Phil Pfeffer asked David to become president of Ingram Entertainment, and David accepted the position. David commented, "I got to effectively run this company and deal with it and Dad got to observe me, at least in board meetings, and that was kind of nice. I think he was happy that he had been able to hang on to me and not lose me because I had talked with him shortly before I was asked to be president, that I really wanted to run my own thing. I was likely going to leave at some point and do something else, maybe in real estate or maybe this or that. We had a meeting about it and talked about it. I remember him saying, 'I hope you'll let me be involved.' So that was, I guess, an admission that he wasn't going to just block it.

"We had a meeting even before that. One night we had dinner at Belle Meade Club, I think, where I told him I thought there was a problem with three boys in this business and how was this thing going to be managed if something were to happen to him? He had said or said to his friends and he acknowledged, 'Maybe some of you guys will be CEOs of some of these operating units.' But he didn't act as if it were a given.

He told some of his friends that at some point he was going to have to do something with the company to accommodate the fact that David wanted to be independent.

Opposite page: Martha and Bronson at Sag Harbour, August 25, 1994, aboard Patsea VI.

"The only reason I wanted to be independent was because I felt that you can have two people run something, but it is very difficult and they have to be of the same nature and thought process. They have to

complement each other. I just didn't see that with me with either of my brothers. I just didn't think there was going to be a good match there. Not that I don't get along with them, but I think that we view the world differently and that's an issue."

Bronson was inordinately proud of his children—no matter how angry he might get at one of them for doing something. When he and I had quiet moments to talk, often with candlelight and wine at dinner together, we almost always talked about our children and how well they were doing or maybe where we needed to nudge one, one way or another.

His tendency was to tell people when they did something wrong, whether they were company people or family people. He had a hard time offering praise. But at Thanksgiving while we were in Charleston one year (we had always gone to Charleston for that holiday), he said, "I want to have a little family talk." The children told their spouses and their small children to take a walk. Bronson said, "I just want you to know, because your mother tells me that I don't praise you enough, how proud I am of each of you." And he went through what each of them was doing.

Frequently, the children will remind me of that: "Mother, you remember that time when we were in Charleston and Dad told us how great we were and how proud he was of us? I'll always remember that." I constantly told them how wonderful they were, and from time to time they said, "Yes, but what does Dad think? Mom, we know you think we're terrific." Those comments made me tell Bronson, "You need to let these grown children of ours know they're A-OK, warts and all." They knew he was proud of them. He just couldn't bring himself to verbalize it.

Ike Robinson called on Bronson about six weeks after our fishing trip for a one-on-one meeting about the Medical Center. Ike stated, "I walked in and I looked at him and I said, 'My Lord, Bronson, what in the world is that on your forehead?' He had a lump on his forehead, just a big knot, looked like somebody had hit him with a jackhammer. I looked at that and I knew that whatever it was, it was bad. Lo and behold, it was bad. That was the first evidence of metastatic carcinoma."

Bronson went in for tests, which revealed that he had metastatic disease fairly widespread and heavily involving his

Opposite page: Fishing in October 1994: (front row) David Hite and Scott Mantz; (back row) Jim Garrity, Bronson, and Ike Robinson.

central nervous system and the brain. Ike was there for the diagnosis on December 1: "I think Bronson asked me to go in with them. On their first visit with David Johnson, after he had gotten some workup and Bronson was to get the word, Bronson and Martha were there together. I never will forget one of the things that David Johnson suggested was irradiation of the brain because of all the involvement, and Bronson asked what effect that would have on his mental processes. David said, 'Well, it may have some effect on recent memory and some things, but probably not major, but it might dull your mental facilities.' Bronson said, 'How long would it be before that happened?' David said, 'No earlier than a month.' Bronson said, 'That is all the time I need to make my arrangements.'"

Bronson contacted family members and told them about the diagnosis, then he dictated this letter to me—slowly but without making a single correction—as we sat in the waiting room of the Vanderbilt Cancer Center on December 6. It went to Denny Bottorff, Clayton McWhorter, Jim Neal, and Joe Wyatt:

> Gentlemen:
>
> As many of you know, I have been having some lower back pain and neck discomfort and in the last few weeks have developed some lumps on my head. Results of a biopsy determined last Friday that these were malignant and extensive CAT scans yesterday confirmed that the back and neck were more of the same.
>
> I have spent today at Vanderbilt determining a course of action that will begin with radiation therapy on the back and neck to be followed by chemotherapy.
>
> I expect to be available a good share of the time through these procedures, but I am going to cut out most of my outside activities to leave more time for this company. I have talked to Chip [Lacy] about it and, fortunately, we are in the final decision making process for a new president of Ingram Micro. Once that is accomplished, he will be accelerating his plans to spend more time in Nashville with the objective still to move next summer.
>
> I wanted you to know of my condition before the rumor mill got started. Fortunately, the company is in good shape and strong hands and I feel good about that.
>
> I am optimistic that my medical treatment will be successful, and that I will be involved with the company for a long time to come.

The next day, December 7, the *Nashville Banner* ran the article "Ingram CEO Being Treated for Cancer" on page 1:

Senior management officers at Ingram Industries have been notified that company chairman E. Bronson Ingram is being treated at Vanderbilt University Medical Center.

"He has cancer," said Sheryl Dunn, manager of corporate communications for Ingram. [In fact, she was manager of marketing for Ingram Book Group.]

The announcement came in a letter written by Ingram himself, in which he said that he was admitted Tuesday to Vanderbilt. He remains hospitalized.

According to Dunn, Ingram has been suffering from neck and back pain for several weeks, and lumps were discovered on his head.

Ingram, 63, said in Tuesday's letter that he would be "canceling outside activities."

An active contributor along with his wife, Martha, to Nashville's charity and arts organizations, Ingram is president of the Vanderbilt University Board of Trust and chairman of Nashville's Agenda project.

The company would not disclose details about what kind of cancer Ingram has or what his treatment plan will be.

"Mr. Ingram is a private man," Dunn said, adding that he did not even mention the word "cancer" in his letter.

"Obviously we're very concerned," she said. "Our best wishes are with Mr. Ingram and the Ingram family. We are certainly optimistic."

With a net worth of $1.3 billion, Ingram was recently ranked No. 56 on *Forbes* magazine's annual list of 400 richest Americans.

Ingram Industries distributes computer products, books and videos, and is the largest privately-owned business based here with 10,000 employees. . . .

Ingram reported $6.16 billion in revenues and $170 million in profits, according to *Forbes*.

Bronson was determined to carry on with his routine as much as possible. He went to the office. We attended various holiday events around town. We hosted the Ingram Scholars for a dinner at our home on the fifteenth, and then we had a company Christmas party there, too. Lee Synnott recalled talking with Bronson at the Christmas party: "We had a chance to visit over in one corner of the room and we were talking about the business and his illness and again he was a leader's leader. He told you a bit about the process and the risk. He also was very complimentary of his Ingram team of managers that in the worst-case scenario, he knew that while he was ill, people would carry on and the outcomes would be indeed very good. And so, my impression was, here the man is obviously very ill, and he's spending that time encouraging me rather than the other way around. I mean, he was just remarkable.

"In the Operations Review meeting a few weeks after that in La Vergne, he was out there as usual. We were going through a fairly complicated financial arrangement, and he wasn't as sharp as he usually was. The usual was instant recognition of what the answer would be. And we, as a group, watched him go through the process he would normally go through, which was instant analysis. You could almost see the wheels turning, though they had slowed down a bit, but bless his heart, he absolutely came to the correct conclusion and it maybe took him three times as long as it would normally take him, but also that would have been about twice as fast as any of the rest of us could have gotten there. Incredible.

"Bronson was a very able four-star general commanding all of this array of activities literally worldwide, and doing it so that his personality shone through. We knew Bronson. You felt like you knew him as a person. You knew where he was coming from ethically and morally, and he was a damn decent fellow. I've seen him bend over backward to help our people to do the decent thing, time after time after time."

On Christmas Eve and Day the tradition was—and is—for the whole family to gather at Alice and Henry Hooker's house for one event and at our house for the other event; we swapped days each year. We did that in 1994, too, and then the day after Christmas, the family flew to Hobe Sound.

Without warning Bronson began to experience excruciating pain, pain beyond what anybody there would prescribe for. We needed to get him back to Vanderbilt for treatment. When we were

deliberating how we were going to best handle the situation—could we get him onto our company plane and back?—David called an ambulance plane, made the arrangements, and reported to the rest of us, "It is already fixed. Here is what we're going to do." There were times when each of the children stepped up and said, "We're doing it this way."

It's the kind of thing that can shake your faith profoundly, and it does. You question, "How can this be allowed to happen when he is so vital, doing so many worthwhile things?" It shakes your sense of answers to prayers. It's something that you finally have to come to grips with. It didn't change my belief in and acceptance of Jesus as a teacher of religious ethics, but it did profoundly affect my sense of the immediacy of prayer or its being worthwhile at all. It didn't negate the fact that, for me at least, there is a greater Spirit. But as far as a direct, personal, anthropomorphic God, it certainly did shake that belief. This was not like praying to pass an exam or get a new toy.

Our last Christmas card together, but unfortunately, Hank and Orrin were absent because of Hank's strep throat; photographed in Charleston, Thanksgiving Day, 1994.

John and Orrin on the Champion Polo Team at Gulfstream, Palm Beach, Fla., March 1995. Martha and Bronson attended to cheer them on. (Photo by David Lominska.)

You have to try to block out the bad times. Bronson had a lot of pain early on and a lot of tough things to deal with. For a while going in that room where there was so much suffering was difficult, but once he had sufficient medication for the pain, it was much easier to cope with the illness. The only thing more difficult than having pain yourself is watching somebody you care about in pain—pain that you cannot alleviate, no matter what you do. As his disease progressed, he did not receive effective relief until he was given the morphine pump.

Clayton McWhorter offered his assistance to Bronson one day after a board meeting: "He was beginning to have some side effects from the cancer. I don't remember how it came up, but there was something about going somewhere. I said, 'Bronson, I'm just across the street. If you ever need me to take you somewhere, just let me know.'

He said, 'You need to know one thing, I can drive myself!' I said, 'Okay.'" Eventually, the treatments caused him to become confused, and it was no longer safe for him to be behind the wheel. The day when he could no longer drive himself was a new low.

On Maryanne Davidson's thirtieth anniversary in January 1995, Bronson went to the office to give her a special award. Maryanne said, "He came here for my anniversary award and he was just tickled to death because he gave me my award but also one of the things I had asked for in jest was my personal parking place and so he handed me a replica of my name. He looked around in the room and he said, 'By God, none of you ever better park in it.' I'll never forget that and he gave me a big hug!"

Martha Denton also attended that event. She had worked for Ingram Materials until she retired, and she and Bronson had developed a teasing relationship over the years. She helped him pick out a boxer puppy and came to the house to take care of the pup's ears. She said, "He kept getting sicker, and one day I went over there [to the office] and he wasn't there and Maryanne said, 'I'm going out to see Mr. Ingram. Do you want to go?' And I said, 'What is it, business?' And she said, 'Yes.' I said, 'Naw, I don't want to go, but one afternoon I'll go with you when you are going on your way home.' Well, he went fast. Every week, I would send him the dumbest cards that you could ever hope to see. Well, he got to where he'd look for them and see how smart aleck they were going to be."

Orrin told his father early on that he would guarantee that if the cancer could not be arrested, Bronson would not have pain—and he didn't after we were allowed to have the morphine pump. Orrin learned how to use the pump, and he was there three times a day every day to make sure that it was working properly. By then, we also had nurses around the clock. I was very fortunate in the midst of all of the misfortune to have grown children who were not only there but functioning and making things happen. We were fortunate to have sons who were strong enough to help move him. Later on, even two nurses on each shift could not manage to lift him. Bronson was a big enough man that that was not possible.

Orrin said, "His memory went so quickly. It was very difficult. He'd zone in and out, and you couldn't tell when he was answering questions. It was good that he lived for six months so that you could deal with the

fact that he was dying, but it was difficult because there were a lot of things you'd want to ask him and he couldn't answer the questions. He stayed at home when he wasn't at the hospital getting chemo.

"I can remember a story I confessed to him after we knew he wasn't going to live. That's when I was about six and John was five. We were watching the *Wizard of Oz* on TV, and Mom and Dad were in another room. We had a fire going in the fireplace, and there was a whisk broom. I caught the thing on fire in the fireplace. John was wanting to play with it. Eventually, Dad smelled it and I heard him: 'What the hell is going on in there?' I heard him coming, and I handed the broom to John right as Dad came around the corner. John got a huge flailing, and he was too busy crying to pin it on me. That was a secret for about thirty years.

"The one thing to me that was really important about Dad was that if he made a commitment, you just knew it was going to be honored. He flat followed through with what he said he was going to do. You could take it to the bank."

Ira Potter first came to work for us as a baby nurse when John was just a few months old. She took some time out to raise her own family, but came back to work for Bronson and me as a housekeeper later on and she is still with me. She said of her early years with us: "They've done so much for me. When I was much, much younger, I'd get in debt for my clothes. I found out where Mrs. Ingram bought her clothes, and I went to those stores and bought clothes at the same places. I'd get way over my head in debt, and I'd talk to Mr. Ingram about it. He'd say, 'Ira, you've got to learn how to manage your money.' He'd pay up, then I'd get back in debt again. I'd go to Mr. Ingram and say, 'Oh, Mr. Ingram, I'm in debt again.' He'd say, 'Ira, you've got to learn how to manage your money.' Finally, I managed to live within my means."

She continued, "When Mr. Ingram was so sick, about two months before he died, he called me to him and said, 'Ira, I want you to promise me something. Just in case I don't get well, will you promise to help take care of Mrs. Ingram?' I told him, 'Mr. Ingram, we're all going to grow old together.' He said, 'Just in case, will you promise?' I promised. Now I think she takes more care of me than I take care of her."

Opposite page: Arnold Palmer, Bronson, and Jack Lupton at Seminole, March 1995. Arnie came to visit Bronson there.

Many people felt compelled to see Bronson and came by the house. Until the very, very end, he was up and dressed each day. He could not speak very well; because of the radiation, his speech was halting. We never quite knew how much he was taking in. It was almost as if he were a stroke victim or had very rapid Alzheimer's. Sometimes we would sit there with him in a wheelchair—and not really know whether he was registering or not—and all of a sudden he would say something out of the blue that made perfect sense. Then it was as though he drifted off again.

I think it was less difficult in some ways for those of us who were there every day than it was for those who came once a week or so because they could see the deterioration. Bronson kept going when most people would have given up. He particularly wanted to get through the Campaign at Vanderbilt, to reach the conclusion and throw in the last amount that put it over the goal. Of course, it went on from there to even higher, but Bronson wanted to provide the bookend gifts.

Ike Robinson recalled the day that Bronson gave the gift to exceed the goal: "Bronson used to say to me, 'Goddamnit, Robinson, you're going to get a lot more from me when I'm dead than you will now.' But we never dreamed how soon that day would come. Toward the end of his Campaign, he called John Beasley and me out to the house, and he asked John, 'Where do we stand? How far are we from the goal?' Well, we were a few million from the goal. He said, 'Well, you just got it, and I want it to go to Ike and cancer.' That was the first money for what has become the Vanderbilt-Ingram Cancer Center. He had already endowed that chair for his mother, the Hortense Ingram Chair, and then he gave an amount that was part of his Campaign to top it off and bring the Campaign to goal. That amount was all to go to cancer. It hadn't been named then. It was only named that after his death. All of a sudden after his death, the Cancer Center was a recipient of a magnificent gift, so he was right."

Bronson's sister Alice said, "It was so startling to see such a strong, in-control man decline so fast. It was kind of shocking, like when my father died." His sister Patricia said, "It was the wrong time for him to die; it was a miserable shame." Bronson passed away on June 15, 1995. He was sixty-three years old.

At his death, Bronson had only two grandchildren: Orrin Henry II (called Hank) (above) and Wilson (left).

Richard Patton, Robin's husband, observed, "Bronson was always there. If there was a storm, there was always this touchstone that was going to be reached out to [by his family]. He was going to set it right. By God, most of the time he could do it. He really could do it."

Kathleen, my brother John's wife, said, "He was very generous to people and family, not just with money. You could always count on Bronson. When Martha and John's father died, my son was at Yale and my daughter was at Choate with a broken leg. They flew as far as Charlotte, but bad weather kept them there. There seemed to be no way for them to make it to the funeral, and they were distraught. But Bronson sent his plane immediately for them.

"Bronson was wonderful about getting all of the family to Charleston at Thanksgiving—no excuses. He had such firm values that he seemed rigid, but we need a touch of that to keep things together."

The funeral services were held at 11:00 A.M. at St. George's Episcopal Church on June 17. The family chose to have the service from the prayer book, a very basic service, with no public eulogy. We asked Rev. Robert Abstein for a special prayer, which he composed for the occasion, even though he had begun his ministry at St. George's only a few weeks before:

O eternal Father, who dost love us with a greater love than we can either know or understand.

We give thee most high praise and hearty thanks for the good example of this thy servant, Bronson Ingram, who hath now entered into the larger life of thy heavenly presence.

Who here, a tower of strength, stood by us and helped us; who cheered us by his care and encouraged us by his example.

Who loved the spirit of competition which enabled him to be a leader in business, in sport, and in the hearts of his friends and especially his family.

Who set a standard of quality for every facet of his life whether in commerce, the arts, or the church.

Who looked not on the outward appearance, but lovingly into the hearts of people.

Who rejoiced to serve all; whose loyalty and integrity was ever steadfast and his friendship unselfish and secure.

Whose joy it was to be of service.

Grant, we pray thee, that he may find abiding peace in thy heavenly worship, and that we may carry forward his unfinished work for thee on earth; through Jesus Christ, our Lord. Amen.

Adapted from Burial Services,
Rite One and Rite Two,
The Book of Common Prayer

As a surprise gift to our family, many members of the Nashville Symphony provided music, from Double Concerto in C Major Adagio by Johann Sebastian Bach, to Adagio for Strings by Samuel Barber, to "How Firm a Foundation," to In Memoriam E. Bronson Ingram composed by Maestro Kenneth Schermerhorn—again quite unexpected. The service closed with "Eternal Father, Strong to Save" (the navy hymn). The burial was at Mount Olivet Cemetery. Orrin had made the funeral arrangements without my ever asking him.

Pallbearers were Brownlee O. Currey Jr., Edward G. Nelson, John Alden Rodgers, John S. Bransford Jr., Toby S. Wilt, Dr. Roscoe H. Robinson, J. Bransford Wallace, Alonzo P. Boardman (Augusta, Georgia), John W. Harris (Charlotte, North Carolina), Arnold D. Palmer (Latrobe, Pennsylvania), M. Carter Stovall (Stovall, Mississippi), Eli W. Tullis (New Orleans, Louisiana), and Dr. Edward H. Wedlake (Pebble Beach, California). Honorary pallbearers included all Ingram associates and members of the Board of Trust of Vanderbilt, Dr. Crawford W. Adams, William B. Akers, Hunter Armistead, John S. Beasley II, Phil Bredesen, Will Brewer, Thomas B. Coleman, Jack Creighton, Maryanne S. Davidson, Guilford Dudley, W. W. Earthman, Sam M. Fleming, Frederic C. Hamilton, Dr. Craig Heim, Keel Hunt, Dr. David Johnson, Sydney F. Keeble, Mercedes Lytle, Hugh McColl, Gov. Ned Ray McWherter, Andrew H. Mizell III, Neil C. Parrish, W. Boatner Reily, Charles H. Robinson, Charles Story, G. Marshall Trammell Jr., James C. Ward Jr., Robert J. Warner Jr., George Weyerhaeuser, David W. Wiley Jr., David K. Wilson, and Ridley Wills II.

I don't know how many people were there—I was numb—but Bronson's sister Alice summed them up: "Both Republicans and Democrats responded in droves. People from the Chamber to governors. MBA people. Old, old friends. Newer friends. St. Paul, Minnesota, friends. Extended family. Out-of-town friends. People from Augusta. People from New Orleans. Hunting people. Shooting people. It was a big circle that he had touched."

All of the family received notes of sympathy, and invariably, the writers commented on Bronson's character: "Bronson went the extra mile"; "he had a punishing schedule but he always had time for his friends"; he "had a positive attitude and belief in the work ethic"; he had a "larger than life reputation"; he was "a valiant contributor to the growth, enhancement, and quality of life for our city"; Bronson had "a strategic vision and fair-minded competitive spirit." Many Ingram associates wrote, "None of us forget that we work for a family business."

This tribute to Bronson appeared in the Ingram Marine Group newsletter in June 1995:

> Those who saw it were touched. Two bouquets of red and yellow flowers had been carefully placed on the sign "E. B. Ingram," designating his parking place. That simple gesture silently, yet eloquently, captured the feelings of many during a weekend of trying to depict who Bronson Ingram was. Much has been said about Bronson's role as a successful businessman, family man, and philanthropist, but not enough can be said about the qualities and core values inherent in his character which contributed to that success and evoked in people the outpouring of respect we saw during the visitation and funeral.
>
> Those with whom he interacted knew he had a presence, bearing, dignity, and simplicity which shaped who he was, who his children became, and how his companies did business. He exhibited hard work, punctuality, service, moderation in habit, modesty, generosity, honesty, honor, sense of duty, and an abiding loyalty to the associates and organizations that he guided with their help.
>
> Corporations are unique structures imbued with the concept of "perpetual" existence—the idea that an

*Opposite page:
A tribute from
The Vinny.*

THE VINNY

Wishes to pay its respects to a loyal supporter and dear friend.

E. Bronson Ingram

1932-1995

enterprise can exist beyond the lives of those who formed and shaped it. Bronson's stewardship always seemed focused on that principle: "Can I build and make something better and enduring out of what I've received?" More than most of us, he had a sense of continuity and history stretching back to the efforts of his parents and grandparents, and a recognition that he was doing something important and meaningful which would last into the future to be guided by his children and grandchildren. Every one of us witnessed this commitment to our marine businesses, through good times and bad.

It's no surprise that this continuity exists. It is a direct result of the values that Bronson instilled in the organization by coaching and example. The core values that make the Marine Group and all Ingram companies stand apart from others in their fields can be traced to Bronson's own strongly held beliefs, value system, and vision of how a company should conduct business:

Treat your customer with promptness, fairness, and honesty; treat your associates with dignity and respect and engender a steadfast loyalty between the company and the associates; conduct business in an honorable fashion which won't give others reason to question your integrity; do your best whatever you do to allow for personal success for the associate and business success for the company.

Bronson lived these beliefs; but beyond that, he instilled these in us and this is the key to why he was different, why he stood taller than others, and why so many people from across the country, from all walks of life, paid him homage when he died.

As Captain Reggie Tubbs and the crew of the *M/V Chip Lacy* stated so well, "For giving us the opportunity to be the best that we can be . . . we give him a long, saddened blast of a riverman's whistle and have lowered flags to half mast. . . . Through these trying times hold your head high because Bronson Ingram's spirit will always be carried on every Ingram vessel that proudly flies the Ingram name."

Several people were interviewed for the Vanderbilt-sponsored video *A Tribute to E. Bronson Ingram*. Here are a few excerpts:

He motivated me by telling me that there was a very large number attached to a program at Vanderbilt and would I take up the challenge and be a leader and raise the funds. If he hadn't been there, and if he hadn't already done so much, I wouldn't have been inspired. I learned that with his inspiration I was able to do something that I probably hadn't thought that I could do.

—Brownlee Currey, Trustee for Vanderbilt University

That relationship over that span of years has taught me a lot of things—one is perseverance, one is the desire to go on and to make things happen. Don't let them happen; *make* them happen.

—Arnold Palmer

I think of Bronson as hard-nosed and soft-hearted. He is a hard-nosed businessman and hard-nosed a bit about community service . . . soft-hearted in the sense that when he met the Scholars . . . he took to them immediately as individuals.

—Hans Stoll, Owen School Professor,
Advisor for Ingram Scholars

Usually you look at somebody that follows you in a campaign and you say, "Well, he ought to do this better, or he ought to do that better." But I said, "Damn it, I've got to tell Bronson he's doing a helluva lot better job than I did." And then I thought a little further, "Being president of the Vanderbilt Board of Trust, he did a better job than I did." I had the opportunity of telling him that, prior to him being ill, which now I feel very good about.

—David K. (Pat) Wilson, Vanderbilt Centennial Campaign Chair

An article in the *Vanderbilt Register*, June 19–July 16, 1995, bore the title "Ingram Inspired Professors and Students":

Professors and students who have been directly touched by Bronson Ingram's generosity honor his resolute dedication to service and unwavering high standards.

"Bronson Ingram set an incredible standard for himself in terms of achievement, generosity and commitment to higher values. The professors and students who hold chairs and scholarships in his name now face a great obligation to live up to this standard," said Arthur A. Demarest, Ingram Professor of Anthropology.

Ingram and his family also have endowed chairs in economics, engineering management and molecular oncology in the School of Medicine. In addition to those four chairs to bring top faculty to Vanderbilt, his contributions include two athletic scholarships, the Ingram Women's Golf Scholarship and the Ingram Men's Golf Scholarship.

David V. Kerns Jr., Orrin Henry Ingram Distinguished Professor of Engineering Management, said, "A generation of Vanderbilt engineering students have benefitted from the vision and generosity of Mr. E. Bronson Ingram and his family. He recognized and created a focal point for the teaching of communications and engineers."

The contribution dearest to Ingram's heart and to which the family has directed memorials is the Ingram Scholars Program at Vanderbilt. Ingram created a scholarship program that requires students to do volunteer work while at Vanderbilt and demonstrate their commitment to continuing community service throughout their lifetimes.

"Young people need to learn that hard work and giving can bring a great deal of pleasure and satisfaction," Ingram said at the time of the program's creation in 1993.

The May 6, 1996, *Vanderbilt Register* featured this article, "Ingram Scholars' Volunteer Work Serves as Tribute to Founder":

The volunteer work of the Ingram Scholars will serve as a lasting tribute to the man and his family who endowed the scholarship program, Board of Trust Student Affairs Committee members were told April 26.

During an emotional appearance before the committee, four Ingram Scholars shared their experiences as recipients of the scholarships. . . .

"He has made an investment in human capital," said Mike MacHarg, a senior majoring in sociology and business administration. "His investment was not simply in endowing a scholarship. He and the entire Ingram family have invested their hearts to this program."

In addition to MacHarg, Ingram Scholars who discussed what the program has meant to them were Nicole Alvino, a sophomore economics and Japanese major; Rachel McDonald, a freshman who plans to major in political science and Spanish; and Zac Willette, a senior majoring in elementary education and service learning. . . .

Alvino, who initiated Project Page linking translators with non-English-speaking patients at Vanderbilt University Medical Center, described the academic seminars the scholars are required to attend. At the seminars, the scholars learn about the non-profit sector and about the people who volunteer in an effort to provide a link between college-based community service and service while in the professional world.

"In the creation of the Ingram Scholarship Program, Mr. Ingram wanted to select students who would carry on his tradition of becoming a business leader and an active contributor to the community," Alvino said.

McDonald, who was rejected for the Ingram program last year, explained how happy she is after being selected as an incoming Ingram Scholar this year. She will spend Maymester in Peru where she served this year with Alternative Spring Break. She'll also serve as a Summer Academic Orientation Leader. "I'm here and I have no regrets. I'm ready to give everything I have to this school." . . .

Willette ended by telling Board members what Ingram's enthusiasm for the program has created in the Ingram Scholars.

"He had a gentleness of spirit and deep faith in the world especially when he spoke of the Ingram Scholars. But let me tell you, the Ingram Scholars share the same gentleness and that same deep faith."

The tributes in words, although wonderful, were less attuned to Bronson and his accomplishments than the tributes in deeds that will continue to be felt throughout upcoming generations.

CHAPTER 10

Unfinished Tasks

The final test of a leader is that he leaves behind him
in other men [and women]
the conviction and the will to carry on.
—Walter Lippmann

Bronson was able to report to stockholders in March 1995, even though his health and mental facility were failing, that 1994 was Ingram Industries' most successful year ever. The company was fourteenth on *Forbes* magazine's annual ranking of the nation's largest private companies in 1994; the company had leaped to that position from twentieth the previous year. At the time of Bronson's death in mid–1995, Ingram Industries employed more than 10,500 associates.

The funeral service for Bronson was held on a Saturday, June 17, and it just so happened that we had an Ingram board meeting scheduled months before for the next Tuesday. The board members needed to know what the family planned to do next.

Bronson had told me in one mellow, unguarded candlelit moment years earlier, "You know, you could run this business just as well as I can if you hadn't taken time off to have all those children." Of course, I did take time off to have all those children and I had not really been part of the organic growth as he had been, but every now and again I had to pull that compliment out and think about that. I had to grab those moments of praise when I could.

In fact, Bronson had also told me, "Look, if anything ever happens to me, I want you to make yourself chairman and surround yourself with the smartest people you can find." Neither of us really thought anything was going to happen to him—certainly not before he retired. You just don't think in terms of someone like him, who had been so vigorous and so healthy, dying at age sixty-three. So, I had been told that I was to be in charge and become chairman and control the family's resources. Bronson had me think that I knew how to do it— or at least knew how to ask the right questions. It was fortunate for me and the family that I had been on site those sixteen years because I knew the people and I knew quite a bit about the businesses.

At the board meeting in June—three days after Bronson's funeral—the members said to my sons and me, "Why don't you all take a couple of weeks and decide what you want the company to be going forward?" I said, "Let us huddle for a while outside the board-room. I think we may already have an agreement." They reassured us that we shouldn't feel rushed, but Orrin, John, David, and I went out of the room for twenty-five, maybe thirty minutes and came back with a proposal.

The biggest part of our business at that point in time was Ingram Micro. Supporting its phenomenal growth was affecting our lines of credit for our barge and book businesses because banks don't want to loan a company more than a certain amount of capital (credit limits), and Ingram Micro was using most of it. My sons and I had talked earlier about how to go forward based upon discussions we had had with Bronson. Just before Bronson became ill, we discussed with him the possibility of taking the whole company public. He was firm: "You're just going to have to wait until I retire at sixty-five. I don't want to have to deal with the analysts and the public. I know I'm not good at that. When I retire—and I'll retire at sixty-five—you all can do whatever you damn well please."

Orrin was president of the barge company, John was president of the book company, and David was president of the video company. They told me, "Mom, we think it's time to take Ingram Micro public, but we would like to keep the other pieces private. We like the busi-nesses, and we don't want to retire at age thirtysomething." I said, "That's something that I also think we need to do, and we had talked about it a little bit with your father. He wasn't ready to do it until he retired, but now that is not a consideration." David also asked to have

Ingram Entertainment as a separate, private business for himself, so he would not be competing with his brothers.

We were at a decision-making point, and we made the necessary decisions. We walked back into the boardroom, and I told the members, "We've decided that we'd like to take Micro public, David would like Entertainment as a separate, private company, and the other boys would like to stay where they are."

They said, "This is amazing." I said, "This is not a snap judgment. Even before Bronson's illness, we had talked about what he might do after he retired. The good thing about having different businesses is that the boys can pursue their interests without being in competition with each other." The board members agreed with the proposal: "If that's what you want to do, let's get about it." Subsequently, the board elected me chairman of the board and CEO, and Orrin and John became copresidents. Plans got under way to separate Ingram Entertainment from Ingram Industries and to take Ingram Micro public.

I did not have a break from decision making until September 1995. I just had to get away and clear my head, so I went to England with my soon-to-be daughter-in-law Sara and my sister-in-law Kathleen Rivers, who had urged us to go on a Historic Charleston Foundation–sponsored tour for two weeks. I guess I was still in a state of numbness after going through those terrible, sad six months from the time of the diagnosis until Bronson's death and the attendant stress and grief and then tending to the company. But I knew I had to return ready to do business. Ingram Industries employed many, many people, and they needed some assurance about their future.

We *had* to make everything work. I think Bronson set me up to be the stabilizing factor with enough knowledge to see my way beyond and advise our children about how we would conduct the business. Our sons and I never considered selling all of the divisions of Ingram Industries and going on to other endeavors. First, we didn't really need the money. Second, Bronson and I never had any interest in rearing children to sit on the sidelines, draw on trust funds, and only play polo or golf or whatever for the rest of their lives. Both of us have had the pleasure of building things. In my case, it was in the performing arts

center world. In his case, it was building a business and
using that power base, if you will, to make good things
happen in the community.

Copresidents of Ingram Industries: John and Orrin.

The irony was that Ingram Micro went public
November 1, 1996, the same month that Bronson would have celebrated his sixty-fifth birthday. It took that long before we were in the
position to have an IPO (initial public offering).

When you get right down to it, I was catapulted from Director of
Public Affairs to chairman and CEO, and Orrin observed, "John and I
had to make a pretty big leap when he died. We ultimately jumped a
couple of positions in the company." As copresidents, Orrin had the
home office, except for treasury, and the insurance and barge companies, and John had the book group and treasury.

Orrin said, "We haven't had much trouble retaining people.
Even in the book company we have very low turnover in the senior
positions. When the dot-com craze was going on, I was concerned

that we might have some retention problems, but we are a family business. I think there is a lot of loyalty on the family's behalf to its associates, but it comes back to us as well.

"We can make long-term decisions rather than short-term decisions. Dad always despised the thought of operating in a public company environment, even though Ingram Industries almost went public. I am so glad that it did not because it would be a much different company than it is today. I don't think it would be as good a company.

"But Ingram Micro at the time was growing so rapidly, we needed capital to make sure that we could stay competitive and make acquisitions. We also needed the public way of rewarding the people in Micro because our competition was already public and had the benefit of using stock options as retention tools. We have phantom stock here at Ingram.

"Dad never would have wanted to tear apart the company like we ended up tearing it apart, but after he died, it worked out fine. Micro went public, and it needed to go public. David got what he wanted, which was the video business. John, Robin, and I got what we wanted." The divisions include the book company, the barge company, the insurance company, and Woodmont Capital, directed by Robin's husband, Richard Patton.

Robin is now on the board of directors, too; her ownership position is reflected in that role. For a while she was so busy having babies and dealing with little children that she was not interested in the business, but as the three children grew a bit older, she told me she would like to know what was going on and to be on the board. I said, "You will be if I can get the outside directors to vote for you, and I think they will. And I'm sure your brothers will be perfectly happy for you to be on the board." She is a conscientious, effective member.

As I explained earlier, boats in Ingram Marine are named for friends or family members or board members. Bronson named one after Clayton McWhorter, who said, "I don't know how many times we talked about going and spending a couple of nights on it while it was cruising, pushing barges. But we never did. We did go on another boat and spend a day, so it was my own education as a board member as to how that functioned, the training of the captains and the whole bit. But that is something we talked about and we'd keep talking about

Our children and grandchildren: Sarah and David with Bronson III and Henry; Orrin with Hank, Virginia, and Aaron; Martha with Reid; Robin and Richard with Crawford and Wilson; Stephanie and John with Christina, Martha, and Alexa, December 2000. (Not pictured: Orrin's wife Sara Ingram, and Lucas Rivers Ingram, born on October 4, 2001, to John and Stephanie.)

it, and all of a sudden, it wasn't an option. From that standpoint I regret that we didn't do that."

Clayton continued, "The good thing about Bronson Ingram and the Ingram family, even though he went through a very traumatic time with his illness, because of their interest and contribution and support of the cancer program over at Vanderbilt, the doctors and researchers have made great strides. They are going to be able not only now but in the future to help others have hopefully less traumatic experiences with their illnesses as a result of the Ingram family making that support possible."

Orrin is now chairing a capital campaign for the Vanderbilt-Ingram Cancer Center. "It became obvious we needed to do a capital campaign. I felt so strongly about it, I chaired that. That is an interesting story. When

PAT'SEA VI

Dad was diagnosed with cancer, we had the resources so that he could have gone anywhere in the world to have been treated. He felt that Vanderbilt was as good as anyplace he could go. I agreed with that assessment. However, they weren't good enough to save his life.

"So after he died, I went back and met with the director of the Cancer Center and said, 'Hal [Moses], if money were no object, what would it take to get Vanderbilt to be the best cancer center in the world?' He came up with a ten-year strategic plan that was designed to get us within the top five cancer centers within five years and to be the best at least in certain areas in ten.

"The first phase of the strategic plan cost $56 million. That is the gift our foundation made to the Cancer Center because we didn't want the research to have to wait on the money. We wanted to get the research going so that other families don't have to go through what we've gone through. And the researchers are doing some fantastic things. In fact even in the gift that we made to Vanderbilt, there is a provision that if there is a cure for cancer and the money is not needed, we can redirect the money to other areas within Vanderbilt. What a great thing that would be to have to do."

Bronson posthumously received the 1995 Distinguished Alumnus Award from Montgomery Bell Academy. His longtime friend Jake Wallace delivered these remarks at the ceremony:

> This year's distinguished alumnus award is awarded to a man who died much too soon, but who in 63 short years accomplished more than most who lived decades longer.
>
> Bronson Ingram was a man that most in this room knew or through business, educational, charitable or family relationships certainly knew about.
>
> The fact that he was so involved with so many important endeavors for so long led many to take for granted that there would always be a Bronson Ingram to lead and to help when critical needs arose. Only now that he is gone, can the magnitude of his contribution be really appreciated.
>
> It is not my intention to recite all his accomplishments, as that would take far too long. The fact that he built in a few years one of the world's largest private companies, that

Opposite page: Martha and Bronson at Edgartown, Mass., Wendy and Boatner Reily's dock, September 1994.

he was on the board of directors of some of America's largest businesses, and that he headed the Metropolitan Nashville Chamber of Commerce all establish his credentials as a superb businessman. In addition he was heavily involved in leading and supporting many other civic and philanthropic endeavors.

What I would like to emphasize here tonight though is Bronson's tremendous and unflagging interest in formal education. From Project Pencil, of which he was a founder, to Vanderbilt University, where as Chairman of its board he among other things led a successful $500,000,000 endowment addition campaign, he was involved in the full spectrum of education.

All MBA alumni should also know how important he was to MBA, and MBA was to him. Like his father before him, Bronson had a deep and abiding interest in and love of our school. I can well remember when he and I were both at MBA in the middle 40's hearing my father say that Hank Ingram, Bronson's father, and Brownlee Currey shouldered both a financial and leadership role at that time, that many felt kept MBA going at a critical time in the school's life.

Bronson came on the board shortly after his father's death in 1963 and he remained until his death this year. He too became deeply involved in the school's search for excellence. He served as Chairman of the Finance Committee for many years, providing guidance and leadership in all areas of the school. He served with four headmasters, and just after he became ill last fall he told me that while he felt all of our headmasters were men of exceptional talent, he felt that Brad would very likely prove to be one of our best because "Brad was the right man at the right time in MBA's history."

To those who may wonder about the void he has left at MBA, I am delighted to report that his son, John, has recently joined the board and his son, David, has taken on the responsibility of Vice Chairman of this year's Annual Giving Campaign, moving to Chairman of that campaign next year. As such he is an ex-officio member of our board. Both John and David are MBA graduates.

In conclusion, let me add a few personal comments about this extraordinary man. He was a great leader. As such, he was very demanding and he was never satisfied with anything short of excellence. But he was just as demanding on himself and he truly led by example. He was as competitive as anyone I've ever known.

When Bronson took on anything, charity, business or sports, he did so with the absolute conviction that he would move it to the highest level of performance. In that regard he made all who worked, or for that matter played, with him better for having that experience.

He was one who had great loyalties. In spite of a tendency to often speak his mind in no uncertain terms, he was incredibly loyal to the people and institutions that he supported and who supported him. Behind that blustery exterior was a man who was sensitive, caring and who had a big and tender heart. Whether it be his family, his friends, or those many organizations he supported, he might sometimes be critical but woe unto anyone who criticized them to him.

Finally, he was just an incredible friend. When you had Bronson as a friend, he was with you through all times, good and bad. Far from the "fair weather" variety who are difficult to locate when times are tough, Bronson was untiring in his efforts to be with you and be of invaluable help when you needed him the most, and the last thing he wanted was recognition. He did it because he cared deeply.

It is with a feeling of great love end respect that I give to his wonderful family, his wife, Martha, and children, Orrin, John, David and Robin, this 1995 Distinguished Alumnus Award from Montgomery Bell Academy.

In addition to gifts I've already mentioned, family funds have been used to further educational goals at MBA (through construction of the E. Bronson Ingram Science Building, dedicated in 1999), at Harpeth Hall (computers and scholarships), at Princeton (the E. Bronson Ingram Scholarship), and at Vassar (an addition to the library).

The November 15, 1998, edition of *Computer Reseller News* reported that Bronson and nine other men were elected to the CRN Industry Hall of Fame. He was called the "King of the Global Distribution Empire." I'm not sure what Bronson would have said about being called a king of an empire; I think he always thought of himself as a businessman. Period.

Orrin and John became copresidents because I didn't want to choose one over the other. They're both very, very gifted in slightly different ways but not in ways that one is a superior gift to the other. When I thought John was going with Barnes & Noble, I told Orrin, "You will become CEO in addition to being president, and I will keep the chairman's title." That was all squared away until the Federal Trade Commission caused us to abandon the deal with Barnes & Noble in 1999. (Barnes & Noble would have acquired Ingram Book Group, and Barnes & Noble would have used Ingram's distribution centers.) It's as if the marriage was called off at the altar, and we are back out playing the field.

Quite honestly, I must admit that the book business is my favorite business and I was not enthusiastic about its going with someone else, but John thought it was for the best. When the deal didn't work out, I was delighted to get the business and John back. He was going to be commuting to New York and be very much involved there as well as here in Nashville. I wanted John to have a proper place in the company to utilize his capabilities, so he became vice chairman of the corporation.

Bronson had a real thing about people discussing companies in terms of revenue line. He always said, "Revenue means absolutely nothing. It is what happens at the bottom line, the earnings per share, that matters. I don't know why magazines continue to rate the size of companies based upon revenue, especially when some of them aren't even profitable."

He made that comment long before the dot-com craze, which has been even crazier because the companies have been valued according to their stock price, and many never have had—and never will have—a dime on the bottom line. Many of them are already out of business. An exception, we hope, is Amazon.com.

John stated, "We're serious people trying hard. We've been given an incredible advantage in terms of having a business, although it has changed a lot even since Dad has been gone. To try to maximize the opportunities we have as opposed to squandering them or be shiftless. That's a tremendous legacy that he has instilled. The values in our organization—I think we are quite proud of the reputation of the company and the family. Not that we haven't had some bumps along the way. But I think it is nice for our associates and people to say 'Ingram' and most people go, 'Wow! I know about them.' And it's

mostly good things, whether it's about the company and the way we try to operate or the family or the company's commitment to the community. I hope they know us as good people as individuals, too.

Martha and Bronson, Charleston, 1988.

"Every month at the book group we have a service award luncheon where we recognize people that have five, ten, fifteen, up to thirty-five years of service. You listen to those people's stories, and you realize that in many cases there are a lot of families that work in our family business. You realize how much they have given of themselves and their time and their family and their lives to our business, and you think, *Wow! That's a precious thing.*

"Even with good people, you've got to make good decisions, and you've got to be willing to take some risks, hopefully calculated risks, and have some losers in order to have some real winners. We've taken some risks. We tried to combine our business with Barnes & Noble. That was a big risk in terms of what that would mean if we did it. Or in this case the government wouldn't let us. That's a whole other saga about how our government works. But we've taken risks and continue to take them and hope that they're calculated and we have good people to execute them and we'll have more winners than losers. We're

constantly trying to look at where we are and what we're doing and try to realistically measure ourselves against what we expect and try to hold ourselves accountable for results."

Orrin reported, "It's the most exciting time I've seen in the barge industries since the early 1980s. It's more profitable. It's not a business that you're going to make a killing in, but it's a steady business. The exciting thing right now is that with deregulation the utilities are all positioning trying to figure out who is going to merge with whom and they're looking at their noncore assets and getting rid of them so that they have more capital to be able to throw at core businesses. We have plenty of capacity to be able to do some investing."

All of us are trying to carry on some of Bronson's passions while pursuing our own, too. Our children are not so involved in their businesses that they overlook civic opportunities. As I mentioned, Orrin is working with the Vanderbilt-Ingram Cancer Center on a $100 million campaign, and he just finished up chairing the United Way campaign. John is working with the athletic program and the business school at Vanderbilt and is much involved with the Westminster School and the Charles Davis Foundation. David is head of the Finance Committee for the Tennessee Golf Foundation (which supports junior golf programs for minority and disadvantaged children around the state) and is a very involved fund-raiser for Montgomery Bell Academy, where he is also a board member. Robin is raising money for the Nashville Zoo, the Humane Association, Rape and Sexual Abuse Prevention, and Harpeth Hall. I never told any of them, "You must do this." They are just doing it, and I'm very, very proud of them, to say the least.

Bronson was on the board of Weyerhaeuser, and I am on that board now. The directors wanted to have an Ingram continuing on the board, since Bronson's great-grandfather was an early investor (1900). I did not know this until I was asked to come on the board, but Bronson kept pushing the directors to have a woman on the board and telling them, "Why don't you get someone like Martha, who is on other corporate boards, because she understands how the corporate structure works and the board structure?" The directors said to me, "You can consider your-self nominated by your late husband. During Bronson's lifetime, we didn't want to have a husband and a wife on the board together." I told them, "You have to understand, I am no Bronson Ingram." I didn't want them to think they were getting his clone because I do not feel suitable to be considered in that way. Their answer was, "We know enough about you; we want you on your own terms."

In November 1995, the Board of Trust of Vanderbilt elected me to be a member, and at the spring meeting, April 1999, the trustees elected me to become chairman of the board. I was on the Search Committee for a new chancellor to replace Joe Wyatt, and I was pleased to participate in bringing dynamic Gordon Gee to Vanderbilt. His appointment was announced in February 2000 as the seventh chancellor of the institution. My role on the board is one more element in the family's commitment to Vanderbilt for the long term.

Bronson's family, friends, and associates miss him, of course, but we're doing our best to "complete these unfinished tasks" of his and to "turn again to life and smile." My four children and I often talk about the fact that it is taking all five of us fully engaged to carry forward his life's work—things he alone handled with such apparent ease.

This is the sum and substance of the man that I married. This is his legacy to his family. We carry this legacy with pride but also with a sense of obligation, and each of us is energized in the process. A rich heritage indeed!

Ingram Family Tree

David Ingram
From Leeds, England
Settled in Southwick, Massachusetts (1780)
Married (date and wife's name unknown)
He and his wife had at least 1 child, David Asel Ingram.

David Asel Ingram (1802?–1841)
Married 1822?
Fannie Granger (1806?–?)

David and Fannie had nine children:
Orrin Henry was the fourth (1830–1918)
Married 1851
Cornelia Elizabeth Pierce (1829–1911)

O. H. and Cornelia had six children:
Mary Pierce (died in infancy)
Charles Henry (1857–1906)
Miriam Pierce (1860–1944)
Fannie Gertrude (1862–1895)
Rebecca (died at birth)
Erskine Bronson (1886–1954)

Erskine Bronson
> Married 1900
> Harriet Louise Coggeshall (1873–1944)

Erskine and Louise had two children:
> Janet (1910–1910)
> Orrin Henry (1904–1963)
> > Married 1928
> > Hortense Bigelow (1906–1979)

Orrin Henry and Hortense had four children:
> Frederic Bigelow (1929–)
> Erskine Bronson (1931–1995)
> Alice Louise (1933–)
> Patricia (1935–)

Bronson
> Married 1958
> Martha Robinson Rivers (1935–)

Bronson and Martha had four children:
> Orrin Henry (1960–)
> John Rivers (1961–)
> David Bronson (1962–)
> Robin Bigelow (1965–)

O. H. Ingram, Bronson's Great-Grandfather

An article in the *American Lumberman*, May 25, 1901, noted of O. H. Ingram: "He comes close to being one of the pioneers in the northwestern white pine business, for he began in the Chippewa valley in 1857. There were, however, quite a number ahead of him, for about the middle of the last century began to be opened up on a large scale the timber resources of that section. When asked how at his age, 71 years, he was so vigorous and active, he replied that it was because he had always worked. Indeed the record of his life is one of constant work at something useful to himself or others."

O. H. was born in Massachusetts, but the family moved to Saratoga, New York, when he was a small boy. His father died, and eleven-year-old O. H. went to work on a farm for board and clothes; he attended school in the winter. Then in 1847 he started work for the sawmill firm of Harris & Bronson near Lake Pharaoh, New York. He earned $12 a month for work in the woods during the winter and $13 a month for work in the summer at the mill. Before long he was in charge of the whole mill. Then Fox & Anglin of Kingston, Canada, wanted to build a mill on the Rideau canal, and seeking the best logging and mill superintendent, they chose O. H. The weather adversely affected his health, and he moved to Bellville, West Canada, and superintended gang mills. When Harris & Bronson wanted to build a mill in Ottawa, O. H. "built this record breaking plant."

Gilmore & Co., of Ottawa, was the largest lumber operator in the world. O. H. received a salary of $4,000 and a house rent free. There he invented the "gang edger which since that time has been an indispensable part of every respectable saw mill." But he didn't patent it, and when someone else tried to patent it, Orrin had proof of prior claim and made it a gift to the public.

Gilmore & Co. offered him $6,000 a year, but O. H. refused and went into business on his own with money he had saved. In the winter of 1856–57 he moved to Eau Claire, Wisconsin, where there was not even a railroad within one hundred miles.

Two fellows, A. M. Dole and Donald Kennedy, joined with O. H. to form Dole, Ingram & Kennedy. They bought a portable mill, and they also began a lumber manufacturing business in Eau Claire, which continued until 1900. From this mill, "equipped with the first gang saw mill of modern type brought into the west, they rafted lumber down the Chippewa and the Mississippi and finally opened a yard at Wabash, Minn., and also one at Dubuque, Iowa, at which latter point they built a mill." In October 1860 the Eau Claire mill burned, and although they had no insurance, they were able to build a new one by spring.

O. H. and others cooperated to build a dam to make lumbering safe and steadily profitable. By 1862, Dole retired from the firm, and two years later, two employees were given an interest in the firm— Ingram, Kennedy & Co. They built a steamer in 1865 and did freighting.

In 1880, O. H. organized the Charles Horton Lumber Company, Winona, Minnesota, and in 1881, after Kennedy sold his interests to Delaney and McVeigh, the Empire Lumber Company was organized with capital of $800,000. This company absorbed the interests of Ingram, Kennedy & Day of Dubuque, and this business was incorporated as Standard Lumber Company, with $500,000 capital.

O. H. had interests in various lumber firms, and "heavy investments in Pacific coast timber through his stock holding in the Weyerhaeuser Timber Company." He was president of Eau Claire National Bank, president of Eau Claire Water Works Company, and director and cashier of Canadian Anthracite Coal Company. He had investments in mines in Montana and Idaho.

"While still an active business man Mr. Ingram has for years interested himself in other directions. In fact, he has never been a slave to business, but has found time and money for the pursuit of reasonable pleasure and for the benefit of his fellows. His recreations are largely in the nature of change of work rather than idleness. He has a large and finely appointed farm in the outskirts of Eau Claire in which he takes great pride. He has a cottage on Long Lake and a sort of private summer resort up above Rice Lake where he entertains his friends, including many men prominent in the commercial world, in politics and religion."

O. H. donated a "free public library to Eau Claire and erected a very fine office building in which it is installed." He was a member of the Congregational Church and the American Board of Commissioners for Foreign Missions. He supported Dwight Moody and the Moody school at Northfield, Massachusetts. He was a director of Ripon College, Ripon, Wisconsin, and a supporter of the YMCA.

"In regard to his early life and the arduous beginnings of his successful career in Wisconsin he remarked recently: 'No other man ever did so much hard manual labor on the Chippewa as I.' This was in spite of the fact that he went there with capital and was always the leader in his various enterprises; but he was one of those men who can never keep their hands from a task which is to be done. And so his life has been one of constant physical as well as mental activity. It has been a busy and useful life."

The Bigelows

Bronson's mother, Hortense, was the daughter of Frederic Bigelow and the granddaughter of Charles H. Bigelow. This sketch of those two men is taken from the *Saint Paul Letter*, written in 1953:

> More unusual than usual is the father and son relationship within an institution, especially one which embodies not only continuity of family but of thought and endeavor. For seventy-five of its hundred years, the St. Paul Fire and Marine Insurance Company could claim that distinction. In 1871 Charles H. Bigelow was appointed secretary of the Company and in 1876 he became its third president. Mr. Frederic R. Bigelow joined the staff of the Company in 1891 and became president upon the death of his father in 1911.
>
> If it is true that experience molds the man in any degree, the Saint Paul, and its policyholders, were fortunate in having Charles H. Bigelow as secretary at the time of the Chicago fire in 1871, and as president in 1906, at the time of the San Francisco earthquake and fire. Surely it could be well believed that it was his experience in the Troy, New York fire of 1862—when his home, among hundreds of other houses and commercial buildings, was destroyed by fire—which gave him a deep and abiding understanding that made him fully realize the responsibility of insurance to the policyholder, and the latter's need for prompt and full payment. This he did but with tears in his eyes at the time of the San Francisco catastrophe, when he ejaculated as news of loss after loss wired in—"After working so hard to build up our strength, this . . ." It was on Sunday that he made this remark as he and Mr. W. J. Sonnen—now retired but still living in Chicago—were carefully charting the losses on a map of the City of San Francisco. He was seeing the entire surplus, acquired so painstakingly over many years, wiped out by one disaster.

Mr. Bigelow left for Chicago immediately upon receiving the news of the great fire of 1871, and adjusted the first loss for the Company. That was in the year that he became associated with the Saint Paul, when he was asked to become secretary of the Company. No doubt, during his association, at the First National Bank, with J. L. Merriam, A. H. Wilder, Horace Thompson and J. C. Burbank, Saint Paul directors and president, these men became impressed with his fitness for the position.

During Mr. Bigelow's administration of the Saint Paul many new coverages were added to the Company's list of writings. One of these was Ocean Marine insurance in 1876. The writing of such insurance by a company so far removed from either coast of the United States has aroused the curiosity of many. They have forgotten, no doubt, that Minnesota's first highways were waterways, and that in Minnesota country, through the fur traders and voyageurs, an extensive fur business was carried on with England and France two hundred years ago—transportation of furs being by water from Grand Portage across the Great Lakes and by way of three rivers to the Atlantic Ocean. In 1876 Minnesota products were still going to sea, as they are today, so why not coverage for them and others by an ambitious young business?

Prior to the time Mr. Bigelow became associated with the Saint Paul, he was interested in many enterprises. Among his major interests were lumbering and the St. Paul Harvester Works, the most natural of pursuits as Minnesota's main output in the 1860's were furs, lumber and products from the farm. He drove the first self-binder which was put into the field by the Harvester Works.

Aside from his business, his family, friends and church were Mr. Bigelow's concern. Loving appreciation was the tribute paid Mr. Bigelow by his family, especially for the hearty "Bigelow" laugh. Mrs. Bigelow wrote that it was eight months after her marriage—when she and Mr. Bigelow visited his family—that she first realized the full force of it. There are many still with the Saint Paul who came to know and enjoy that laugh through their association with Mr. F. R. Bigelow.

Less reserved at home than in his business, Mr. C. H. Bigelow was ever thoughtful of his family's comfort and welfare. The garden was his pleasure, but he built a washing machine for his wife, and provided many other conveniences for their home. It was not beneath him to stitch a seam on the machine when his wife was enveloped with the family's sewing. Travel, at home and abroad, stood high on his list of pleasures, not only for himself, but his family. This was important to his business of insurance, as it was to his interest in his country.

In 1902, Mr. Bigelow wrote the Honorable W. R. Merriam—Minnesota Governor from 1889 to 1893, then in Washington on a federal appointment—to the effect that he believed Oklahoma should be granted statehood and that Indian Territory should be attached to it. It was in just this way that Oklahoma became the forty-sixth state in 1907.

During Mr. C. H. Bigelow's term as president, he was able to build up the assets of the Company from one-half million to over seven million. To him goes the full credit of the Company's financial structure which made it possible for a small company to survive two great catastrophes, to earn the sound financial reputation it enjoys today. Though some new lines in addition to Ocean Marine and Hail, were added during Mr. C. H. Bigelow's presidency, the great expansion in coverages occurred during the administration of his son, Frederic R. Bigelow. That this was so, was inevitable for during that period machine industry came of age, and presented problems with which one of Mr. F. R. Bigelow's forceful, dynamic personality was best able to cope.

In round numbers the manufactured products of the nation, in terms of money, amounted to one billion dollars in 1849, to eleven billions in 1899, and sixty-one billions in 1923. Allowing a margin for error, those in 1919 engaged in trade and professions were about equal to the entire population of the northern states in 1860. In the words of an eminent historian, this was the era in which "ingenuity gave a pneumatic drill to the miner underground, electric appliances to the woman in the kitchen, a tractor to the farmer and a radio to the child." It was also the age of the automobile.

Though the Saint Paul wrote five of its most important lines prior to 1894, more than twenty-five lines were added subsequent to that time, with most of them offered during Mr. F. R. Bigelow's years as president. Some of these the Saint Paul pioneered, one of which is the direct result of Mr. Bigelow's vision and courage, for it is peculiarly suited to our present habits of living. It is the Personal Property Floater, the writing of which is yearly increasing in volume. It was this policy, and others like it—the all risk lines—which made the Saint Paul, shortly after the close of World War I, a nationally known company, to become so advertised by her representatives all over the world.

The Mercury Insurance Company organized in 1925, and the Saint Paul Mercury-Indemnity Company in 1926, subsidiaries of the Saint Paul, also pay tribute to Mr. F. R. Bigelow, for it was during his regime that they were organized. Certain statistics do as much: The capital stock of the Saint Paul was increased to an amount twenty times greater than it was in 1911—from $500,000 to $10,000,000. When Mr. Bigelow took office as president the surplus was well over $2,000,000; when he died, it was $43,176,244. And in 1920 the Saint Paul became a world underwriter.

Though Mr. F. R. Bigelow's father, then secretary of the company, contributed to the plans for the Saint Paul's first building, three of the four additional buildings fall into the list of accomplishments of Mr. F. R. Bigelow.

Mr. Bigelow was ever interested in the social activities of the men and women of the Saint Paul and liked nothing better than joining with them on parties and picnics, especially the latter. On these occasions Mr. Bigelow proved to be one of the ablest of the baseball players, and no one had more fun at the game than he—in shirt sleeves trying to make a home run.

Sports stood high among Mr. Bigelow's interests. On his desk for many years there stood a figurine, a sturdy figure of a Scotchman bent over in putting position, and he had just started for a round of golf when he was attacked by his last illness. Football and bowling were other games which he followed, and he never missed a Minnesota season of the former sport. His interest in horses went back to his youth, but business came first. When he took his first job with the Saint Paul, he often came to work on horseback. One day, expecting to remain but a short time in the office, he tied his horse to a lamp post and called one of the boys from his work to hold it for him. Becoming absorbed in the business of the moment, he forgot his horse and went about his appointment on the streetcar. The office boy held the horse for most of the day.

Mr. Bigelow's sense of humor was also a source of pleasure to his associates.

One day in having a friendly discussion of a problem with a young woman associated with his office, he asked if she never made a mistake. She said yes, but that she knew when she made one. Six months later when Mrs. Bigelow came into the office one day, he took her to the desk of the young woman and in introducing her said, "This is the young woman who knows when she makes a mistake."

A "Merry Christmas" wish developed into an incident which he never forgot, one which he enjoyed to the end of his days. It was Mr. Bigelow's habit to walk through the office and extend greetings for the holiday season in person. In shaking hands with one of the men at Christmas time, long ago, when this chap was still a mapper, Mr. Bigelow said "Merry Christmas, Jack," and before Mr. Bigelow's lips had closed on the last syllable, Jack responded with "It's up to you, Mr. Bigelow."

During the depression of the thirties, Mr. Bigelow was still president, but as he was out of the country part of the time, many of the problems of those hectic days fell to the vice president for solving.

INDEX